Voices of Nature

The Postures of Light

Juniper Urieh Pearson Good

Acknowledgments

I thank my Mother for giving me this life and holding space for me, always in love and light. I thank my father for his suffering, sacrifice, strength, and resiliency to always be there. I thank my sister for her companionship, her reflections on growth, and her ability to keep me on my toes. To all of my extended family, living and passed over, I would not be me without you.

To my Great-Grandfather Harold Gene Hunt for being a man of God and setting an example that has been emulated throughout our entire family. To my second dad, Joe Ray Garcia, for his support and presence, we give thanks.

Green Briar, my birthplace and alternative school for families that appreciate nature and permaculture and want to raise children off the land. Thank you to GB Khalsa, my midwife for catching me and assisting my mother and father as they gave me this opportunity to breathe these words.

My Uncle Dan Ratuta, founder and facilitator of Crestone Healing Arts Center, 14-plus-year Sundancer, great friend, and spiritual teacher—the Yoda of all Jedis. You have helped me conduct life-giving energy and certified me as a healer, allowing my force of nature to receive a certificate of qualification.

My Auntie, Sue Beck, an accomplished kundalini yoga teacher recognized in the community and of the yoga alliance. Spreading yoga in high school helped me and many other high schoolers to grow into strong spiritual beings. Sue Co facilitates Crestone Healing Arts Center and is married to Dan.

My uncle, Alexander Kofi Washington, and My auntie, Isaline Simms, for introducing me to Tasunke Witco and delivering me to the tree where I could affirm and make my vow and commitment. Thank you to Kofi, his Music Jah Kings and his African teachings and heart.

In memory of Karen Acher, our beloved teacher and founder of the Crestone Charter School. She assisted all the youth of Crestone, recognizing each student as being different. Karen and Mark recognized my differences, allowing me to find inspiration in education through QI gong. Karen knew the creator did not give me the mind for books or traditional academia. We need more teachers like Karen.

Mark Mikow, my high school teacher, an amazing man of many talents. So humbly changed my life, lightened this path for me to walk, and passed the qi gong to me to carry.

My Sundance family, for allowing me to learn from them, pray with them, and better understand my life, and all our Earthly relations, the opportunity to surrender myself to the essence of nature and the many spirits. You keep me on the good road and help me to do more and talk less.

Specifically, I want to thank my good friend, elder and teacher of medicine, a holy man, Nolan Yellow Kidney. To all of the Yellow Kidney family! For you have helped the lives of many, all we can do is offer that back to you.

In great memory of Gerald, Ice Bloodline and Carrier of Tasunke Witco Sundance, Crazy Horses Sundance, you will always and forever be acknowledged as a great leader. You have always given your heart to your people. Rest in peace, dear Uncle. Know that Tasunke Witco will always be with us and we will always dance strong for you in the Moccasins you gave me. For you allowed me to dance and to confirm my walk with WAKAN SKAN/Sspommitapiiksi.

My SR. Priest Kwame Alahooty and his priest family for welcoming me, recognizing me, and initiating me. The Adogbe families that received me and fed me.

John Milton, founder and facilitator of Way of Nature, world changer, environmental protector, Rites of Nature

Hanne Strong, the Founder of Manitou Foundation and the visionary of Crestone as a spiritual Pilgrimage point and a universal spring of healing and the essence of nature.

To my dear brother, Arnold Villanueva and all his hard work and prayers. He welcomes me and teaches me so much. It is a gift to know you and to work alongside you. Your support of the works is undeniably appreciated – with love and gratitude to you and your beautiful family.

My dear friend Angelino Cabrello is acknowledged as the key component to the success of Voices of Nature reaching the public. More importantly, Angelino offered me friendship, support, service, kindness and ethics. Without Angelino, VoN would not be what it is today. He's a great team manager, leader, and communicator. All the best to you, Angelino!

To Hambone Publishing for their services and abilities to help me and so many important books make it to your hands. We hope to continue working together on our future books as I refer and recommend Hambone to any author. They are professional, helpful, knowledgeable, and supportive. Most importantly, following through with their word. With respect to Hambone and the whole team, it has been a pleasure to work alongside such professional advice and creative people. Big thanks to all the helping hands at Hambone.

Dedications

This book is written in dedication to SSpommitapiiksi/WAKAN SKAN the above peoples and the great sky networks longing for the relationship we all once shared. Awaiting us to again recognize and listen deeply to the great spirits of the sky. May it be a time to return to you and build strong relations again. You are the one who has allowed Juniper to spell out the Voices of Nature. You guided him in all things he's done, keeping him safe and sound on his global pilgrimage. You have filled me with too much excitement at times, and I'v feel so high. We give all our thanks to you. As, I, Juniper, can come down from this long journey. Things are becoming clearer in my eyes on how to perceive nature and all the beautiful boundaries of her atmosphere. Without the connection to WAKAN MAKHA Mother Earth and WAKAN WI Father Sun, we would not be able to decompress from these tough times, and we would not have the opportunity to talk through our traumas or share our gifts. This book is dedicated to our elemental families and all of our relations in our widespread universe. In dedication to our early ancestors, the Earthly indigenous peoples, the reasons why we are here today. May we remember.

SANKOFA. African proverb: "it is not a taboo to come back for what is rightfully ours."

May we be unshakable in our connections as once before.

Table of Contents

Writer's Disclaimer

I've never liked books, never liked to read, and would never refer to myself as a writer, and I ask you not to view me as a writer for I mainly liked to observe and listen, and I appreciate the story of evolution. I'm here as a witness to West Africa, Asia, Latin America, Europe, and the U.S.A. today. I am a global traveler, a global observer, a global activist, a soldier of poverty, a council and friend of junkies, a hustler of love, an uncle to all children, an ally, and a spokesman for the people's people – the voices that go unheard. All self-proclaimed of course and Uncertified in most areas. Anyhow it is time to sing, it is time to stand out, it is time for your show. I like to joke and I could rant about what time it is, who we are, and what we need to do to see change. I really want to know where you stand and what you think, if you care.

I hope this book can paint some good pictures through stories and experiences. I'll do my best to extend an emotion, a perspective, a vision, and possibly a mission to you.

This book may be dull at times and sharp at others, this book could provoke sadness and hopefully instill happiness. I hope you can laugh with me at the state of the world; I hope I can portray difficult topics with a grain of humor, and if not, well, it needs to be talked about and for me, it's time to share. My Dad always said if you want to reach a lover or family, writing can be the best way to do so, and since I've embraced the world as my community and have brothers, sisters, uncles and aunties, nieces and nephews, Grandmas and Grandpas all over. I guess I'm just here as a bridge, a reminder that love is everywhere, I see love in all things and to love is to tell, don't let another era of silence come over us. Express yourself, love yourself, and communicate what you witness with love and awareness.

Without further ado, a book written by a kid who never liked books, I, Juniper Urieh Tree, apologize for any misunderstandings or miscommunications in my travel study, even with clarity comes uncertainty. I'm doing my best to speak from the people who spoke to me and relay what my elders have said to me. I am no longer myself; I am a human being speaking on behalf of other human beings and nature. I no longer travel for myself or for a glorified vacation; I'm traveling to shed light on things people may never hear about. I'm here to tell you what is happening globally through some simple observations. With some years of walking the global road on my back.

Dialogue, ideas, conversations, and feedback are welcomed.
Email: naturestemple108@gmail.com
Website: Naturestemples.com

Introduction

In this book, we will be weaving in and out of personal stories and experiences that have benefited my cells. We will be looking into the history and her-story, looking deep into the collective trauma and globalization of our new world. Going on mental field trips into a time when human beings lived in harmony with nature when we heard the voices of nature altogether. In this book, we will stop from time to time for some 'energy yoga' or 'qi gong.' This is a self-help book, a recipe for cellular remembrance. A book written in hopes of elaborating our remembrance of who we are. As we dive deep into the darkness of human manipulation, slavery, and genocide, the colonization of not only our lands, peoples, but our minds, we will be looking into the power of human beings as we rise from the darkness together and step into our cells of light by actively **opening, expanding, absorbing and transforming** our traumas and emotions of our mind, to imagining the self as light. We will be sharing wisdom from many elders and teachers. Voices of Nature is a recipe book of foundations for building spiritual success.

Looking into Human Permaculture, the benefits of tribalism, and how we used to support each other in community and vision. This book intends to expose darkness and bring light. Imagine a world full of people conducting love and light, a synergy of a collective mind, and many of us know the darkness. I'll be sharing personal stories of my darkness and what I've seen in 15+ countries, looking deep into the global machine that is supporting some much more than others.

We will highlight Indigenous spirituality and the power of the four races of man before globalization. Sharing vision of how we as mankind can reconnect to the voices of nature, nature of self, and nature itself, to live in harmony as one people. This book will discuss some prophecies and ideas of peaceful revolution. There are so many global issues. This book intends to inspire and invite action. As they say in Ghana, we are all one family, one heart, one mind, and we need to support each other in the ways we can, in the ways that we used to, the ways that many of us have forgotten. A reminder of how far we have come, and how far we have to go. This book is about acceptance and questions, a book to reflect if you feel, asking the self, who am I? How do I want to live? Where will I be? Why do I want this in my life? This book is not intended to divide but to respect one another's choices and honor one another's path. It's a cross-coloration of religious study and deep study of self or cells and the human mind, body, and spirit.

This book is written to share imagination and perspective. We will be going over the simplicity of nature itself and how the nature of self is a mere reflection of what we witness every day. We will talk about our daily bread, what we ingest, and what our grandparents and forefathers ingested. Looking into a meditative practice that can be perceived as a prescription, we will be talking about light and the very controversial conversation of En Lighten Mint as we break it down into a daily prescription given to you by no one other than your father, sun, and mother Earth. Nature reflects the golden mean ratio. Looking into quantum harmonics and the structures of nature, the miracle of sunshine/fire, air, water, space, and Earth produces a perfect environment for life to thrive. We will be asking ourselves who and what we really want to spend time with as we all find ourselves in houses and with phones, screens, jobs, bills, and trends. It becomes easy to predict that our elemental and ancestral family, the spirits if you will, may disregard us. We may not be aware of our relationship with them, but the voices of nature are speaking to us. Are you listening? We can simply ask ourselves. Being honest with the self, reflecting in the self as nature stares you in the eyes every day, the beauty of her color, air, and light.

Can you see yourself as a conductor of energy, becoming an antenna for nature itself? Do you feel that you are a tiny sun? A sun-born child. Do you feel your smile throughout your body? Do you find yourself in awe of nature with your hands raised to the sun? Well, if you don't, I hope by the end of this book, you will feel gratitude for each of your breaths. As you have come so far, birthed by the darkness and warmth and love of your mother, delivered into the most chaotic and distracting time in human history possibly. We are gentle on the cells for we did not create this world; this world was created by man, steered by the patriarchy – the control, the rule, and the day of the masculine mind. Is this happening as a product of nature? And do we have the ability to change our course of nature? Maybe it's time to live in the heart once again and get back to nurturing and supporting each other, sharing and loving one another. The voices of nature are waiting for you to listen, smile upon her, lay your head down, feel Mother Earth, and rejoice with our elemental and spiritual family. To offer them love and attention, to become stewards and representatives of nature, as we once were.

This book is written to address the voices of the people who are going unheard, the people in poverty, the people on the streets, and the ones who ask for money. This book is written for animals, oceans, and sea life. This book is written to the spirits and ancestors. This book is a tool to come back into our original postures.

I'm here, representing Mother Nature, speaking the voices of nature that have been speaking to me. The Earth and its inhabitants have been speaking to me.

We are all the same children of the sun, products of the greatest union in our universe from the fires and waters of creation, from darkness to light, from lost to found, from there to here.

Chapter One
Dualities

I never thought about writing a book; this came to be through journaling. A traveling tool to help me reflect on where I was going, where I had been, what I was feeling, and what ideas were coming through. I had been traveling with friends and partners for fun and rest, for adventure, and mainly to build the confidence to travel alone. I started with an easy trip and invited my dear friend to come along at that time. We set out for Thailand, Cambodia, Laos, and Burma, now known as Myanmar. As many travelers know, Thailand is a major expat destination and gets some of the world's highest number of tourists. It is indeed a beautiful country with so much to offer. My friend at the time was an Iranian American; she had a passion for her people, was an advocate and activist for LGBTQ and women's rights, and educated people about the struggles of immigrants and people of color in the United States. As we sat by an amazing waterfall, full of nature, the first duality of the trip was acknowledged in the light of the sun and the amplification of nature, a joy that filled my body. My friend revealed her feelings about current situations. This was during the time Trump was elected as president, he was banning any Iranian immigrants from entering the country, and families were being turned away upon arrival. Her heart was with her people. The connection and beauty of her thoughts were like waves crashing on the beach; it became a theme for us on the trip. We continued to watch waterfalls, and international expats juggling, playing games, and living their best lives with no judgment. I've been that person, and every time I go on a trip, I accept that I am a patriot from a country with a much higher currency.

The uniqueness of this insight was to acknowledge that while many people are suffering and being refused human rights and equal opportunity. Many of us are just watching the waterfall or enjoying the works of our forefathers, not really thinking about how many people lack the opportunity to do what we are doing. So many people are struggling to get out of their country if they desire to, simply because the currency is not in their favor. I'll use Laos and Togo as examples, both colonized by the French, one country in Asia and one in Africa. When you ask the ATM for 200 US dollars, the machine spits out 1 million Kip in Laos or in Togo 1 million CFA. A jackpot for anyone with a Euro or dollar. How much work for Laotians to make 1 million? Which is only 200 dollars. We all know how much a plane ticket costs, usually over 500 dollars. Some small perspective for those unaware of this, is that half our world has been mined and stripped of resources to build. Leaving so many countries impoverished. While Western society is spoiling from too much, others are left in despair.

Duality is tough in that since we say that we support all lives, for all lives to have equal opportunity and freedom, that's a no-brainer. I hope!

However, the other side of the coin reveals that the hole is dug so deep that it's hard to find the bottom of the pit. Stolen land resources and technology, giving life to westernizing parts of the world for comfort and accessibility. The reality is present, for any colonized country is actively having to rebuild families, emotions, infrastructure, business, and resources in general.

It's a lot to think about; I intend to not overload the reader with problems of the world but to take some moments and think about the world in the last 400 years. What comes up for you?

We will do our best to go from waterfall stories and great experiences to real-life problems and how we are all a part of it. This book will be filled with stories but is mainly a study of what has happened globally and how we as humans can steer and create a world we all want to live in. So, at the time, my travel companion was looking at two feelings: supporting her people or going with the flow and enjoying her vacation. As we decompressed over Thai tea, pad tai, and eye-opening sites, we had to acknowledge the emotional polarities about the world we were witnessing. Human behavior is to come to the rescue if empathy is present. We feel we can accelerate change, this rings true in many historical times, highlighting leaders of movements and great change. We all know their community was behind them, and they were all organizing together. In every hustle, you have positions, and we all have separate and important roles to play. By supporting each other, we will arrive at our collective goal. Being just her and I, we decided our team was small, and even though we glorified flying back and helping the Iranian people, we stayed put; the waves of thoughts persisted throughout our trip as we explored and learned some amazing things, things I still think about almost a decade later.

It seems that duality is present in every topic and thought of the human mind, even in nature. Simply, we have male and female, sun and moon, light and dark, rich and poor, black and white, and so forth. One important aspect to look at in this study is what natural duality is; for instance, the sun and the moon are part of nature that man identified as opposites and even deemed one masculine and one feminine. Seems that there was duality before mankind, hence the naming game begins. As humans evolve, so does the vocabulary and the creation story. I feel it is important to be aware of some man-made dualities, such as rich and poor, good or bad. I tend to leave it up to the individual to decipher what is rich or poor. I've met plenty of people who actively choose to exit the system that is fueled by money; in society, most success stories have to do with how much you can make and unfortunately, how much you can own or possess. With only the self to decipher, which avenue to walk and how its viewed based on the simple ideas of what we were given, good or bad, less or more etc.. I see how not viewing things as bad or good and right or wrong could be difficult in the world we live in today. The older I get, the more I just flat-out say that is not good, and call it out. I like the philosophy; instead of being bad or good, there's life-giving and life-taking. Simple things you do that make you feel good are life-giving; say drinking a healthy green smoothie gives you life; we eat simply because it gives us life. The more you see in the world, the more you will recognize that it is still a game of survival of the fittest. Someone may take from another because it gives them life but the other person is now left with less. That's where good and bad come into play. We can throw some of that hippie-esoteric shit out at some point; we just need to be direct and firm in our inner standings about how we have gotten to the place of westernizing the world. In early America, and I'm sure all over the world, as colonization was rampant, there was the duality of the "civilized" and the "wild." I could use the colonizers' word for an Indigenous, as there were many. They called us savages, primal; even the word Indian is a product of the naming game.

Appearing that the vibration and spelling of words hold power and have put us against each other, I'm actively working on using the words that are preferred and generally feel good to address one another. Of course, it is important not to take things personally. We can feel love and hate in a joke, and sometimes there's unclarity. We can have a conversation about it, and we also know when someone is being disrespectful. That is usually a good time to educate and invite them into a space of humility and let them know it is not okay. Seems that this is a large part of what collective healing looks like. The target to shoot for is love. Of course, there would be acceptance if love is fully present for one another, no matter your background or beliefs, religion, or color.

One of my elders said to me, "What is knowledge without understanding?" Then I asked myself, "What is understanding without a feeling?" Some people learn from knowledge in books and physical study, which leads them to fully understand a system. Without the knowledge of building a house, you would never get it finished; you wouldn't understand the steps. On the other hand, some people come to learn through a feeling, offering an in-body experience and recollection. You may walk into a room and not know a thing about it. However, your body is receiving information, and you slowly start to understand what happened. A sensation is naturally occurring sometimes, it catches us off guard. An empath or psychic feels on a deep level and sometimes tells you knowledge about yourself or a place that you have looked at in books or taken a lot of time to know or understand.

I've arrived at a feeling, that we all can psychically tune into each other's feelings, and each other's emotions to feel into another's trauma story. This would also reveal a level of care for another human being. Now. I've met many people who feel similar to me. Usually, we share the same feelings, a world full of empaths yet possibly thrown off guard due to global broadcasting and the disassociation of our self and nature. I'm sure if you take some time to think about the last 400 years, how far we have come from tribalism and living with the land, stewards of Mother Earth, guardians of the lands. We were elemental beings; when I say that, I mean actively engaging our elements. Of course, today, we can argue that we are still engaged. My feeling stems from my observations of society today and the priorities of mainstream movement. I'm sure we can all agree that when you take something, there will be a reaction. I'm sure even the big oil hounds, supporters of deforestation, and large corporate leaders are dealing with similar waves in their minds. Did we take too much? Is our Earth mad at us for not supporting her? If, for some reason, they are not thinking those thoughts. They are the product of a colonized mind; one cannot colonize another until they have thought it over and know or understand how it will happen.

That's why they say knowledge is power. Still, without feeling and sensation, they won't ever understand the damage that they did. They will continue to do to our fellow human beings, animals, trees, and all our Earthly relations. One who seeks knowledge over feeling is in danger of greed and jealousy and may even learn to hate. If love is to care, to hold accountable, to move through difficult times, love is to overcome together. A feeling that grows when you arrive at the point of greatness, such as loving feelings for a place, a person, or an experience. So is the opposite of love, hate coming from a lack of feeling, withholding information, a lie to gain, an action with no remorse. The duality of love is lacking the feeling? A sense of hate has been outsourced in our world. They even gave this complexity of human nature a name. For a good reason, we must also name the "bad" more than the good, if we speak on these terms. When I share my opinions and observations, I usually include this group of people that many young people and I refer to as 'them or they.' They that have lacked love for our Earth, those that have lacked love for our fellow brothers and sisters, lacked love for our animals and our oceans, our forests and rivers, they are the ones that started the naming game. They are the ones who have consciously used words and dualities to divide us and create disagreements. They have us all talking; they have our elemental family talking to us as we see shifts in our weather. I don't like blanket statements and do my best to stay away from generalizations. However, it seems that there is a global shroud that has been put upon us.

They are so powerful in their knowledge and understanding. They know so much about the human mind and body that they planted ideas. Seeds that have grown into realities. I'm not trying to bunk or throw shade toward technology or advancements. However, it seems that it is becoming more and more evident that people are getting more stressed and diseased than ever. Are we as a collective, under a spell of natural and very exciting progression that leaves some of us fully engaged with robots, WIFI, GMO foods, and factory farming? I mean, I can order my extra big chicken wings on my iPhone right to my door and have a robot vacuum on my floor. Write a book on AI and so much more. I hope you find some humor in this read. I catch myself laughing out loud at the sites I see and hear in the world as we know it, mainly in America.

This brings us to the elephant in the room. Everyone is talking about it: Is nature the source of our healing? Is being in nature the key to true relaxation? It seems that we are living in a world of forgotten wisdom; nature is the opposite of the man-made world that we know. Once upon a time, nature was all we knew, but nowadays, it appears that we haven't been listening to our elders and our ancestors, and we haven't been listening to our elementals. Is this true? Are we really listening to ourselves? Maybe we are listening but cannot act on it because the comfort is just so nice, and the hole is so deep. Is there even a bottom? Can we come back to our psychic selves? I truly believe this is based on this feeling, a feeling that comes from my environment, an environment that has been ruled by nature, guided by the elementals. Some say we become what we eat, and where we live will reflect us. I am simply a representative of my environment, a spokesman of our elemental family. They have raised me alongside my parents. I give thanks every day for the spirits of nature and affirm nature of self.

Regardless, if you were raised in nature or the city environment, you can always connect to nature and the nature of the self. Look up to the sky, rejoice in the reflection of spaciousness; the energy of the sun and the sky is present in all our environments. It is very possible to become an adept of nature in the city, we are all a part of this great human experience, no one can really say the heights of the human capacity in the city cannot be accessed, for nature is there still, the elements are still there. In my own experience, I observe myself being filled with my environment, whether I'm in nature, chatting with the birds, breathing with the trees, drinking the fresh mountain waters, communicating directly with the elements. Or I'm living it up in Mumbai looking into the latest fashion, exploring rooftop parties, and exploring a neglected aspect of myself, a suppressed part of my human nature, to pamper myself and actively find pride in looking good for myself and others. I've learned a lot about myself in the city, I've learned about fitting in and becoming a blender, and I've learned about finding faces of different social statuses. I've always found it the easiest to connect with street people; they are open and happy to approach you, even if you're not inviting them into your space; they want to converse with you, and maybe even want something from you. Dealing as a human, we acknowledge our desires to connect, indulge, laugh, and play. We all crave intimacy, whether that's a personal conversation, sex, or a quiet time in a sacred place.

It seems that there's a theme amongst city dwellers vs. country dwellers. I found myself wanting to look more beautiful in the city, buying new shoes and accessories to enhance my look. We can take accountability for wanting to be seen. To be seen and recognized feels good. In the country, we find celebration in other aspects as well, such as how your tools are kept and how you keep your farm or your homestead. It really comes down to authenticity. Do we operate from a space of superficiality, cover-ups, hiding our wounds and our trauma stories? Maybe we are naturally expressing ourselves by giving off messages, setting healthy trends, and showing our peers a fun way of dressing up or even uncaring. I've never been one to care how I look, often wearing the same clothes for weeks, not brushing my hair and pretty much fitting the bill of an organic hippie. In my environment, the trees are not looking at my features, the animals do not care to hear my voice as humans do. I embraced nature and allowed myself to be as I was. Nature is naturally beautiful, and most people won't even begin to critique how a tree leans, how a leaf falls, or how a mountain is shaped. It just is. I find myself in awe and acceptance of the constructs of nature. Nature is accepting. By taking time to build a relationship with nature you are building a relationship within yourself, how you accept yourself, how you find beauty in your shape, your form, and your uniqueness that is you.

Nature is a non-judgmental space for you to feel free, feel beautiful, and realize that you reflect many aspects of nature. Our body is composed of elements, we are water and blood, and we are flesh and bone. We consist of a complex inner verse, mirroring our solar system, our organs are like the planets, our bones the constructs of gravity holding us up, and our meridians and acupoints reflect lay lines and powerful places in our universe, connecting to different stars even could be similar to placing extra attention on certain power points along the body. The less time we spend with external entertainment, the more time we will inherently spend inside our body, becoming more familiar with the constructs and blueprints of our bones and flesh. We can even pause and take some time to acknowledge our skeletal system.

Bone Breathing

Part 1.

- Starting at the top of the head, close your eyes if it feels natural, see your skull, see the constructs of your face bones, cervical spine, clavicles, and upper ribs, and allow for your energy and awareness to gently scan the skeletal system. As you see your thoracic vertebrae and rib cage, see the whole spine as it connects to your hip bones and your sacrum. Allow your awareness to continue past the hips into your thigh bones, the kneecaps/bones, envision your tibia and fibula, your ankle bones, bones in the feet your metatarsals, and tarsals. Imagine the bones in your arms, allow the awareness to reach your fingertips, if it helps you can even look at a picture or skeleton doll. For some small moments, see yourself as just bones. The structure that holds your muscles and allows for the constructs of your body to vine around.

Part 2.

- Affirm the health and the strength of your bones. Breathe into your bones. Imagine healthy happy energy entering them and surrounding them with each breath. Simply imagine your breath, breathing life into your bones, and hold your awareness on your skeleton. Slow repetitive breathing. This is an inner yoga posture for bone health, allow yourself to feel no judgment. For this is your nature of self, your natural construct, your own creation story.

This simple meditation is great for building body awareness and becoming familiar with your infrastructure, posture, and alignment. A beautiful space to build a relationship with your truest self, without judgment.

"Speak to Your bones for they are holy and hallow, Invite the good energy to flow through your skeleton before being buried or burned at death."

Only in a human mind is there a level of judgment that can close us down. We are emotional beings, and our feelings rule our day, our judgment of self will either uplift us or keep us down. So, the feeling I'm expressing is coming from nature, the natural beauty that lives within all humans. However, it seems that due to the lack of connection with nature, there is a larger space in our minds to judge ourselves and others. Not only have we cut down so much of our forests to make way for cities, roads, and golf courses, the list goes on. We have chopped down our standing relatives, the bones of nature the infrastructure for so much life, and homes to diverse plant and animal species. We have put up billboards and advertisements regarding the latest fashions and make-ups, or even affirming depression with drug stores and suicide lines. Is it possible that there is so much depression and high rates of suicide simply because we were also part of the diverse species that lived amongst the trees and made our homes alongside them? On top of that all, the other layers of judgment could amplify sadness. We see so clearly in the human world what is cool, sexy, or trending, it seems that the focal point has become outside of the self. What we can physically see in one another, our weight our skin, our products, and accessories. As I look for my partners, I see that I want to be a certain way to attract a similar reflection in another. In one view, we could say that most pampering of self comes simply because we want to be seen and celebrated as the beautiful people that we are weather it for the self or others. To find our mates to procreate and continue the original human creation story.

Recently, I've come to some new inner standings about my standards of beauty and why it took me over a quarter century to realize that it is not only important to be well-dressed and clean for our human family. Yet it's most important to be clean and put together for our ancestors. Some say cleanliness is close to godliness. Now, I know some readers do not believe in a higher power, yet even in yourself when you feel good and high in life, could that be perceived as a higher power? It seems that people who are living their dreams, indulging or experiencing, the things they want truly, are accessing their higher power. An individual who is dealing with emotional blocks and feels stuck or bound to some old attachment that is holding them back from their power, the power to feel happy, to feel joy and bliss, the power to create. We can even see how being clean physically and energetically for yourself without the faith of a higher power could still be a great benefit to yourself. This is not to say that a person with less is not experiencing more, I have always looked up to Saddhus and cave Yogis, living deep in the mountains and forests. Their physical appearance may not be as such a concern in contrast to the modern man or woman. They have offered themselves to the nature spirits, to the ones who do not judge, leaving only the space for their inner judgments.

To look deeper into the idea that nature is a container for immense growth like the rain forests in Costa Rica where the plants flourish year-round, some areas in our planet are very balanced regarding the elements. When water, air, fire, and Earth are equally present and equally clean there is an amazing amount of growth. The space, the fifth element, the container and source of our elemental family will transmit such mana or source that you will shout out with joy. Raising your arms to the sun and the sky, for those who know the feeling of being fully supported by our family or friends, it's a joy to be in such love and closeness with our elemental family. When we are connected and in love with the sky, and the sun, planted firmly on the Earth and in reverence to her with each step, an event takes place, where our duality births a third aspect. The aspect of "chi… energy."

An elder of mine once shared a dream with me. He shared the dream with his friends and medicine men. It was a dream that consisted of information that was important to the listening ears, a dream that lent more insight into our collective and inner standings. The elder then continued to say that if you are experiencing a dream or vision, it is important to share that, so that we may all share the awareness or message.

I only speak on this topic simply because I am witness to the divine reception and conception. The marriage of two dualities of nature coming together in my awareness, was a dawning similar to how realizations appear in your mind. I was not trying to see anything, I was simply resting on a rock smoking some herb, my mind was relaxed my body was resting, and my being was gently smiling as I sat in nature, in no judgment, in the company of two dear friends. I spotted a winged one, that flew so high in the sky, was just a bit bigger than the size of a period. The bird was a messenger telling me to look deeper into the sky, as I gazed into the sky, I witnessed the birth of light in my sight. I'm going to stop here with the writing for a moment, I do not speak much of this day as it is one of the most special days in my life.

So, I'm going to paint a picture to further explain the conception that has birthed so much in my life. It seems a beautiful way to share is through art and imagery.

"Sky Dancing"

A day not to forget, a sight of such beauty that will hold you till death. On this day, living color has led me forward since.

I have engaged in a relationship with something higher than myself, something that I was told I should not try to understand, something that is to be simply observed and loved, something to feel. Now I may be a crazy person, I may be in devotion to something that is nothing more than a self-perceived hallucination. Yet my relationship with this energy supports my happiness and keeps me active in most things I do. It has been one of the hardest things to talk about. I've kept quiet about it mostly sharing my experience with close friends, lovers, and family. I don't know much about this energy, I find some level of understanding, yet it is the feeling that keeps me in devotion. The beautiful thing about devotion and human beings is that there are billions of us in devotion to different things. The feeling that a person receives from being in reverence is the true beauty here if it is supporting their reality and giving them life. It may not matter whether you believe in someone else's devotion, if it adds to their life then why create problems? This is also a beautiful platform to let go of judgment and the pointing fingers towards someone with a different belief or tradition. To honor each other in whatever it is that gives life.

Devotion comes off to me as an interesting aspect of a human being. In India, I witnessed a worshiping and devotion that seemed almost frantic, a bit excessive. Yet so beautiful to see how many families came to the Shiva lingam to offer their flowers, gifts, and prayers. I'd never been around so many people so passionate about their gods, I sat amongst many people as we looked onward into the crowd of thousands of devotees. It was during Maha Shivatri a celebration of the Hindu gods and honoring of Lord Shiva. Of course, there were people from all over India coming to show their regards to Lord Shiva. The Kumbha Mela had just finished as well, and many Saddhus and devotees migrated to the city of Varanasi, the city of Shiva, to continue the prayers and celebration of life.

I'm sharing a bit about devotion and worship because it has played an interesting role in my life. Originally, I was an atheist as a youth, and then finding myself in awe of something that felt so good yet did not understand what was taking place. Knowing that if I spent an hour a day in awareness of the energies, my days would be simply better. I accept that I am in reverence and relationship to an energy that is omnipresent, an energy that is auspiciously in the air in the elements. One story that I've come to appreciate was shared by a Babaji, he called himself Ruddrock. Ruddrock is the seed that is worn on malas, a holy bead. Regardless of his name, he was a friend to me and offered me some chillum and some tea, I could see that he was dressed up and playing his role, I was entertaining his show. Now, just to paint the picture, there were hundreds if not thousands of Saddhus all camped out along the ghats of the Ganges River, the holy river of the Hindus. You could start at the beginning of the ghat and start to see the Maha Shivatri taking place. The deeper you walked, the more people and Saddhus you would encounter. Now there are many types of Babas and Saddhus, mostly, the Naga Babas naked and covered in ash. You could approach different camps, some Babas calling at you to come sip tea and smoke chillum, some Babas you even have to watch out for, and some are also just dressed up and putting on a show.

So, after walking around the ghats, I visited the same Baba to start a friendship, smoke chillum, have some tea, and enjoy the presence of the colorful environment, and of course, the muddy yet beautiful Ganges River. One day, Ruddrock started to talk to me about Shiva. He said, "Shiva is your papa, Saraswathi and Lakshmi are your mothers, all the gods are your uncles and aunties, your family." Ruddrock said, "The more time you spend with your papa, and your family the better your relationship will be." Seems that rings true, even human to human the more time we spend with our mother, the closer we will be. When we meet a new friend, we must actively make time to build that relationship. If you want to get to know yourself, you must actively be building an inner relationship getting to know your inner constructs such as your bones, flesh, blood, etc. I'll never forget that day as I left that ghat and Ruddrock. I began to view all this devotion differently. I saw that everyone was singing to Shiva, they were asking for his presence to be with them as they were giving their attention to him, a strong bond.

It was in the city of Shiva. I embraced myself as a spiritual devotee, although I'm not Hindu, Buddhist, Christian, or Muslim. I see the reasons for which we go to pray and why we take time out of our days or weeks to go and spend quality time with whatever energies or spirits bring us comfort. However, you see or feel something that offers you joy. That could be the self, in some views, the higher power that one may feel is emitted from oneself to honor oneself and to worship oneself. There's nothing wrong with that. In fact, it seems that was a very common thing to do. Some believe that we are the gods, we are the kings and queens. With a healthy ego, I could support those individuals, some sects of Rastafari believe that there is no higher power and that the best work you can do is to serve yourself, to eat ital meals, veggies, and fruits, and to be free in our expression. To know that Jah is in all things and when we breathe, we are with Jah. Jah is within us. So, whether you believe in Allah, Jah, Christ, Tonkashila, Voodoo, Ram, Oden, energy, or yourself – you can always choose to spend time building a healthy relationship.

It appears to me that in some African and Asian countries I've visited, there is more of a rawness in devotion. A more vocalized delivery and possibly even more persistent action, could this be because they are uncaring about what people think? Maybe they are putting on extra for an outsider to witness, or perhaps they are just in their element of suffering and calling for help. They are focused on their relationship with how they see a higher power and the effects it has in their daily lives. In the USA today, it appears that we have lost sight of a lot of our rituals, through oppression and assimilation. Our connection to nature seems to have been pushed farther away, now having to go to nature parks or national parks, this is all over the world, preserves and world heritage sites, recognized and protected by the governments. It appears that it was not even our choice like we did not mean to push ourselves away from our ancestors and our relationship to nature, higher powers, and even ourselves. It looks like the system, at large, has crafted an amazing maze of choices. The wildest aspect of this is that they left the choice up to you. Mostly, besides our four races of Indigenous families, who were made to learn English, assimilate into Christianity, and live in the white man's world, a global epidemic. American Indians were not "legally" allowed ceremonies or way of life until just recently in the 60s and 70s. They began to allow the people who lived here first to pray as they once did. Yet even on the tribal lands, we still have indigenous choosing church over ceremony. Again, appearing as a result of our oppressor. We all have big choices in our lives. If it rings true to you, that your environment plays a large part in who you are. Once you understand the food you eat and the information you ingest, it will become more obvious to you what and where you will go.

It seems that the naming game and the world of manmade dualities have enhanced the difficulty of accepting and prolonged the journey through the maze of finding ourselves. There's just so much information and so much propaganda. Everywhere I go, I feel like the conversations are the same.

There seems to be a puzzle that many people are trying to understand, it appears to me that the plan is working out. We may be fully happy being a part of the system, we may feel grounded and connected to the constructs of the manmade world. In that case, there's not much to do, maybe just enjoy the creation of man and stop complaining? It seems the reality of the manmade world in contrast to the world of nature is drastically different. The choice is up to each individual, at this point in my life, I have accepted the number of resources it has taken and will continue to take to support such a mass amount of consumption and material gain. The industry has been taking from the Earth and vomiting the waste and excess into our lands, oceans, rivers, and sky. Can one really be happy knowing all that has been put into this world? Coming away from the singularity of nature, arriving at the polarity of city and forest? Wi-Fi connection or connection to self?

So, the big question in chapter one is are we able to sit still anymore? Are we able to appreciate Earth in her stillness? Is it possible to imagine a world where we have our garden and our simple homestead, without the need to go shopping for the latest apparel? Would we still feel beautiful if we lived in the opposite of the manmade constructs, the forest? Would beauty be as important if we all lived in the forest? Maybe the ideas around beauty and social norms would shift. These are just some simple questions that come to mind as we explore the duality of two different walks. Is it realistic to continue as we have since the industrial time? Does our Earth have the capacity to manage the countries that are still building industry and infrastructure, while managing the level of consumption and waste?

I'm a supporter of anyone's choice, I may offer some advice or simply education. If we know our body is a small universe, we can see that one can only manage so much before one of our organs or inner planets gets out of harmony and then creates a whole domino effect. Sooner than later our organs and energy reservoirs begin to drain, our meridians do not flow as strong, and slowly we become slow and stagnant, as we all are in preparation for death. It seems realistic to look at our solar system and Earth the same way we would investigate the human body. I know just based on recent documentaries and even news that the scientists are becoming worried, and the ones who helped us to get this far in our human advancements are working now to figure out new ways to produce similar products with new more sustainable ways.

I'd really like to think that love is not lost in the human heart, the home of our spirit, our connection to our ancestors, and the antenna to receive frequency and vibrations from our elements and surroundings. I'd like to believe that the love will outweigh the hate. It appears in the masses there's a lack of feeling for our oceans, rivers, lakes, and underground water. In all indigenous communities I've been around, they have a name for the spirit of water. I'll use the Bon Buddhist naming game. The Naga is the spirit of the water. Being raised by the water Naga, we would go there often to spend time, rest, play, hydrate, and swim. My father and I would build alters or shrines to show our appreciation to the spirits. As a child, I thought the world consisted of clean water like this. It was not till I was a young adult that and started to get out into the world and saw the

15

contamination firsthand. Now after visiting four to five of the seven continents, I'd say that there is a mass mismanagement of waste and contamination of our waters. I'm sure most of us know that already, but to witness some of this stuff firsthand makes your heart heavy. I'm very grateful to hear about some of the latest ideas to help manage the trash and the pollution that is affecting not only the Earth and water but our elemental family is compromised and directly impacted people in larger cases than we have seen in many generations. In the USA today, you may never know the hardship that people go through. I feel I have a responsibility to at least speak this information into the air.

Being a person of love, it is a duty to share. I do not travel for vacation; I travel to listen to people and their needs as well as my own. I travel to submerge into a sensation that I hope to extend to the reader. Love is to work through difficulty together. Love is to believe in one another. I want to believe in them or they, the ones pushing the constructs of a manmade world. I want to know that they are not so full of hate, that they are human still, and that they are connected to their spirits and their hearts.

May their dualities find a balance, and may their hearts feel connected to their spirit. May the hate or lack of empathy be laid to rest. May they come back into singularity, or even better rest and ground into the dualities of nature, asking to be graced by the greatest reception. May we be connected to the Earth and the sky and may we see the birth of light in our vision.

To the ones who lack the feeling of love, may this space find you.

Chapter Two
Hope

Hope is a word that I've heard some people say they don't resonate with. Hope to me is almost a feeling that comes from recognizing the beauty of something so fantastic that it naturally shifts your perspective from doubt or sadness to a sense of joy and grander awareness. In my personal experience, hope enters my mind even when completing a large project such as building a house or a business from the ground up. At times, it is easy to feel despair and a lack of support, and you can find yourself on the floor looking up at the world asking yourself how in the world am I going to get this done? Or even shifting from depression to happiness. I think many stories along our historical timeline have given a lot of people hope or at least a comforting feeling.

Dr. Martin Luther King Jr. was a revolutionary speaker and leader in a movement, his speech and his ability to deliver messages comforted so many people. We saw a shift happen as the movement for equal rights and justice for people of color grew. We are still witnessing Dr. King's dream extend into present-day America. An amplitude of energy has been expressed by young people in America of all colors standing up for people of color and even apologizing for their ancestors' actions and the cruelty they imparted to their fellow human beings. I think it is so beautiful for a human being to identify aspects of embarrassment or shame, to ask the creator for forgiveness and to speak it out loud, to let it be known that they have been hurting inside or have felt a sense of hate and kept it all balled up. It is also beautiful for a person to accept apologies when a human being is opening up a space for inner and outer healing, becoming vulnerable in their emotions. What a gift it is to witness and also comfort them and to say that even if forgiveness is not there, there always is an appreciation and gratitude to express such deep feelings.

The global trauma is so deep and feels so heavy. I think that part of the reason for writing this book is to air out some of this toxic and undeniable past. It is easy to wallow in our sadness, victimize ourselves in our bodies, and constantly shame the self for doing or not doing something that could have helped or possibly shifted that scenario. In some situations, it seems that our actions can change an outcome. However, looking back into history, we can see a dominating force spreading throughout the world. A power, hungry for control and rule. Guns play a massive role in our global history, the ones with the guns, of course, pull the trigger, and the ones without get out of the way. It seems that within the last 400 years, the globe was dominated by indigenous life, all the way from Australian bushmen, to European Pegan, indigenous Tibetans, the tribes of Africa and South America, and all of Turtle Island, which some say is the entire continent from chili to Alaska. The globe was natural, the people were natural, and the original naming game was active, all indigenous people I have spoken to have told me of creation stories, or great migrations. They have told me the names of their gods, their spirits, their elements, and their love.

This is an era of time that I have romanced for the majority of my life and even felt like a stranger in the world we are living in today. In a way, we can be grateful for a universal language that can be spoken globally, and definitely made traveling easier for me being only an English speaker, unfortunately. However, this evidence reveals that whoever started spreading English, and the culture of English, may have carried the most guns and implemented their ways of power throughout the world. Yes, indeed that is a strong statement to make. It is not even a certain statement; I'm just looking into the global evidence that I've witnessed. Part of the evidence that is very present now is that the United States, the most recent massive land mass that was colonized is home to more guns than I've ever seen. In the majority of the countries I visited only military personnel, and officers carry guns, you don't see many toy guns even. Part of the peace and harmony you feel in these countries. Even though the media, portray Africa and India, South America as dangerous places, it seems that the USA today has more violence, gang activity, mass shootings, and racial tension than anywhere in the world I've been. Looking a bit more dangerous?

The evidence we observed suggests that the true "WHITES," the white supremacists, at the beginning of the takeover of this beautiful country, were the majority of the so-called founding fathers of this new world, are slowly starting to look like the ones who were part of this planned genocide and blanketing over our old traditional ways of life. The ones who brought guns and many mechanisms of disruption to the inhabitants of Turtle Island. The ones who paid others to go "red skinning," the ones who tried to completely wipe out the original genes of our tribes all 600 plus of them. That's just in North America. After years of bloodshed and too many deaths, our First Nation people were moved onto the reservation, literally had their livelihood, culture, and traditions stolen, their lands stolen, taken from the WHITES. Just imagine all global tribes! Just how many clans were removed from their inhabitants and placed into an outlined environment. I've found myself disgusted with this history and upset that our school systems do not talk about it from the perspective of our indigenous family. The books would read a lot differently if Crazy Horse, Sitting Bull, Black Elk, and our real fathers of this land wrote the books. It saddens me that most of our youth grow up today singing an anthem that was sung after a genocide. I have never sung that song and still today as an adult, I will respectably take a knee.

I feel that it is not too late to change the history books, especially those that are handed out in school. That history is still unfolding, and it could be a great benefit to go to the people who were affected directly, the people who were firsthand told by their grandparents about the experience and the hardship they went through as Natives and Africans. Just going to a reservation, you will hear stories if you listen, you will learn about a feeling that is still present in the land and the people who carry the wounds of their ancestors, from the hands of the oppressors. You will hear first-hand the difficulties of drugs and alcohol, the stories that my brothers share about their brothers and family members, and the reasons why we all gather around the sacred tree every year to pray for our sick and wounded relatives. The first time I went to the reservation. I went with my Sundance uncle, and me drove up to Wounded Knee South Dakota to the Tasunke Witko Sundance, directly to the house of the Sundance Chief, Gerald Ice, Tasunke Witco himself meaning Crazy Horse, a direct bloodline of the Crazy Horse family. At his side was another chief, a direct bloodline of Black Elk. It was a humbling moment in my life to be in the presence of such men. At times I did not know what to say or how to act. Most of the time I just did as I was told and followed my uncle around.

Before going to the wounded knee, I had a dream that I was at a Sundance, I was learning what it was to be at Sundance. In my dream, I saw a man pierced to a tree, he had no tent and slept on the ground. I also saw different people in different places pierced to different trees. My dream was all over the place, it was a look into what I had only heard about. After seeing it in my dream, I was even more humbled to arrive at the grounds of Sundance that was to take place in one month. It became very clear to my uncle and me that we needed to step up if we wanted to see the Sundance happen. At a Sundance, you have many roles, and many people to fill those shoes. There are sponsors, supporters, helpers, cooks, builders, firekeepers, Sundancers, singers, leaders, and even more unseen aspects. We build an arbor with a center pole, that center pole is the sacred tree that we pierce and pray to, the component that connects the Earth WAKAN MAKHA to the sky peoples WAKAN SKAN. The sacred and holy networks of Earth and sky spirits. Different tribes build their arbors and pierce in different fashions. However, all Sundances consist of certain roles, as we all need to be present to make it whole, or holy.

I guess I'm sharing this story not only to educate individuals who are not familiar with the native way of life let alone Sundance, one of 7 ceremonies, but to also share a story about hope. Sundance is a four-day ceremony that consists of fasting from food and water and praying and piercing throughout the four days. There is singing and drumming that fuels the dancers to keep praying, asking the creator to help us, the supporters are there to hold space for dancers as the days go on, and on. Sometimes dancers start to fall due to exhaustion. I've witnessed people die in these ceremonies. I'm also sharing this story because not only is it important to talk about the original "church" of this land but also to look at aspects of hope.

The day that Uncle and I verbally affirmed to Chief that we were here to help get the arbor built, even though the helping hands were few, we stepped up on that day. It was a day of hope. As we knew the time was now. His eyes teared up you could feel his sincerity and trust as we all took a moment of silence to take in what had been said and agreed upon. After that morning, we went to work, days of fetching timbers and bows, digging and tamping, and hammering. Days turned into weeks and after almost a month of hard work, we could stand back and look at the beautiful structure we had built. The Sundance took place and I think the most satisfying part for me was to see the Chief Tasunke Witco in his full traditional dress move around the arbor, dancing for his people, his land, and his ancestors for Crazy Horse.

This is a story about how hope turned into a reality. Now, I'll agree that hope with no action is like shooting at a target that isn't there. If you have no aim, then what is there to hope for? It's kind of like prayer, do you believe that you can just get down on your knees and pray to God, this idea that there is a higher being than you and that he will bestow upon you? I've never been one to believe in this idea, I only began praying after going to Sundance. I'd never had a great relationship with God or prayer, as the church was pushed on me. Every time I'd go, I felt like a reject and a sinner, I actually decided I liked being a reject and felt fine to sin in the eyes of their god. For me, I was giving myself life by exploring so many new ideas and concepts. Karma was once prescribed to me as habitual habit, so it seems that you are the creator of your reality if you like that definition of karma – you can look deeper into what that means to you. I have learned to view karma in that sense, it means that you take full accountability for your reality because your actions are creating it. I also like this idea of karma because it somewhat takes this idea of higher power out of the picture, if that helps you feel better about hope and prayer.

I've really embraced prayer since I started Sundancing, now being a carrier of prayers for my family and people who ask me to carry their prayers to the center pole. Anyone wise at a Sundance will say to you, the four days in here are the easiest days of the year, the ceremony is a 365-day-long prayer, until you come back to the center pole, back to your fasting, back to being present with the creator, back to yourself. Those 361 days you will be challenged by the temptations of Whiteman's world, the world of addiction, consumption, and many avenues to walk, the world you were born into. You can imagine how pure life can be in the arbor, fasting from everything, well besides some tobacco, laughter, sleep, and prayer.

It feels good to be telling a story about a very real and important aspect of our natural life, our original ceremony, and to also be speaking about hope, an aspect of life that some say is lost or others don't like to use. I guess I'm writing about hope because I'm watching my actions affect my communities, and I'm watching my communities affect me. The things that I once saw in my mind materialize through hard work and devotion. I can start to see reality looking like I had hoped, how I see my life in my mind. I can rest in a space of gratitude simply because I'm choosing to see life in love. Self-love creates gratitude and gratitude creates bliss and true rest, the rest of the mind and the body. Hope may be useless without action, action may have no purpose without reason, and reason needs a purpose. It appears to me that whether or not there is a higher power, there is a choice to be proactive to co-create our reality.

Your emotions may mold your face, which then wears its shame around for weeks. The power of a single emotion or feeling can be strong, it can elevate us to the heights of understanding and can leave us feeling crushed like tiny particles of rock longing for its original shape. That is why prayer and meditation have become very important in my life. After 15 years of meditation and visualization, seeing and affirming the self I want to be, I can allow myself to rest in a space of ease. Not pressuring myself to meditate an hour a day, but to be in a space of bliss and awareness of my 15 years of awareness building. I can relish in my habitual practices and own my karma.

Building spiritual awareness is kind of like building a house. First off, you need to have a solid foundation, you need to anchor yourself or your house to your foundation so that when a power surge or strong winds come through your body or your house, it won't be hindered. It's important to get to know your walls, get to know the substance of which your insides reside, and take shelter. As we stated earlier, our bones are the constructs of the human body, similar to studs in a wall. We want to affirm the strength and the longevity of our bones. In building body awareness, we want to examine our energy channels that are similar to the electrical wires in your house that allow power to travel from one outlet to the other, to turn on a light switch. Our body consists of 13 main channels or meridians, which are responsible for moving and transferring energy to our organs and parts of our body. The house is the body, behind the wall or the skin is the complex inner standings of the inner blueprints. Yet that we have lived so long without giving time to look into what is there. Only a builder knows what is hidden in the walls and the roof of the structure, similar to a yogi who has spent years of his or her life looking into the finer aspects of the human blueprint.

It has been quite fun to be building my spiritual body and being, alongside building my physical home, my house of spirit. I've thought at times I could write a whole book on the similarities and crossroads of becoming aware of the constructs of building physically and spiritually, which could be seen as the same. Any builder knows the feeling of looking at a picture or seeing something in their mind and then being able to materialize it. It is one of the most satisfying aspects of my life I've experienced. A funny component of myself is that after ten years of building on my home, finding comforts on my couch, having flush toilets and hot water, and amenities that I should and do take full advantage of. I still have a very loud voice that echoes in my mind. To go to the mountain, to leave behind the comforts. Nature calls to me and comforts me in many ways, it always has. It seems that this is also where hope comes up for me due to the inspiring stories of great yogis and sages, adepts who spent 12 to 20 years in the mountains learning the constructs of nature and nature of self and coming out with what most of us would call magical abilities – some call siddhis, yogic success.

I guess that is where the aspect of hope is present in my head and could be in yours too. For example, before I built my house, I'd hoped I could build one as a teenager, I imagined it and felt excited about the idea. The outcome was the inspiration, and the hope came from the curiosity of what if. I've been dialoguing with this call to nature for as long as I can remember, there is such a curiosity there, there is a romanticized image of self, and there's a curiosity about our human potential. Do you ever wonder if this is it? This life that we are living, even your dreamiest job or perfect relationship, is this it? Do I stand alone in the feeling that there is something inside a human being that when accessed is activated?

My curiosity has already led me down the rabbit hole, deep enough to say I believe in miracles or magic. I mean the fact that we are living in a solar system on a planet that inhabits life due to the perfect distance of space to this massive ball of fire we call the sun, to be situated between other planets that may or may not affect our rotation and our position in our solar system. In quantum harmonics, this reflects the golden mean ratio. We can see the golden mean ratio in all aspects of life, it is a large aspect of curiosity to go deeper into our inner and outer standings. It is easy to get caught up in a cycle of complaining about how the world is not perfect and how unsatisfying things may be, however, when you take a deep breath and feel your body expanding and contracting as you inhale and exhale, your heart pumping blood in a beat a rhythm – you feel the miracle of nature.

Even now if you are inspired to put the book down and take some moments with yourself to just feel.

Inner Smile

Part 1.

- Invite long deep breathing. Breathe into your navel and even into your sex organ/root chakra/VMA. Allow your breath to travel throughout the body. Imagine your body expanding as you inhale, contracting as you exhale. Slow the breath. See if you can inhale for a duration of 20 seconds, hold your breath for 20 seconds, and slowly exhale for 20 seconds. If possible, slowly let your breath out and let go of things that do not serve you. As you inhale, invite some positive feelings into your body. I like to breathe in the qualities of JOLKA. **JOLKA** stands for **joy, openness, love, kindness, and awareness,**

Part 2.

- Open the pores of your skin. Imagine your skin as a sponge absorbing the surrounding space and whatever qualities you are consciously inhaling. As you hold your breath affirm the sensation growing in your body. For fun, imagine your heart smiling gently. Imagine your happiest feeling when you are physically smiling. Allow that feeling to fill your heart. Allow your other organs the same access. With your imagination and affirmation, see your organs happy and healthy. Take time to breathe into each organ. If this feeling is resonating in your heart, you can invite this gentle smile to fill your entire body from head to toe. Allow your lips to smile, and feel a sense of awe in your body. Allow yourself to rest in this inner yoga posture.

This meditation is good for General health, organ health, relaxation, and emotional balance and much more.

"The feeling of a true smile could be monumental in all moments."

In Chinese medicine, our organs are said to play a large role in our emotional self. We can even look at our emotions to see what may be happening on the inside with our organ function, organ health can also reflect our emotional status. It seems that it would be important to get to know our organs just as well or even better than our bones. Our organs really are a great example of the golden mean ratio, the whole human body is a working and living miracle. Fragile yet durable, known yet lost, the human being ranges from the adept yogi in the caves that have not ingested food or water in years, to the human being that is supported by machines and modern comforts. One of the hardest parts about being a human is recognizing that we are all born with differences that shape who we are. Some births are very simple and effortless while some are intense and of course, end in sadness and miscarriage.

It seems that from the moment our father's sperm enters our mother's ovaries, our imprinting begins. There is a great study that my elder has spent many years of her life looking into pre-natal and post-natal imprinting. It seems that this could be a massive topic to look into regarding the next

400 years as we are procreating in a time of such external focus, and 400 years of generational trauma imprinting. The simple life of sitting on your porch with no Wi-Fi chewing on a stick, and tapping your foot, is something of the past mostly, to experience that you will have to go looking for it. I'm pretty sure once you get there you won't be taping long. I'd say as young adults today, we should take some real time to think about how we want to conceive babies and also where and how we will raise them. I hear a lot of people say they don't want to give birth to babies in this climate of complexity. I can see why that is felt. However, I feel so much hope for humanity and by that, I mean, I'm very curious about what I'll see in this lifetime. I support the believers, the ones who think that we can clean up our Earth, act better for our children, end the war, and find better ways of creating resources. Most wars start from auguring over resources or fighting for lands, so yeah, I'd say it's a lot to hope for. However, I'd rather take some action and speak up about some topics I just can't look away from. Even if no one cares to listen or read, I'm still curious enough. I still have hope that I'm not the only one thinking these thoughts. I hope I'm not the only one who is feeling empathy for our extended families in countries where food and clean water are not as available. I hope I'm not the only one who is going to take time to prepare before procreating.

I think the reason why some people don't like the idea of hope is because it can go on and on just as I did there, hoping for this and that. When in fact we simply need action, ideas, and plans; belief and hope will only get us so far. Dr. King believed in his movement and his people did too, he gave his life to his cause. People were hoping for a man like Mr. King, people who believed in him. He offered hope and became the action, he was the voice, he was the dream. He spoke out for something bigger than himself. A reality that gave hope for the next 400 years that we may love each other as one, that we may celebrate all lives, that we may help one another, that we may see eye to eye. We extend our gratuity to these activists, saints, leaders, and chiefs – to the true spokesmen of the people, to the original roots that have helped so many people grow taller and stronger.

Now, I'm not even sure how to vocalize what I'm seeing in the world. There is a sadness in my being after experiencing the world. I don't want it to eat me up and depress me. I've always believed we are alchemists, transmitters of energies, ingesting others' emotions and exhaling positive vibrations, positive words, laughter, and light. I guess if I look into this more, I've taken trauma stories from five different continents, connected with five groups of people, and felt, and witnessed their lives. I've taken that with me, I still see the faces of poverty, and I still remember the trash slums from trips ten years ago. Every time I'm in the ghetto or slum I can sense a feeling of peace and acceptance or at least have memories of smiling with friends. Alchemizing all these experiences into a space of surrender is healthy for me to do because the chance of global change is slim. I guess I have hope and believe it is possible. So, I wonder what we as people want to do in our lifetime, if we feel there's a reason for a revolution, and if we feel that this has been enough. We the people are the shapers of our history.

The idea of a revolution in the USA is a scary thought because there are so many guns and violence and there seems to be a large group of people who lack feeling and can kill and take life without thinking twice. If a revolution were to happen in the USA, I think it would be a quiet one. One way would be people leaving the cities, leaving the system, showing the government that we do not need many aspects they offer, and showing the corporations that we are sustaining on our own. The funny thing about this is that we would be going back to the village style where we build all of our homes close by, we grow all of our foods close by, etc. On the other hand, the people living in the village now are possibly tired of it and want to move to the cities and live in the Westernized comforts. This is where I start to let go of any outcome and settle back into the thoughts of everything is as it is, the historical timeline has happened and left us all slightly lost or grasping at things we don't have.

It seems that there are some very silly rules in place, like the system wants us to keep consuming so that their business can continue. That is why I ask the question, is it time to revolt, to recognize that it is like a mother who will not let the child be himself? Is the system nursing us along like a helicopter parent? Constantly bringing us new suggestions new drugs, new cars, new versions, new thoughts that bring us even farther away from that good old simple life. As I write this book, I'm thinking about the reasons why revolution is due again. For most of my life, I've listened to people upset at the system. I've heard a lot of people talk about a reset. Is it time for land to be simply land, unowned yet again, for people to just be sovereign in their person, their personal connection to self and nature. A taking away of boundary that was placed on the land and us as an outline and possibly to control. The revolution would be hard on many people and when I think about it, I think many people would not be interested in going off the grid back to the village, and back to working the fields. If we really look into this life, we can see the amount of work and action it will take to be sufficient. It may look like a division of land and people, some stepping out of the system, some staying in. Realistically, Its hard to really see how anything can happen, the pit is just so deep that the bottom is almost impossible to see. Will take some major actions.

I think technology can rescue us, and I have hope for our scientists. I don't believe all people of power operate from hate. I have a feeling that many people are actively working on new ways to move forward while considering the Earth and its inhabitants.

I'll just drop one more food for thought here before chapter two ends. Both the Hindu and Native American philosophies, if I'm not mistaken, have a similar view on cycles and change. In both cultures and beliefs, they look to the four-legged cow in Hinduism, and buffalo in the native way of life, both are saying that each leg represents a time and an experience as the animal gets older, the legs begin to fall off as well as the hair. Some people are saying that there is only one leg left and little hair – that would mean we are arriving at the end of the cycle. To be fully honest, I've heard so many things in my life I can entertain it all and support people as I see it offers them joy, but the majority of the things people say, I call them hippie myths, passed down information, read or heard, known but not understood. Until I feel something, I'll remain in a space of gratitude and appreciation for my sights – for my sight has been blessed with beauty. The older I get, the less I feel the need to entertain this grand show and just go with the feeling and sensation that has been growing for over a decade now.

Chapter Three
Oral Traditions

The Hopi prophecy is a prolific storyline, revealing an immense amount of development and change. Human exploration may or may not have to do with the progression of their projection of what may come to pass or what we are already seeing. There is a film with no words, I'm unable to recall the name. The film portrays the timeline of creation and destruction, taking you on a journey of naturally occurring events. The time of coal and rail road's built, the time of early America becoming a western world. It shows the building of skyscrapers, the building of roads, and bridges, and the number of cars produced. The businesses in the streets of New York City, the industries that our mining our Earth, the fossil fuels escaping into the air, the heat of fire, and the power of water. It reveals climate change, an intensification of elements, it takes you to the end of a great period when things become still, and nature prevails once again.

It seems that in every cycle of our Earth, there is a massive shift that is usually elemental. Looking into the Earth's timeline, we can see that in the beginning the Earth was covered in water, there was little to no life, oxygen was created by single-cell organisms, and after the oceans build nutrients and diversity of different elements, small life started to move about. Our Earth has been through so much as we have seen land masses form from underwater volcanic activity, seems that fire, water, air, and Earth have always been a massive part of the Earth's creation story. That's common knowledge in most discussions. It is fascinating to look at the process of land and life growing. It is amazing to think about a mountain growing or shrinking. There are young mountains and old mountains. Similar to people, we grow as youth and as we age, we hunch over and sometimes literally shrink.

The Earth has been a landscape of water, fire, ice, and possible things we do not even know about as science can only reveal or let alone guess what has happened. It's not like any of us lived to see the ice age or witnessed the meteors that wiped out dinosaurs. Currently, I hear people conspiring about the moon being fake, the Earth being flat, and our timeline being a made-up story. Being open to these ideas is a good thing, absolutes are dangerous. To think something is true fully may have consequences, more so mental limitations. Whatever lends people happiness is it. Honoring each other's thoughts and processes is a gift to give to another, as I said, I've heard it all at this point, I don't even quarrel in debates, I support other's thoughts and continue with mine. As stated, what we ingest is what we will become. That's just my philosophy, maybe you can think of another thought and ingest their teachings and remain in your truth. I'd say that is the strength and openness of a spiritual being. To be able to listen and witness but not take on other's story. For what brings one happiness may bring another distress.

I find gratitude in my natural encounters as I'm sure you do as well. Our spiritual discernment will grow with the many things and people we navigate throughout life. I've been graced by the presence of Rinpoche, medicine men, Voodoo priests, and most importantly, nature. For nature has no words, nature can only lend you a feeling, an insight into the unspoken. The direction I've received from my teachers and elders, the practices that were prescribed to me, are tools to help one engage with nature and elements more. For in nature, there is color, color is everywhere we look; in nature, there is sound and a humming frequency, similar to many modern-day meditations where people chant 'Om' and 'Ah.' I like to look back to our oldest people, the ones who did not have a language yet because they were still discovering sound. They were organically listening and reflecting on the sounds they heard. Maybe a feeling they felt delivered a sound, such as 'Ah,' to me 'Ah' is a sound of resting or relaxing after a hard day of work. There are irritable sounds we make today like shouting in pain, and sounds of discomfort.

The mind is an amazing mode of transportation. We can close our eyes and see ourselves in a completely different time and environment. It is very fun to visit someone far away from you. Closing your eyes and projecting your energy into a room or a space, seeing different people, possibly people you don't even know. Sometimes I like to visit jails and prisons, say a quiet hello to my brothers locked up, and offer a gentle smile. Even if they do not feel or know that you are visiting them, you are affirming to yourself that you are with them. I often do this when I'm traveling. I close my eyes and see myself sitting at my altar in my home, viewing the garden, and saying hello to the fish. Instead of using Facetime to connect, we once would connect through spirit time. Listening to a call and responding accordingly.

It seems that this is an inherent practice that all people are practicing and even originate from. Even when we think about who we are becoming, we are closing our eyes and looking into our future moments, as we prepare to give a talk or play music. You can see yourself there, it's part of becoming comfortable as you are making ready for a display. The mind is the mode of creation, birthing your thoughts and wants into reality. Someone told me energy is information, and that is why I allow only traditional teaching into my space or downloads from nature. If I allowed the hype and the diversity of spirituality today, I think I'd feel lost. I'd be still looking for something to really ground me, allow me to be in peace, in harmony, and acceptance of myself. This is why I feel the importance of actively going to a direct lineage or finding a teacher who has passed down the practices, songs, and information from a predecessor. Some oral traditions have been passed down for hundreds, if not thousands of years. There has been true evidence that these ways of life are strong medicine. In all oral traditions, I've learned about a mythical and magical aspect to take time with. The native Americans talk about shape-shifting into animals, placing their consciousness into another being, and calling upon great spirits to come to assist them with healing, I could go on about the stories I hear at the reservation, and things I've personally witnessed. However, the invitation is there for you to go and get a look for yourself, when you go don't be a stranger, introduce yourself, and tell the people you encounter why you are there, that you are coming home, coming to listen. Part of my understanding of Sundance's prophecy is that all people will come back to the center pole to pray, that Sundance is for the yellow man, the black man, the white man, and of course, the Redman. All human beings come back to the center pole to listen to nature, Tunkashila Father of creation speaks to us as human beings. May it be a remembrance of magical lineages, as the old ways are still resonating and building presently.

In indigenous Buddhist tradition, the stories are similar, the carrier of nature and practice will be sustained in remote locations for long periods. Ancient yogis Exploring the universe from the cave, I've heard beautiful stories of these adepts of nature, achieving fantastic success, flying, whether that's physically or energetically, being seen in two different places at once, projecting light into a room, and changing an atmosphere. I've heard of Monks/Llamas who have ingested so much light that they are actually imitating a shine of light. Many of these traditional practices are passed down and hidden away for many reasons. One big reason is that they are powerful and a human being who is not used to this engagement, may go into confusion, inflated ego, and possibly go crazy. It seems that in the '90s and early 2000s, teachers from Nepal, Tibet, and India started to come to Western countries to spread these teachings. Some teachers have even been ridiculed for sharing too much of their traditions. On the other hand, some holders of lineage do not welcome outsiders without invite and may keep their practices to themselves.

I respect this position; it is their oral tradition passed down by the old people who found it originally. That is the beauty of oral tradition and the difference between going to a breath workshop or going to a monastery or a Sundance. Though I'm grateful for the courage and openness that spiritual leaders grow through to share something that changed their lives and if it is enmeshed in their flesh, they are impacting many lives. That to me is a small miracle, it may not sound as cool as flying or bi-locating yourself to new destinations but is possibly more beautiful because it spreads energy and awareness, that some adepts kept to their selves, rightfully chosen.

In Pagan culture, you hear of the magic and the stories of Oden and Thor. You read about magical beings. Many Pagans would use mushrooms to connect deeper with nature and to communicate with the spirits. There are also accords of sages and hermits that dwelled deep in the forest and would speak to the animals and relay messages to the people. It seems that they too would become so close with animals and nature that they could extend their energy to another creature such as a bird and see from their view. When I was a child, I used to play with that exact idea, I called it the bird's eye view. I would see a bird flying over me and I would think about how high they were and what they were looking down upon. I'd allow myself to feel the bird, to imagine myself in the sky. In my mind, I was seeing a vast landscape of desert, looking down on the small details on the ground. Nowadays, I find myself doing this with airplanes. I'll imagine who is on the plane, what they are doing, where they are going, and what they are seeing as they look out the window, do they see me? Sometimes I imagine I am seeing them.

In West Africa, I've heard miracle stories of the Israelites migrating to Ghana, the promise land they say. My senior priest told me the story of his ancestors as they carried their voodoo spirits.

29

Voodoo meaning spirits of nature, many spirits they carried with them from Israel through Kemet and the heart of Africa until they reached the oceans of West Africa. Kwame told me that when his ancestors got to Volta Lake, a very large body of water that borders very close to Togo, their final destination point. The voodoos/spirits formed a way of crossing the water, creating a bridge to pass safely over the lake. Kwame showed me where his forefathers built the Shine house for the specific spirit that helped them cross the lake. He also spoke of the power of African spirits, stating that they are some of the strongest spirits. The healing work that I heard about was just as profound as the medicine men back home and the stories that I heard from my friends and family about up-close experiences with living saints and adepts of human beings.

The reason why I appreciate all indigenous traditions is that it seems that they are working directly with the spirits of nature. They may have different names for these spirits and sing them different songs, to celebrate them or ask them to dinner or for assistance. It seems that all Indigenous peoples prepare food for their ancestors and the spirits they are working with, dressing their best and cooking the most organic and beautiful meals, we cook for them first, and we offer food and drink to our great spiritual family. We are asking nature to bless our food and our drinks. All my elders and indigenous teachers state very clearly to not mess around with these teachings for they should only be used to do healing work. As you know the mind is powerful and can manifest so much, without healthy thoughts and practices, it will be easy to slip into a space of distress and jealousy. Instead of sending healing energy, you will start emitting your feelings. Therefore, all true medicine people keep clean, they stick to the protocols that were passed down to them, sing the songs that are specific to different spirits and prayers, and never question the power of the great spirit.

It's also very interesting to look into the aspects of our ancient ancestors in how they worked with plant medicines and different minerals to engage with themselves and the spirits of nature. From South American ayahuasca ceremonies to North American Peyote meetings, to Pagan mushroom circles, to Tibetan and Indian soma. The great Padmasambhava or Guru Rinpoche of Bhutan and Tibet, was a saint, to say the least, he was a rebel of the monasteries in some texts. In some texts I read he would ingest an array of substances to invoke vision and sensation in his body. Guru Rinpoche's handprint is still left in solid stone in Bhutan. He is said to be the lotus-born master, birthed by the light and the elemental family similar to other stories of great saints appearing in human flesh. It seems that all of these beings were elemental adepts and in close relationship to the elemental family, contained by the birther of all life and space.

It is clear to me why when I look into the spiritual community I don't know how to engage. I don't want to come off as an egomaniac or a know-it-all because I simply don't know much at all. I come from the forest, from a community that has explored drugs and spirituality. I enjoy living in the mountains and engaging in simple things. When I get into the spiritual community, I am usually greeted with a salad bowl of words, the latest trending practices of breathwork and yoga, singing bowls, and crystals.

Veganism has seemed to be one of the biggest debates of the 20th century, seems that veganism has become part of the spiritual community. I've heard vegans state that meat is low vibrational and other passed comments that to some ears would just not be received, possibly laughed at. Since I appreciate Rastafari and can understand why they do not eat meat or animal products. I can see why, also looking at the environment of Rasta they are surrounded by fruits veggies, and fish, which could be a stereotype. I guess when I think of Rasta I see reggae on the beach under coconut trees, I see red, yellow, green, the colors of the mango, the color of the sun, the color of the trees, and the color of the blood of mankind.

If you're not a Rasta then it seems you may fall into the two main categories of vegans, not to categorize you. But to simply look deeper, we see there are people with actual eating disorders who cannot process dairy products, and then there are the people who choose not to eat meat or dairy products because they don't want to support the animal industry, and they just overall may feel better. I guess there are many types of vegans, diets, and trends that many dabble in. Every time I've been given vegan food, I feel amazing and it tastes delicious. I'm not against vegan eating and the majority of the time I'm striving to eat leafy greens and things I can grow in my garden.

I guess I'm talking about honoring each other. When you travel around the world or even the country, you will be offered all sorts of foods, of course. Depending on the context of eating, it may be respectful to yourself to not eat the food, and even acknowledge that the meat is very high vibrational and has even been blessed by great spirit. In voodoo and other indigenous ceremonies, we sacrifice an animal, and the animal does not go to waste. We prepare a plate for our ancestors and allow them to bless the food with their presence, and then we chop the food and digest the amazing meal from this amazing animal that gave its life to give us life. It seems that today it is very easy to offend one another, even looking into a relationship between two people, there can be discord simply because a diet or a religious belief does not align. To further that thought, it's the view that is passed down from family member to family member, generations of seeing food change in front of us. The story of each individual unfolds and crosses paths with another. My experience has opened me to their story and their family's ways of life, their habitual habits around food, and general intake, which is essentially the basis of growth. That could be one reason why we call certain people our soul mates, souls that find each other to offer a reflection and a difference of being. The meshing of two components often births new inner standings and can help us grow mentally and spiritually. These relationships are cherished by most people.

This brings up the thought that if we can be open to all walks of life and meet each other with a want to understand their history, and their trauma story, then we could say that we all look like soulmates. In some texts, it says that we all come from the same land mass and that at one point we were all one people. Many people believe that Africa is the home to the beginning of human life, looking back into the Earth's storyline we could imagine Africa, originally known as "Alkebulan." Meaning mother of mankind, possibly all inhabited on this one land mass Alkebulan. All land was connected, if you look at a map of the world, you can almost see where land masses fit together like perfect puzzle pieces. Pangea's separating of land, the shifting of tectonic plates and now, the 7 continents surrounded by water. Is this a look into why all indigenous communities similarly view nature? Evidence of a similar way of life. Could these ancient creation stories of Pangea or even Lumeria, and Mu possibly be the predecessor of Pangea? This study sheds light on the similarities of ceremonies and their relationship to the spirits or elements of the lands, assisting the lands to move and change to support a more diverse life. It seems so many things are downplayed. It appears that in history something powerful must be destroyed, we can use Jesus as an example. Of course, we all mostly know the heights that Christ reached, and we all know what happened in that story. If they repainted a picture of the story of Christ, why would they not do that in other areas of human history? Christ is said to be Jewish from Israel. In some texts, they say the Jews were darker skinned but not African, and the 12 original tribes of Judah were the true Israelites. The cross-pollination of Africans and Israelites is where my curiosity about Christ grows thicker. Viewing Christ as an ancient indigenous person connected to the spirits and self to the Earth and all Earthly relations. Then hearing stories Kwame my SR. Priest told me in Ghana about his Israelite ancestors carrying their voodoos with them. Voodoo spirits lend a hand to a singular Christ or even a community all holding hands together in connection and sharing the magical ability to alchemize atoms and particles. Could it be that this powerful character Jesus and the original tribes of light, of spirit. We can see that the swastika, voodoo, and King Nigghast, amongst many people or spirits even symbols and words of power and great fortune have been taken and then turned against us? In this creation story, I'd like to believe that Mount Zion was the promised land for the original Christ and the 12 tribes of Judah, tribes of light. Just as Other Tibetan clans would practice deep in the mountains. The rainbow spirits are scribed in text all around the world.

I'm no historian, I spent most of my time in history class messing around as I did in almost all my classes. I did enjoy the history fair and took it upon myself in middle school to produce projects about the trail of tears and the struggles of our Indigenous peoples, and also highlighted the evolution of basketball in context to the first black American basketball team and how we saw basketball go from the majority of lighter-skinned people whites to being dominated today by people of color. I guess I've always been distressed by the history written from the colonial perspective, and how I've been actively finding myself learning firsthand from the mouths of the people on the other end. Learning the history of the people and how they see the evolution of humanity. The more I travel and hear, the more and more it makes sense that, our indigenous people had a strong relationship with nature, which lent them a power, a power to connect with not something necessarily higher but maybe around and with them. The great networks of energy. Something that allowed them to live in harmony with nature.

So, was it that when an outsider stepped foot onto that land they didn't understand it, or was it a person from within the land that wanted to change it? There are many unanswered questions. Could it be someone, who began pushing us away from our original way of life and wanted to hide or suppress the richness of the life once lived and thought it would be clever to create a new story, painting it a different color.

This is all hypothetical conversation rooted in a study of world travel. Looking pretty clear though as we submerge into indigenous cultures, we can see that they have been suppressed and even intentionally attacked. Made into a taboo, some people look at voodoo and indigenous ceremonies as witchcraft and something too wild to understand. It's hard to talk about this, on one hand, we have direct lineages strong in tradition and culture, and on the other hand, people who have ingested so much modern information that they don't understand us. It's been the hardest thing to reconcile, how to bridge nature to a people who have not been in touch with the spirits of nature for so long. Not by their own doing but by the passing down of their family's ways and the prevalent subliminal messaging that comes with the colonial and Western world.

The naming game is still happening as there is a new word for walking barefoot foot, a new word for sitting in the forest. What this tells me is that we have been so disassociated from nature that we are taking off our shoes and walking into the forest to "ground." In the time we live in, I guess this is a large step in getting back to our original selves. Even though I may not fully understand why a person feels more grounded with a rock in their pocket or more spiritual because of the crystal they carry. It benefits them, that is where they are at, at this point, I offer them a celebration. It shows that they are devoted to at least giving their body attention. That's the main message, to love yourself, do what makes you feel good, and enjoy the things that make you laugh and smile.

A wise woman once shared with me the word miracle, a noun meaning amazing occurrence, deriving from the Latin word *miraculum,* meaning an object of wonder. Looking more into the word *miraculum* derives from the word *smeirnos* meaning to smile. Could simply smiling or sharing a smile or maybe the sensation or feeling that is followed by a smile be a small miracle in a day? I've always viewed miracles as massive healings or magical abilities, so it was nice to come down to the simplicity of a smile. I end my prayers as I stated before and will continue to state and pray as it is a mantra, a repetition I offer to the world even if it is quiet and unheard. I say that I pray for us to smile upon each other, to extend the feeling of a smile to others, others whose days are not as sunny, not as full of laughter, food, or family. To those without I extend the sensation of a smile. To all of our relations, may we feel the sensation of a global smile. The image in my head is beautiful as we all rest in that joy a smile offers and a sense of awe felt in the body and the lives of people and creatures all around. Not to say it is felt, maybe where there is no power there is no sensation, maybe it is part of my healing.

Let's take a moment. If you feel inclined to do some spiritual work together, these practices are altered yet passed down to me from direct lineages. With humility and sincerity, I will share only. We can put down the book, let go of our present thoughts, and go inward to that space in chapter two. The inner smile.

JOLKA~ Joyous + Open + Loving + Kindness + Awareness

HRIH
Part 1

- Resting in happiness and peace observing the body and all living sensations. Allow the breath to become prolonged and full. Inhale energy into your body, maybe the qualities of JOLKA. Maybe just pure bliss, maybe some color. Inhale those contents into the body and hold your breath. Allow your body to receive life-giving energies/information. Exhale the energy out. Allow yourself to breathe in this way, as many breaths as you want. With each breath cycle, allow that sensation to grow. Allow your body to feel the living sensation of the contents you actively breathe in and pack into your flesh and bones, blood and water. Inhaling for 20 seconds, holding for 20 seconds, and exhaling for 20 seconds repeating the breath in this manner, qi foundations in tack.

Part 2

- Now as you rest in this posture of qi, see the world from above. Like you're looking at a picture of Earth from space. Dial in on your loved ones, family members, and friends around the country, and the world. As you continue to breathe in nature, health, and happiness, exhale and imagine your breath filled with life-giving contents to travel through the air, encompassed with pink light. Use breath and intention to direct the energy into the heart of your loved ones, into the waters, into the trees into as many relations as your awareness can contain into your space. You can use the syllable HRIH pronounced 'hre.' Slow your exhale and chant or vibrate 'hre.' The vibrations of JOLKA radiating light and love into the air. Send the love to your ancestors and let them know that you are with them and that they are in your awareness. You can also imagine a singular being in front of you or you in front of them…. As you rest back into yourself, affirm your love, your inner smile. Give gratitude to your spirit and your life. Rest in your foundations of chi.
- This meditation is good for special awareness and actively building good karma, inviting more health and qualities of life-giving substance into your being. This practice is great to do in the morning or before bed.

"HRIH is a source of, light, vibration, projection, color, and bliss,
to breathe instant bliss is to radiate and embody HRIH".

Space is, of course, a very vast term and subject. We are all living in space, our solar system is in space, and naturally, space is just present. The ingredients that make space are vast and colorful. Space is the carrier for so much in our world. I like to think of space as I think of wi-fi signals traveling through the cloud, and messages reaching one another's phones, that's how I look at energy and working with energy. As we cultivate energy and information, we can actively send it out to one another. The best example is two lovers who are far in distance but close in spirit. When they think of each other and send one another love, the relationship is still growing, the love is still felt. I've had many lovers across the ocean, and as hard as it was to be away from them, I think of them during their day, I go to them and allow my presence to be with them. Sometimes they reveal that they had dreamt about me or woke up thinking about me strongly.

One of the funniest aspects of the world today is to look at the truth and the power of our indigenous family and the spiritual technology that they practiced. Nowadays, scientists want to test them and finding that yes, an energetic current of information can be shared between two people at vast distances. Scientists are finding that our auric field is changing based on our environments and the spiritual works that certain people are exercising. The part I laugh at is the part of ignorance a colonizer had, to just trample over such an advanced connection to nature, to literally pave the way and concrete a new world and way of living. Then slowly start testing people who are coming back to remembrance, only to prove the power of nature and nature of self, yet again. It's not really funny to be fair, I humor myself though. A good friend of mine said to laugh at the difficulties in your life, if you can laugh about it, I can probably move around it. To lighten the heaviness of the world, I think I've created an interesting aspect of my own trauma story. Laughing at things that might not be so funny. I'm also just a giggle person and love to find a way to share laughter. Even laughing at things I shouldn't, merely to continue a vibration. I'm working on new responses and inquisitive replies.

Laughter is similar to a smile. I've laughed my way into an altered states. One time in Sundance, an altering place to be anyway. My friends and elders, medicine men were preparing to pray with their pipes, they had asked me to hold the Curtin so that they could be in privacy, as they gathered around, preparing to sit and pray. Our good brother stumbled and almost fell, he was caught by a good friend, caught and held up by our brother, his pants slid down and those cheeks came out. Not your face cheeks either. The arbor was already filled with roaring laughter, joke after joke, laugh after laugh. This moment set it overboard as we all paused and then busted into laughter, that type of laughter when your teacher is telling you to be quiet but it's just so funny inside that you can't help but laugh. I think we laughed for about a solid 5 minutes. As we were laughing there was an audio that became present in my ears – a laughter from above that disassociated me from my body, I started feeling light and funny. 'What's happening? Am I here right now?' kind of feeling. The similar feeling of your first time being high on mushrooms. That laughter was a sign to me, a good omen of our ancestors and the spirits we built the arbor for, to be with us, celebrate with us, share a laugh, and share love with us.

The people you pray with, I find you stay with, your spiritual family.

My friends and fellows be happy with who you are, if you are not around authentic oral traditions, know that you are with nature, and nature is with you. Remember that the salad bowl of words can be dangerous. An elder said to me once that the English language is the most dangerous language of all, full of words that mean the same thing, full of unknown spellings that you may not realize you are a part of. My Sundance uncle who introduced me to this way of life, introduced me to many elders and concepts. He always said, "As a Sundancer, we must speak gently for the plume that sits on the end of your eagle bone does not want to be ruffled."

Speak gently, tread lightly, know your intentions, and do your best not to ruffle someone's feathers. Of course, unless that's what they need. Sometimes it is time to interface with a brother or sister to extend love and care by expressing your concern. You never know sometimes it might push someone over the hump of depression or suicidal thoughts. Sometimes we just need to laugh at ourselves.

There is a beautiful state of innocence I see in the communities today. There is no right or wrong way to do anything, it is between you and the creator. However, certain ceremonies and practices need to be respected. Some are very potent and can give so much life or take life from a being. So, if you are exploring some areas without guidance, let the spirits know that you are practicing, that you want to build new relations, and you are inviting the voices of nature back into your presence. For there is great work and relationship to nature, sometimes nature will drop a practice on you, or a new awareness can dawn upon you. If you find yourself in a circle of wisdom passed down orally, listen closely, and be humble, it is a gift to find yourself surrounded by the wisdom of walking carriers of prayers, songs, and the old stories of how things came to be. The great organizer of all of life. Some elders have been listening to the voices of nature for a long, long time. Some even are graced by their forefathers who listened and received, the ones who lived their lives in coloration to nature.

Chapter Four
Practice, Meditation, and Great Work

The great work was first expressed to me by a humble man, my high school math teacher, who was also a friend, elder, and spiritual teacher. He mainly expressed the importance of the great work as a way of existing. By more closely observing the self with awareness while working makes it easier to reveal your habitual postures of thought. Going through the steps of your daily routines at work, possibly Forgetting about our breath, the constructs of our body, and our awareness of the self. An opportunity to tune in, during our busy days of work. It may not be about being in retreat, where you have all day to observe yourself and do your practices, that sounds extremely rewarding and relaxing. And may be necessary depending on your ambitions for growth. It is definitely a goal of mine to arrive at a place of true resting and retreating. However, that's not very realistic for most of us, as we are dealing with financial strain and have children or family to actively support, or even habits. No matter what kind of job you have whether you work in an office space, drive vehicles, do construction labor, or really any job you do, you can do your meditations and practices that feed your life-giving energy, even if you are multi-tasking there's still a sensation that can be felt. Of course, it could be less equivalent in contrast to a full retreat where you only have one task, at a time and can fully feel or focus on sensation.

I know from personal experience that even at lunchtime I can feel drained, uninspired, and ready to go home. In my younger years, I would smoke ganja all day as a reward to myself and to keep my job exciting, part of my trauma story was habitually smoking after I completed a step of the project. So, as I got into construction, I would always look forward to finishing a step of the build so that we could sit back, smoke up, and get ready to hit it again. It seemed that laughter, jokes, and smoke filled the job sites, and that eased up the day. They were some of my best days. Some of my teachers encouraged me to stop smoking ganja due to the idea that it can lessen the connection to self or our inner standings. Now we all know everyone has their recipe for success. It depends on your level of awareness, and how you feel about your body's awareness. You may feel solely satisfied with your bodily awareness and be able to stay in your routine without thinking about what else lies beneath your skin.

Due to the inspiration and change of mind that my teacher shared with me, I will always state that my main line of work is qi gong/energy work. Although working with the nature of self does not pay the bills, it pays off in your discovery. So, my passion for life is to actively integrate into nature. My uncle describes a human being as a mobile source of energy conduction, a waking flesh bag of water that amplifies energy. Simply put, we are mass conductors of energy, amplifying all things that we ingest, from food, and water to knowledge. This is why the math teacher told to me, be very careful and mindful of what I do with this practice and study. He also stated that you need to be actively experimenting with 'chi.' As energy workers or alchemists, we need to be actively testing ourselves and putting our practice to use. So, with this view, as I began to build my house, I had the freedom to do and be as I wanted to, with no boss and no job site rules or dress codes. Most every day I'd wake up, meditate, and go to work pretty much in what I woke up in – shorts, no shoes, no shirt. I enjoyed working barefoot for many reasons, mainly because I was raised that way, in my youth I walked most places barefoot. Our local stores allow you to enter, I could go to school without shoes, so by the time I was a young adult, it was just part of myself. Also, it helps you build body awareness and ground awareness, you don't want to step on a nail or hot piece of metal. Being barefoot has always helped me walk mindfully around cactus and prickly objects. It allowed me to slow down and step gently, when I wear shoes, I notice that I'm moving faster and not looking where I step nearly as much.

So that was part of my experimentation. Other aspects of my experimenting were to see how aware I could be of my breath and my body. In massage school, our teacher would refer to our practices as foundations, in school and even in high school, we would stack foundations, adding different layers to our awareness until we were basking in a beautiful image of self. So, the idea is simple, get into your foundations and see how long you can stay or rest in the posture. Observe yourself when your energy shifts. I think it's beautiful to be aware of your body, and it's more beautiful to actively give love and attention to your body. Doing both these things together can be monumental in our emotional experience and even raise our physical energy level. It was such a joy to be free to explore constructing my body awareness and physically learning how to build a structure. My building mentor, an older brother to me, we would work all day, smoking and talking about different aspects of building houses and building ourselves.

At that time of building my home, I had a 1976 Chevy Nova that I traded to him to help me build my house. I'll always cherish those moments of living in my family's school bus while we built the greenhouse disguised as a house. Since I traded my car, I would walk a lot, it's about 5 miles to town via trails, and this was also part of my practice. If I was not working on the house, I'd wake up sit on the cushion for meditation, and then set out for town, taking time to walk, I'd incorporate my practice into my walk. I got into walking meditation a little bit with the math teacher and then more in Thailand when I did my first Thai poly vipassana, we did a lot of walking meditation. It took me about 1-2 hours sometimes three if I'd stop at the creeks to let the dog get a drink, enjoy a smoke doing and my best to stay tuned into my foundations along the way. My favorite practice is sky gazing and sky eating. The beauty of walking through the forest without traffic or much distraction is that you can look into the sky most of the walk if you like. So, along the walk, I'd go in and out of thoughts to feeling sensations, until I'd reach the town and then run into another, and recognize conversation would take over my awareness, maybe even more than the marijuana.

What I'm attempting to do here is to paint a picture of the difference between meditation in your home versus practice, as you go to work or interact with society. That is the difference between work and great work I feel. Until we arrive at a true resting point and retreat, it may behoove you to start implementing the practice of awareness in your daily work routines. Implement a little more care, love, and gratitude for your body as it moves and carries you through your day. Invite a little more intimacy into your connection with yourself. It is easy to take the grace of our movements for granted until our body is stiff and slow. Don't wait to connect to yourself and your community, time is passing us daily, and the opportunity to see love in our actions is a daily choice. It is our daily bread, as my teacher would say, to choose what we ingest and want to relate to. To acknowledge what we give and receive regarding our body, mind, and spirit. There are many good things to give to ourselves, we all know them. Eating healthy, exercising, meditation, general self-care. Without discipline or understanding, we will go through the motions in life without noticing the self's growing sensations resulting in dullness or lack of inspiration. Eventually, arriving at a feeling that is harder to shake, than if we maintain ourselves and clean ourselves daily like we clean our house or prized possessions.

I've really grown to appreciate the works of Ayurveda, Indian medicine and way of life, a nature-based relationship to self. Ayurveda is the study of preventative medicine. Using herbs, minerals and various treatments to maintain a healthy status of health. I wanted to study in India, so I looked into different schools around India, however, I ended up leaving India to renew my visa and headed for Sri Lanka. I found a program that I was able to attend, it was only three weeks of study and wasn't the experience I was looking for, although it was a good introduction, I was able to retain some treatments and practices. With my knowledge of herbs back home, I figure I can offer some regional Ayurveda. As we grow to know more, whatever it is you study or practice you must be persistent in your pursuit. I have a common issue of getting too excited about too many things and finding myself neglecting things I'm very interested in. Seems that nature deals us our hands in life, as we read deeper into our hands, we will see how we can best manage what we were dealt. Usually, our gifts arise as we accept ourselves. Some people find their natural talents early in life, many child protogines we have witnessed from naturally talented musicians, athletes and artists of all kinds. Channels of effortless ability.

Some children are born into the great work, incarnated, and recognized beings that live the majority of their lives serving up the teachings that were passed down to them. Living in a beautiful retreat space. It may be a controversial topic to touch on, it's tough to talk about the beings that are renowned and respected. Straight up recognized as reincarnated peoples, souls that have lived many lives and remember things of their past lives that allow them to be recognized in their present new lives. Due to their understanding of human suffering from their previous lives. Removing all obstacles and creating a channel for pure source energy to incarnate yet again in the flesh. These accounts show up in ancient Egypt, Tibet, India, and many others as well.

However, it seems that suffering changes and, in each century Lends a new aspect of suffering. The conversation can simply stem from the idea of one who sits upon a thrown or in a retreat, who has the comforts and the services brought to them. Never really having to grind with the working-class people. We can look to the story of Siddhartha better known as the Buddha. Most of us know the story of the Buddha, being raised in the walls of the kingdom, having a pure and beautiful youth, effortless bliss, and play surrounding him. Until Siddhartha reached his teenage years and began to wonder what lay beyond the walls of the kingdom. It was in those years that he left the kingdom to have a look into what was happening, and how where people living. What he witnessed was what led him to his path of love and compassion for all people. Siddhartha went around and uplifted communities everywhere he went. The story is still told to this day, as it was told to me.

I got to witness something of a correlation at the monastery where I started writing this book. I was graced to be on the same grounds as his holiness of the Bon tradition, as well as many other holy people. Now we all know what the Tibetan people have gone through recently, as China invaded Tibet and pushed Tibetans out of their homelands into neighboring countries, such as India, Nepal, and Bhutan. So, we can look at both sides of the walls of the monastery. The displaced Tibetans had found home in India and built beautiful spaces to initiate monks and be in devotion to their gods and spirits. I was there for Losar, the Tibetan New Year, a grand celebration that went on for days, full of traditional drumming, chanting, and dancing. Many mantras and prayers were recited, and so much great work was taking place on the inside of these walls. Powerful prayers that traveled through time in space. You could feel it in the air, I'll never forget the trumpeting of their horns and clashing of symbols. And the deep tones that the monks would recite in their daily prayers.

I spent about two to three weeks there, having nothing to do but rest and reflect. I'd circumambulate the main temple, and sit in the main temple sipping yak milk tea, allowing for the power of over 100 monks chanting prayers to enter my body and ears. I'd walk up to the stupa being constructed, watching the men lay each brick and eventually spread mud. I'd observe them during their smoke breaks and found a connection to the working-class people. Builders seem to enjoy the smoking of herbs, I sure do. Each day, I would do my rounds visiting the same places, same practices, and same prayers. I'd bring my flute to the stupa being constructed. It was at the top of the hill, there was a large cinder block wall covered by prayer flags, such a beautiful place to look and listen, the wall separated the bush from the monastery. As I looked beyond the wall, I saw some small homesteads and families playing cricket, hanging laundry, and going about their daily activities. One day, some kids came to the wall as I played my flute. The kids climbed over and sat upon the wall, I remember watching them watching me, prayer flags blowing in the wind. After some time, they came over and began to play with me, I had a small ball in my pocket. We kicked the ball and played the flute as they all took turns blowing sound through the bamboo stick.

The kids all had shoes that were either too big or too small, their clothes were slightly raggedy. These kids were free, they would start fires and throw rocks from the top of the hill into the monastery. I had to step in as Uncleji a couple of times and tell them to stop doing that. "Ka ha hey,

41

mamaji, ka ha hey papaji?" Asking them where their mother and father were. I spoke little Hindi, and they spoke little English so we would communicate with games. They would ask me for money, "Paseo, Uncleji. Paseo, Uncleji." They would repeat "Money, uncle. Money, uncle." I started to bring them chocolates and fruits from the monastery's guest house, I started to wonder who else might support the kids, or if the monastery would be more upset about these kids being in the walls. The Tibetans were receiving many meals a day and had everything provided. Their families most likely sent them there to be supported in that way. Yet the contrast was evident, in my mind, why just a wall away was poverty and more of a struggle so apparent?

That's where the dialogue gets more interesting. Coming from the struggles of poverty and hardship for years or even decades to finally arrive at true peace and happiness finding true gratitude for simply what you have. There is a strength and resiliency that comes from having nothing. Finding joy in the minimal aspects of living a life on top of a remote mountain. On the other hand, coming from comforts and conveniences being readily available, arriving into young adulthood after years and decades of having so much, plenty of comfort and peace yet a lack of resiliency, potentially spoiling only to come to find practice and meditation. The journey of finding true joy and gratitude for simply yourself. Maybe the struggle is less or looks different, but both avenues come with insights and setbacks. With healthy reflection, both avenues can put you in a state of Nirvana/blissful mind. I've met young monks who initiate and take a vow to later get out and end up in the streets. It seems that both paths will prepare you for life. I'm not the one to say that either is better than the other. I guess, I'd just like to see "Holy people" support the people who have not been dealt all aces. To the people who would appreciate being served chai occasionally.

If you are a street yogi, then you are actively doing your meditation throughout your day. The street is your retreat place, the sounds, and chaos, the street is your experiment your Alchemization of turning chaos into peace, minimalism into riches. I love the street Babas, I love the idea of finding peace in chaos. A truly spiritual being does not rely on an outside source for mental gain, nor the comforts or accessories. This awareness will keep you strong, with a natural endurance and powerful mental toughness. The practice has been implemented, and the devotion to self-development and acceptance is evident. Although you would see a lot of begging Babas and rows of beggars lined up. You would see just as many street adepts as nature adepts posted up displaying their devotion to the great work. They show us we don't even need a retreat house to do it in. You can simply sit down anywhere you are, and do the great work.

In one perspective we could say that meditation is the action of awareness, and practice is a way of life as we navigate through our daily actions and life. Are you acting in awareness, are you breathing, speaking, and moving in a meditative manner? To me, practice is developing a natural and effortless expression of all things we do in life. The more time we spend in our meditation the more we realize how good it feels to rest in the inner postures of happiness and color that is produced from our mind. As we balance ourselves in our polarities, our dualities of masculine and feminine, the yin and yang components of ourselves, the more we allow for this space of rest, the more potential we have to witness the birthing of our energy. Sitting in the commune of our sun/sky and Earth/moon birthing the awareness of energy. The living sensations in us and without, above, and below us, the more time we spend in this spaciousness the more effortless it will become to let go of the man-made or self-projected comforts. We will realize that we are with our original father and mother and elemental family members. This state of being natural grows on us just like any other relationship we form. We will find ourselves wanting to stay in this space, moving in this space. The bliss that is felt in this space is undeniable. It may take years or decades to reach this point. In Buddhism, they say it can take lifetimes to reach a space of enlightenment. I'd like to think that it could also appear out of thin air. The sensation or feeling that space offers could be momentary. It has been an unavoidable aspect of my life. The beauty of color and the auspiciousness of space is liberating in itself. Nature will extend its hand out to you. Maybe nature has been waiting for you to extend your hand out to her. Maybe that is all it takes. Love and surrender to our father and mother. A coming home party to celebrate our original family, our original house. Maybe it is time to clean ourselves off, shed some of our man-made traumas, and allow our mama Earth to recycle our unneeded waste. She is indeed a master of Alchemization.

I know that the word enlightenment can be just as triggering as the word god for some people. It seems that we have put enlightenment up on a pedestal. A place that is so far to reach. If we break this word down into three parts or three syllables. The word reads 'en lighten ment.' As I read those three words, I reflect that 'en' means 'self,' 'lighten' means 'to become light,' 'ment' means 'to coat or to mint' as we would put a gold plate on a sculpture or coin. I've been actively looking at this as a simple yet slow process of alchemy to add a substance, in this case light into a container/conductor, our body the container, and the minting or meshing of particles. Actively inviting light chi into our human structures. A potential scientific process, or a natural happening. In this observation, we could almost simplify the idea of enlightenment. This may be taboo to some who revere enlightenment as a far-off feat. Which indeed it is and of course, there are many ways to perceive enlightenment.

In Buddhism, the talk of the rainbow body is also a big topic to look into. I'm fascinated by color, and in devotion to the rainbow. The particles of light that are emitted from our sun reside in the sky. I've taken it upon myself to devote my life to the sun and building my rainbow/energy body. Even if these stories are to entice an individual into devoting their life to something that has not much physical evidence. I am captivated by the stories and Well, it brings me great joy and gratitude which turns into love, similar to the devotees at the Shiva temple. It gives them joy and love so I'm not going to interface with them and tell them it's a story. Many of the religious stories are grand and hard to perceive. So miraculous, living saints or miracle workers, it makes it even harder to believe. Yet I have been one to get invested in these stories. Traveling the world going to powerful places that these stories derive from, wanting to learn more. As beautiful as all this devotion talk and worshiping of gods are, it also brings up the question of religious oppression. To say that it takes lifetimes to reach enlightenment, or that you need to pray at the church and accept Jesus as your lord and savior, or that you need to withhold from any sex, these things dont make sense to me. It seems that some of these books or ideas maybe even stigmas are due for an update. Our laptops and computers offer updates every year. Our PlayStation is always updating. Many things that we see in the world are updating. Yet the dogma of religion seems to be focused on what was stated when Christ lived or Buddha. Super yogis/men who walked with great spirits. Made into the modern-day stories of glory. Is it time to update these images? Update our image of self.

This is also where some suspicion comes up for me. Why are we not listening to nature? Why do we place so much trust in a person who speaks nicely? If the person is not showing sheer signs of being a saintly person, then why would we give so much attention to them instead of ourselves? Have we been lost or forgotten to communicate with our first family? Is it that we are afraid of change? Or maybe we have hyped up the second coming so much that we are all just waiting for the arrival of this great avatar. Is it an avatar we are waiting for or is it simply ourselves?

We are all children of the sun. In Kemet, the sun god Ra is the giver of life, the giver of light. In my mind, Ra is the father of all life. And we are the sun, literally a reflection of him. All people consist of water the amplifier of all energies, as the scientists say, and the spiritualist feel. Earth's creation story, which we chatted about earlier, was very present in the evolution of all things. Water being on Earth and fire being in the sky perhaps. The sun reflected so much light that it penetrated the waters of the Earth and yielded life, color, and diversity.

Are human beings the microcosm of the macrocosm? Can you imagine what it would be like to have a tiny sun, a small orb of light living inside of your body? Can you imagine the feeling it would spread through the body? If light is energy and energy, is information, could you imagine how many new thoughts would be produced let alone feelings that course through the blood and chi of your waters? I am simply asking these questions because it seems that these are some of the practices of our ancient ancestors. Some of the practices that have been kept silent, why? Because they are too powerful for a human of today to comprehend, would it throw us into a loop or unground us? We all know what happens when one person gets too excited and leaks their chi spouting out all their secrets and exciting information. I know I've done it. Usually, when I do that unconsciously, it does not manifest. I've found myself doing that to impress or to feel like my ego is stroked. At this point, I'm opening up, a feeling that could benefit others, now in service to you, I've seen and felt enough to know this is a selfless action, an action to uplift human beings.

There could be many reasons why these practices or ways of life have been hard to access. However, it is also apparent that humans will go up and down, all around until they come back to the center. I think if we survived starvations and genocides and still be competent, adapting, and healing through it. I think we could take a little light. Energy alchemy is a slow process and takes a lot of focus and devotion. I can see why the Buddhists say it could take lifetimes to build your light body. Let alone understand how to do so. The aspect of oppression is still strong in my mind. I've heard that simple statement repeatedly by so many Buddhists. The Christians say we cannot enter the doors of heaven until we have invited Christ into our hearts. Then they tie Jesus to Christ and then all of a sudden, you're invited to worship this picture of a guy you can't even trust due to the fraud of the nations and the history that we have been digging into. "Shout out to the true Christ" with love and sincerity I do give you Praise.

When I've been to church, I have to actively translate what the preacher is saying. When I put it into my terms, it makes plenty of sense. Invite Christ into your heart. Christ's body and rainbow body are the same to me and so in my daily practice, I'm inviting light into my body. The more I do this practice, the more I can see the kingdom of heaven all around us, the Buddhists and Christians start to sound similar, all energy with different information potentially streaming from the same source of creation. So, let's take a moment and add another layer of foundation to this read. We are starting to stack up awareness of our qi gong foundations or postures. If you have felt moved in the past chapters when you put the book down for some small time to digest, what you are ingesting and sitting with yourself. Let's take a moment to actualize, if possible, what we are talking about. I think you can take it.

Sun Inside

Part 1.

- Allow yourself to close your eyes if you feel moved to do so. Invite that bodily awareness to amplify. In your mind's eye, see your skeletal system as before. Become aware of your organ. Feel the living sensations of inner smile in the body, heart pumping blood, lungs expanding and contracting. Sense your organs smiling functioning in health. Sometimes a pulse of your body will surface. Allow for that sensation of awe to grow in your heart's center. Gently smile from your heart, radiating happiness in all directions into the water in your body, flesh, and bone. From the top of the head to the fingertips and toes, allow this sensation to flow through your body.

Part 2.

- Now in your mind's eye, imagine a tiny sun, an orb of light resting in your heart's center/solar plexus area. Take some time to contextualize. Ask yourself what color is the orb, what shape or form, the texture and personality of your orb. Imagine this orb just like the sun in the sky. Feel the warmth and heat of your body. Imagine rays of light spreading through your organs, your bones, your flesh, and your skin. Allow yourself to relax deeper into this inner posture. Breathe deeper into the parts of your body that lack attention from time to time. Allow the qualities and sensations to be affirmed. Allow yourself to shine, just for fun see yourself as light. Be as bright and as beautiful as the sun you see in the sky. Bring light, life, and warmth continually to all your relations

"Resting in the warmth of your own sunshine."

One thing I really appreciate about Buddhism is that it offers physical meditations and practices to incorporate into your daily life. There is a great book named Tibetan Yoga, written by Ian Baker, you can hear him talk about his book on YouTube as well as his travels and ventures in Tibet and Nepal. If you enjoy these meditations, I'd recommend his book. A good friend gave me the book with an ounce of mushrooms to go with it. See, the monastic monks are taking prescribed applications from their Sr. advisors, and then there are the rebels, the cave dwellers the mountain yogis. I have always rebelled and questioned the prescription. My math teacher is one of the only people I let my guard down fully, allowing for energy guidance to bless me with blissful sensations. There was no dogma, there was no hagiarchy, just two human beings sharing in a bath of mentally projected imagery, affirmed by the living sensations of the body.

Most of the things that he shared with me come from Tibet. Yet rooted in the origins of universal energy I come to find. Named by the global tribes differently and practiced very similarly. Has helped me corollate qi gong/energy work as a universal way of connecting to all Indigenous ceremonies I've participated in. I may not know the names of all the spirits or the songs, yet I've been Graced by WAKAN SKAN or Sspommitapiiksi the above ones, the network of light, the spirits of color. Guided me to the Sundance tree to pray and confirm, took me to the Bon Po's place of practice at Menri Monastery, home to strong rainbow spirits the "TIGLY". Dropped me in the middle of the Adogbe voodoo village, Tribal lands in Togo, West Africa where I was initiated by Kwame my SR. priest, it was he who recognized me as his rainbow brother and priest, a carrier of "INEDO TOGBE" meaning rainbow voodoo spirits, spirits of nature of color. In Lakota, we call these spirits "WAKAN SKAN" and in Amskapi Pikuni blackfeet we call Sspommitapiiksi. Above ones and holy sky networks. Guiding me to Indigenous lands around the world to learn the many names of what is channeled through my waters and hollow bone. First, offered to me in the mountains in Crestone an adolescent, not knowing a name to call them. Now we know their presence is felt all around the Earth, and can start calling them by their many names. See the spirits are happy when we speak of them in good ways, when we can recall how our forefathers called to them. Humbly, I state my claim, and welcome my responsibilities, take my vows, Creator holds me to the great work and the great awakening after a long sleep, as our old peoples were laid to rest, today, we are struggling to remember, slowly waking up to all sacred networks.

I was also guided to not take substances, for meditation at a peak is more altering than any substance. All networks in awareness may be too grand for one to perceive.

However, a friend gave me the book Tibetan Yoga, talking a lot about the assistance of plant medicine, even Guru Rinpoche using datura and other plants to enhance vision or to connect with the spirits. The book Tibetan yoga has inspired me to open up again to mushrooms. As I have pretty much quit smoking cannabis, I do find benefits in mushrooms. Mushrooms have affirmed a lot of my spiritual works and have helped me find a voice in song and vision. I'll share some of my acid trips and mushroom journeys in this book. They enhanced my life as a teen, showing me some things that made me burst out laughing similar to the laugh in the arbor – a laugh from within a laugh that erupts out of pure joy and an altered state. Whether high on substance, high on experience, or vision, a feeling is to be celebrated and remembered. I'll never forget those moments.

I hope this chapter has revealed some interesting aspects, grown some new thoughts, and that the stacking of foundations is interesting for you. For me, these playful imaginary images have led me in my life. Of course, I get sad and feel many other emotions, yet I always rejoice in the sky and find effortless devotion to the colors. The great work has become my purpose. It seems that so many people get lost simply because there is a lack of purpose. So, either have some children find a good partner, and settle into raising something, if not a family then raise yourself, high to the sky find purpose in your connection to your first family, and enjoy the coming home party as you celebrate the sun, the Earth, and the elements.

In Bon Buddhism there are three main practices, sutra – the renouncing of drugs, alcohol, and sex, and simplifying life, a lot of monks practice sutra.

Tantra is the practice of bliss, meditation, yoga, self-care, and things that bring you joy and give you life.

Dzogchen is said to be the highest form of practice. Dzogchen is a state of effortless bliss, an outcome of so much practice. Living, breathing, and moving through life in aware action. We could compare Dzogchen to a highly connected being, so connected to their Hindu gods, Ram, for example, a blissful expression if you feel very connected to Ram or Shiva then would you need to practice. Is this possibly one of the reasons why in the study of Hinduism, there are not as many meditations spelled out, in a certain format, more based around your awareness of your god family that lends you the space to be in love and see love in all life. This is very similar to Dzogchen, living in love and effortless bliss, a feeling that all is in harmony, any hardship will be greeted with love and able to alchemize into grand feelings. We could say that Shiva's or Krishna's consciousness is very similar to Christ's, Jah's, or Allah's. It seems that they are present and consistent energy all carrying a different name of godly presence. It seems we could view them as frequency, vibration, and color, or simply spirits with a name. Nature was the reveler of this particle of light, to me, that is partially unnamed, or in another look named 100 times all around the world by ancient traditions. There are very few books that talk about the raw form of these orbs and these colors. In the book that Ian Baker wrote, he exposes some depth of how color is regarded by the Tibetan people, they talk about togel vision, an aspect of a human being that is said to emanate through the heart. If I'm not mistaken, the text states that if your heart is very open and full of love and awareness, it will project outside of yourself and you will start to see more love in your surroundings, your eyes will be full of color. The emanation of orbs will be seen and felt. When I became devoted to the orbs, mesmerized by their beauty, I was grateful to have a friend and student of the orbs himself to console in. He said that these orbs are called Tigle. It's been very hard to find any information, mainly knowing a couple of yogis that we can dialogue about Tigles. Tigle, Deriving from the Indigenous Tibetans possible.

It seems that these orbs play a massive role in nature and the nature of self. I feel they are the key component to building a rainbow body or Christ's body. I've also heard accounts of orbs being talked about by my Sundance family in both Wounded Knee South Dakota and Blackfeet country. In Adogbe Voodoo and language the orbs or sky peoples are named Inedo, I learned that the rainbow is also a very strong spirit in their traditions. Regarded by our early ancestors around the world pre colonization. It's even more interesting to state the miraculous stories of these people and places and how the rainbow is in their conciseness. Could it be that by surrendering the self, letting go of the world as we know it, and the identification that we have been looking for as we try on different hats and roles in our lives? By stripping down to simply identifying as water flesh and bone. Identifying as our original self before the buffet of subliminal messages and the dangers of the English language and all that comes with it. It becomes clearer to me that if I arrange myself as I do my home, clearing the dust, organizing the important feng shui of my home, and getting rid of extras, my house naturally invites more relaxation and allows me to rest in more peace and inherently I'm able to create more energy effortlessly. It seems this concept would be very applicable to the human being as well as arranging ourselves in a certain manner, offering up aspects of self that are not serving us to make space and reservation for a grand engagement and reception. These orbs find comfort and appreciation for a container to grow. A caretaker and a spokesman, for if we say, *Aho Mitakuye Oyasin,* recognizing and thanking all our relations in Lakota, the orbs would be included in this relationship saying thank you to all aspects of creation.

It seems that all beings look for shelter or space to reside. I believe things are starting to make a lot more sense. It simplifies our lives, allowing for the analyzing brain to turn down, the left brain to rest, and the right brain's intuition and feeling to stand tall as it once used to. Is light or auric engineering beginning to look more practical? The understanding of a process.

I've been told by different people that the rainbow resides in different areas of Earth and space. I've been told to love them and make space for them in my life, I've been told to sit with them as I would with my parents and loved ones. To build a strong relationship, I was told to invite them closer, I was told to extend the invitation to enter my human being.

Chapter Five
Building Family Relations

Looking into the variations of creation stories and the evolution of human reproduction, we can postulate many aspects of our existence and where we truly come from. The possibilities are vast like stars, some are said to be descendent from the stars. Some believe we started as other forms of two-legged, possibly evolving from prime mates or Neanderthal-type beings. Humans have been depicted in portraits bread or crossed from animals throughout history. The spectrum of our existence is infinite it seems. I ask myself if these stories are depictions of our human imagination. I ask if our imagination and projection of mind can manifest in the physical. The structures of imagination? Can we materialize our visions and thoughts? Does one feel the importance of knowing where we originate and the beginning of human time? Possibly more important the magic or merit if you will, that is still strong enough to be remembered today, after 400 years of globalization, westernizing of the world. Our population today exceeds 8 billion, and many of us feel the remanence of a deeper connection to the Earth and something that may not be higher than us but all around us. With more people more complexity, more difference. With all that we have been through as a species, it is safer than ever to release all our anger and sadness our traumas, and give it back to the oppressor who imposed upon us. It is time to reclaim it is time to remember, SANKOFA African Proverb: It is not taboo to take back what is rightfully yours. It feels like they have been domesticating us. Replacing the laws of nature with the law of man. The weak man and jealous man to control and rule over another fellow.

As written by the *European Scientific Journal* (ESJ), The Seven Laws of Nature are as follows: The Law of Attraction, The Law of Polarity, The Law of Relativity, The Law of Cause and Effect, The Law of Rhythm, The Law of Gender and Gestation, and The Law of Perpetual Transmutation of Energy….

If you are interested in more ideas of viewing natural or universal laws, refer to the writings of philosopher Thomas Hobbes.

We can travel in our mind to a time when our human family started very small I'd imagine, yet very much connected to nature, it would appear the connection between humans and nature is strong, evolving from nature itself. At some point along the human timeline, the idea of God or creator was adopted into the human mind. Now not only mankind is living with animals and elements, but the god family is introduced, or possibly more realistic, the spirits of nature that spoke to man. Maybe the idea of spirit came before the idea of God in the mind of an ancient human, but there's no evidence. So, it's a thought to ponder a fun space to play around with different ideas of how we came to be. Not sure if there are too many creation stories that support the timeline of when mankind started to worship or at least communicate to a source of something outside of the self or something in the air, something that spoke to them.

In my thoughts, it seems that ritual was practiced, as a way of talking to nature and offering some currency whether that be voice or physical gifts. It appears that the spirits of voodoo are very old, and the tradition has been around for thousands of years, to offer physical food and offerings to the spirits of nature, and still very practiced today. If human life indeed originates in Africa/Alkubelon, as people say, it would make sense that these were some of the original practices or rituals of our human timeline.

In that era of time, I'm sure there was a different name or even an unspoken feeling. It seems it was not so much a practice but a way of life that was so natural, a sense of innocence – so pure, so natural, so beautiful, maybe our early forefathers have been in such effortless service to spirit simply because they were fewer people to speak to. Would it be that our early ancestors spent the majority of time with Papa Jah or Papa Shiva as Ruddrock spoke by the Ganges River? I can close my eyes and travel back in time to that era and put myself in the shoes of a being that spoke no language yet, operating with sound and vibration similar to a whale or dolphin. I could see myself looking up at the sky and communicating, asking for more. Another ceremony of Indigenous Americans is called humblacha, or vision quest when one goes into nature for a vision. Spending 4 days with nature, to allow animals to visit, and hope that great spirit will speak to us. Protocols are in place and very from region to region, people to people.

I can put myself in the shoes of our early ancestors and see that most of life was a vision quest. If you listen to the stories of people who go on vision quests you will hear how the animals and spirits spoke to them. It's always beautiful to hear the vision questers share their experiences, as it lends us all insights and understanding of the big picture. It appears that our ancestors were asking nature to guide them forward in their evolution. Our ancestors became rich in the currency of awareness and connection. Their relationship with great spirit was so authentic and untampered. To me, it was the glory days of two-legged existence, until the spirits of our individual were guided to take more than what was needed or to harm another for their gain. In the story of Adam and Eve, when they ate the apple and gave in to their desires. From that point onward, we see the evolution and downfall of this period that was flourishing. A time when people were in such reverence to Earth and the ocean, their ability to work with the land and to sustain themselves. From then till now, there has been so much devastation, all a natural happening of evolution similar to Earth's evolution. It seems that the more humans wanted to rule the land and the relations of land. The more rules started to appear, my uncle said to watch out for man-made rules and constructs. For the constructs of nature, the law of nature is what our ancestors knew and lived in correlation to. Not owning land, living in the land just as an animal, building shelter, hunting and gathering like the squirrels and birds. Living in a current of natural energy.

It is easier and easier to see the demise and downfall of our originating desires and wants for more. My meditation teacher used to say that if you don't know what to ask for in your meditation you can always ask for more, the magical more. Is more an okay thing to strive for? Well, it depends on who is asking and what they are asking more of. One could be asking for more health, happiness, awareness, and connection. On the other hand, more could come in the ways of greed and control, domination and consumption. The tables turned from being a humanity in reverence and gratitude to our Earthly family members and sky spirits, with honor to the grander families, all living beings. To a world that operates out of control and rule. A world fueled by consumption and a want for more, more material gain, more recognition, more power of self, more land, and more possession. Before states were states and countries were countries, there was no need to possess land for it was not owed by anyone. It was simply a miracle of life shared by all life, a space to explore and enjoy the natural environment, ruled by the days of the sun, a place of stillness of the night, a place of reverence and curiosity of stars. Humans struggle with stillness, today. We are constantly looking for more stimulation, for some entertainment, something to take our mind away from the stillness. Because our world is so based on convinces, instant heat, instant food, and instant gratification, it takes away from our work. Back in the day, we worked so closely with the elements, making fire to cook, hauling water to drink and bath, gathering wood for shelter and fire, and breathing deep fresh air as we moved through our day being mostly naked on Earth. We heard the land speaking to us and the elements guiding our days. Our purpose was simple, to chop and to eat. I've always been taught to chop wood and carry water. To work for what I reap, I always love watching people in villages fill and carry water, I appreciate every bucket bath I take, for months on end I've bathed with buckets, only using a couple of gallons or liters of water. We are not accustomed to cleaning the self in this way in the Western world. Yet the majority of the countries I visit, this is common. Of course, you can go to the highly developed places in all countries, the capitals, and find a shower and hot water, yet that is the life of the wealthy ones who went for the New World, the desire to live what some would say an easier life. While some have lived full generations of chopping wood and carrying water, building healthy bodies and minds due to the constant devotion of cleaning the self and preparing food to nurture us, some have lived generations at this point of modern conveniences, producing children that don't even know where ketchup or milk comes from. I've heard stories of school children who do not understand how the milk got into the carton, not knowing that it comes from an animal another major topic of modern-day, factory farming. A good friend of mine educated me about a film that his father made and produced alongside his crew, the movie is titled Cowspiracy. Cowspiracy is exposing the inhumanness of the cow industry. Of course, in India the cow is holy, most Hindus do not consume meat. So, my friend and his father being a part of these traditions brings a beautiful cultural understanding to the conversation. Their want to create a vegan village and a sustainable farm is a beautiful dream, to me, it falls in line with the revolution that is already taking place. I love my friends like this because it shows that many of us are sharing energetic thoughts, and our psychic abilities are coming back as we push the system away from us, the system that was pushed onto us, such as the cattle industry was also pushed onto this land, cattle were not even native to our land. The devastation of the colonizing mind, the mind of greed, and want for more hit our lands like the meteors hit the dinosaurs. There are photos of piles of buffalo skulls documenting the slaughtering of our buffalo. To American Indians, the holiest four-legged was nearly wiped out. If you know anything about Redman, you will know how important the buffalo was and still is, nurturing our bodies with their flesh making tools with their bones, and tipis and cloths with their hides, medicines in the organs. Our First Nation people honored this animal so much. Not only was the buffalo the source of life for humans. They also grazed the grasses and offered fertilizer for new growth and food for other microbes and life. My insides cry as I write this, as our people were pushed out and killed off so was our life support. The colonizers brought cattle and other non-native species, cut down our trees, and overgrazed the fields, they brought unbalance to our world.

The cattle farming then got way out of hand, with cows becoming diseased and sick, and mass amounts of manure, that is not able to be spread out. Due to factory farming and containing an animal. The amount of GMO feed given to a cow is not the same as it used to be. The amount of methane that cattle farming is giving off impacts our atmosphere. I've heard crazy stats showing that cattle methane is higher than car and industrial output. It seems that on the one hand, they are doing their best to feed a mass population of people, and on the other hand, they are just money-hungry. Anywhere there is fast food, there is inhumane cattle farming. So, the cow is becoming sicker and its DNA is changing because of the GMO feed to get bigger, more cows, more meat, more money, a lack of empathy for our animal family. As a result, we are dealing with the highest rates of obesity, diabetes, cancer, heart attacks, and high cholesterol in the majority of our human world. I cringe and feel for the cows and every time, I drive by a cattle lot or am passing a cattle truck. A lack of empathy, a want for more. This is active hate, if we look at hate as a lack of feeling, is there remorse felt by the cattle owners? Is it that their mind is plagued by greed and a lack of understanding of what they are producing? It reminds me of a drug pusher, like obviously the product is destructive it brings harm, but the distributor is high on his supply. Until he feels the death happening inside himself, he will not know the death that is taking place in his cow or his client.

I'm very grateful to my friend's father for exposing such inhumane industry. Another great film just shared with me called Watson I believe. A documentary and story of a man Paul Watson, who exposed so much and created a society to protect the seas, the whales, and all of sea life. His organization is called Shepherds of the Sea. His organization started as a grassroots and is now an international and global platform for protecting the seas from illegal fishing. Factory fishing is just as nasty as cattle farming and could be even more impactful as Mr. Watson states in his activist voice. If the seas are dead, we are dead. As I was going over the creation story of Earth in previous chapters, there was a growth that provided oxygen to enter the air and birthed so much and possibly all of life that we see now. Watson stated that this is still the case, the seaweed is the trees of the sea, the lungs of the ocean. He explained that the whales are the farmers of the oceans, like the buffalo they travel through the oceans ingesting tons of Phytoplankton and then fertilizing the oceans with food for more life to grow, food for a diverse species of ocean life.

Just like our Sundance ceremony, there are many crucial roles to play, each person coming together to make a more effortless motion of creating a house for the great spirit. We can see that our ancestors learned that from nature as all animals and life forms have a reason for their existence. The winged ones play a major role in the growth, the diversity of plant life, and the ability of plants to grow thousands of miles away from their origin. As they eat seeds and plants, fly and poop them out into new areas of land. The birds like to enjoy the company of buffalo, all land creatures interface with each other, and all predators are grateful for their prey. In survival, you take life to give life, it is a sacred part of life. The animal is a great mirror to look at a healthy aspect of taking life. A lion kills effortlessly and may or may not feel pain or empathy for the prey that he pounced upon. It was simply hungry and jumped, in nature and moderation this seems to be healthy and part of the cycle of life as blood, bones and flesh also play a huge role in the soil becoming more fertile. It is when one takes too much and throws off our balance of nature. There's a name for this person, in Lakota the wasi'chu, the one who takes too much, a colonized mind. So to the chicken and the egg, so to say, which came first, was it the chicken or the egg, the man or the woman, the desire or the balance? Whichever it is, we are here now, tears and blood have been shed. I'm not going to leave the chicken out of the conversation, that would be like leaving the Native Americans out of the history books, not acknowledging that during a time of white and black segregation and implementing black-only bathrooms and white-only bathrooms, our original people were not considered in the conversation. This is the heaviness of the history and of what people call a "Great Country."

Deep exhale, letting go of the pains and traumas, deep inhale. Inhaling gratitude and joy that we are all here together, they did not succeed in wiping us out, for the spirit of our ancestors is always with us and no man can kill that.

So, just to take another moment to acknowledge the chicken, dealing with the same difficulty as cow, fish, pig, and all other animals experiencing such hardship. I'm not sure what an animal is experiencing emotionally. I've heard that elephants are one of the most emotional creatures on the planet, their memory is so strong, similar to a person when you witness death or trauma, usually, we never forget. We will carry it around until we heal that relationship and recognize that it happened and that some things we cannot change, and also may behoove us to accept all things. However, I don't usually believe in can't. I believe we can.

Now that we have looked into the reality of our animal family and our elemental family, our human family, and even our god/spirit/ancestral family, let us bring awareness to a more invisible family member. Some refer to them as hungry ghosts, duppies, or lost souls. Whoa, so much love for all the family members listed, so much love to the family members that have passed their physical bodies on. So much love to the bodies that have been buried and burned, drowned in the waters, went back to the elementals. We give thanks for your lives and for getting us here. If we look at three main aspects of human beings or any two-legged, four-legged, winged ones, or the ones that swim, we all have a mind and a body and an energy body, our toroidal field just as Earth reflects to us. So, we know where the body goes, and the mind rests, yet the energy – where does it reside after physical death? After years of waring and colonizing, massacring of our fellow human beings, we could reflect on how much energy is lingering on the Earth, in the air, and space. Whoa, this is a lot to bring into our awareness I know, and I apologize if I'm bringing up too much. Or triggering a trauma, or response to arise. However, it may be the first way to let go. To surface and talk about it, to reassure that there is love and security in your being, to validate the trauma, and then to allow for that to rest. We chose what to carry and how long we would like to carry it. It is our mind that tells our story, organizes, and gives us choices to present to the outside world. The capacity of my mind has extended into the ethers, into the spatial particles, the energies that go unseen, honoring families and souls, energies, ancestral timelines of our family trees. Cycles of life and death.

The Tibetan Book of the Dead is another great book to look into. It talks about hungry ghosts, souls that are lacking and even looking for a vessel to live in, similar to the orbs of light we talked about in previous chapters, and will continue to. If your house is not kept clean or simply no one is home well a wanderer can come right in and make themselves at home. Pretty clear and simple, if you're not grounded and, in your body, cleaning and maintaining yourself, foreign energy may be hungry for a home. You may be to. I'm sure we have all felt afraid at times in our lives and not known why, or felt a presence that was unsettling either around a person or a place, the energy is almost palpable. When our high school teachers took us to an Auschwitz camp in Germany, you could feel the spirits lingering, the heaviness and sadness of the people were still present, and suffering still felt. The slave dungeons in Ghana, you can feel it in the whole of Cape Coast. The massacre site at wounded knee, the hanging trees in the south, the jungles of Laos where more bombs have been dropped than anywhere in the world, and Agent Orange spread through the air. The streets of Cartagena Columbia and the un-moderating cocaine spirits. These places hold an energy, and sometimes that energy follows you. You can feel the presence of ancestral souls.

I've been visited by spirits or energies off and on throughout my life. What would make a ghost or spirit, an energy feel hungry? This visitation showed me some hunger, I was in Columbia, and I tried real cocaine for the first time. As I went to lie down to sleep, I crossed my hands on my chest, and as I fell into a lucid world, I saw myself from above looking dead, my hands held a beer can. I looked available. I then came back into the view of looking up at the ceiling, feeling my beer can still, I realized I was asleep because I did not go to laydown holding a beer can. Lucid I was visited by 3 faces, these faces were white and withered, the faces of old and drained men. They moved around my vision like balloons on a string moving in the wind, where these hungry ghosts I'd been told about.

When I was a small boy, like age four, I started having seizures, and on top of that, I was seeing and feeling things that provoked fear. I felt bad for my mom as she witnessed me unconsciously seizing, foaming at the mouth at times, and then lying completely still as a corpse as she described the situation to me. I would come to and tell her that there were spirits outside of the house, they wanted in. I can't remember much during this intense time; however, I remember the feeling of being scared. From a young age, I'd developed some strange sights, there were experiences I looked back on and asked myself, was that a dream, a vision? Why are there strong memories of moments I struggle to explain? After age 7, I'd say I went on living a fairly normal life.

Until I was 16 when my sight and my feeling came back into my inner awareness and inner conversations. That year, I started to witness more color in my sight, the orbs the day I was in the mountains. Magical things have happened in the mountains of Crestone, things I can only see and feel, have great respect and carry them with me quietly. At the age of 16, I was also approached by one of my best friends' moms, she is a medium and a psychic. One day she pulled me aside, she said she saw me driving in my car and felt, or maybe saw, a vacancy in my eyes. I was puffing plenty of ganja at the time and that was her concern. She offered me a session, I decided I would like to hear her out, a chance to get to know myself more and to hang out at a best friend's house. She went on to tell me some interesting things. She told me my energy came from a faraway star, Serious B, composed originally of fire and ice. That was interesting because I'd been told that before by other people who identified as Serians, not hippies but yogis, adepts of energy. You know hippies and their ideas though, you can usually decipher what's what. I like the mythical aspects of human beings. I've met people who say they're from the plea dies. I've met people who said they came through a vortex. Some people are more grounded than others. The two people who shared this information with me, I have great respect for and see them as grounded and wise people. She continued to say some nice things about me. She spoke of blue energy that was there as an assistant or an ally. That was also interesting to hear because my dad used to tell me as he would walk the river beds as a child alone in the woods that a blue American Indian possibly an ancestor, or guide would meet him sometimes. I wondered if that had any connection. I believe in family ancestors and guides, or ghosts that follow us. Past on like carpentry, or an ancient trade or ability.

She then went on to tell me that there was a hungry ghost that was enjoying feeding off my energy. She even gave this ghost a name so that I could remember him. After the session, I realized that I was starting a friendship with Hector, the hungry ghost. This may all sound funny, and lucrative, but I'm merely just sharing my experience as a human being. The ghost was also connected to my past as my birthplace was home to some heavy spirits. There was drug use, child abuse, suicides, and deaths, and children buried there. It seems that when these ghosts or even traumatized people have not received an apology or at least taken time to air it out or clear the space, the energies would wait around till it is loved, till it is filled with life-giving energies. Just like any relationship when there is love present, it's easier to pass the difficulty by and go on with life. Without love and attention, those traumas may or may not subconsciously affect our day-to-day lives. It is easy, even in the human mind to ponder and ponder, wonder and wonder, looking for connection and acknowledgment.

She said Hector was coming around when I was using cannabis. He was coming to peek at me, similar to how the faces in Columbia greeted me. Not scaring me but leaving me with a funny feeling – a feeling of not being in my body as much. A feeling that I now look at and can say I was lacking attention to certain parts of myself.

Looking back at the days, I smoked a lot and didn't have as much purpose. I can say I did fall into a drain, a dullness. Could it be that Hector was picking up on my energy not being as contained, my house not being as clean? Or could it be that it is all mental, a projection of thought that becomes validated? It's hard to say if there are ghosts of our minds or actual beings floating around us daily, accumulating in environments of heavy trauma.

I've watched my friends become what I think is possessed by ghosts, due to too much drug use, either ending up schizophrenics or in the streets, trying to make sense of where their energy went and managing the new information that has entered them. Some say energy is information as stated could that also be a different view of the spirit of mind or souls of collective trauma? or a story that may plague us with confusion and may contaminate our original thoughts and connections? It appears that whether we are talking about a place or a person, a tree, or a rock, energy can linger or reside. Can either give life or take life, be celebrated or neglected. It's easy to sweep it under the rug unacknowledged. It seems that is human nature… human history swept under the rug hiding us from the nature of self. Our respect for ourselves and other beings was replaced by selfishness to numb the pains or things we have done in our past. The selfishness of a killer or a junkie with a family, not realizing that he is not loving himself, therefore he struggles to love his family and, in the end, sits alone in his selfish habits and feels a certain way. Is that why I feel so much sadness when I travel the world or sit in a man-made cave recognizing the trauma and disrespect our mountain received and the heaviness I feel in my hometown? I'm so grateful for the tools I've received in this life. I'm not sure I could be happy after witnessing so much.

This chapter is obviously about coming back to commune with all our family members to be actively building a relationship with all relations, to grow awareness, even into spaces that may be unseen or unfelt, for once you witness a feeling or a sight it is with you. I see light everywhere, there are rainbows in the sky, the sky is everywhere and even if I cannot see them in my close vicinity the feeling affirms their presence. After learning about Hector, the hungry ghost, and feeling his presence, I feel hungry ghosts everywhere I go and can even sense when someone is dealing with a ghost. This is a lot of energy talk, subtle things that may make the reader question my sanity. Spiritual beings are on the rise, coming back to our senses, maybe some readers will feel gratitude that they are not the only ones who are asking why. More of us are starting to think and act in building our awareness and developing feelings for all of life, seeing love in all aspects. It's time to forgive ourselves, it's time to embrace each other. We are merely products of our ancestors, we are all fighting to get back to a place of resting in deep joy and connection to nature, becoming still, self-sustainable, and elemental once again.

This was a heavy chapter. It's nice to decompress a little and acknowledge some of the beauty we see as our family and recognize each other. I feel a sense of psychic abilities coming back to us. I sense we are listening to nature more these days because what else is there to do when there is so much suffering in the world? In our past, and our history, we cry for assistance, we cry for attention to nature. We have to give love to nature to receive love from nature just as in any relationship. The silent communication is here. I know a significant number of people getting tired of the world as we know it, the want for a life that was once upon a time, mythical and magical. I can see us coming home. I can feel our collective healing. I invite you to check out what some of these activists are working on and how you may be able to get involved. There are so many actions that are needed around the world and in your local communities. These people are soldiers of spreading awareness and action.

I'd like to end this chapter with a prayer instead of a meditation, and who knows they are kind of the same. To me, Prayer is to see a positive conduction of energy/information and to simply hold space, consciously and intentionally. For that will bring life-giving energy. Meditation is to envision a feeling or image in your mind you desire to feel. So, if you don't like prayer then this is just another meditation or a simple affirmation of global healing.

Prayers to the great Networks

Dearest creator, great spirits of nature, of the rainbow networks, we ask that you may be with us, we ask that you may see us in our suffering, we ask that you may assist us in our surrendering, the lending of our ears to hear you when you speak to us. We ask that you may grace us with your presence in our lives. We ask that you will be with the weak and the sick, that you may be with the corrupt and the rulers, we ask that you may humble them, help them to make quality choices for their people, the people who are hungry and impoverished. Great spirit, we ask that we may feel each other, we ask that we will remember together our responsibility and relationship to WAKAN MAKHA Earth and WAKAN WI sun, to the rivers and oceans, bodies of water, To WAKAN SKAN we ask to see our reflection in you. We ask you to be with the animals, we ask that general love will fill the air and find lost souls. We ask that you fill them and allow them to rest. We ask that the spirits of nature will receive us and pity us for our shortcomings and our stubbornness to listen, we ask for your guidance. Great spirit, allows us to be closer to our ancestors. We ask that we may serve you in the best way as you have served us with such a beautiful life. We offer you the love that grows in our hearts as we engage in the divine union of you, the nature of light, as we invite you back home into the heart. May we rest together as one family. Great rainbow spirits, guide us back into the kingdom of heaven, the temple of our truest self.

We offer you the growing sensation of the gentle smile and light that lives in our heart center, we extend this smile to you, great spirit, as an offering and affirmation to you. To all animals, all spirits, all ghosts, all elements, and all aspects of nature.

ASE AHO AMEN

We extend this smile to you and a little extra love to those ASSHOLES, we can all be assholes. Not to call names but to identify the things that we know we are working on, and we all know depending on the individual, the weight of their story may result in more eruptions, which is a great space to recognize that we have lots of work in that area. The compassionate view is to also recognize that someone contaminated our original thought, and we are all in the process of clearing our waters in a literal sense. So even though I joke about assholes, I love you, I understand that we are all victims of this globalized world I can be an asshole also. It is a choice of how we carry ourselves. So much has happened amongst our human family being stolen, killed, and put against each other, we can validate what has happened and as a family, the hope or prayer that we may see, the synopsis of the world we see today was very well planned and stems from the evil of the ones who devised and outlined how they would do it. I believe asshole would not be the appropriate label for these individuals, to be clear I'm refereeing to them as the ones who need the prayers the most. We have full reason to speak up and speak out about how we can do better. Accepting that we are here now. The simple notion of growing out of this together is to liberate and ascend into love, peace, and inner standings of our magical avatar.

One family, one awareness of all our relations, we extend gratitude. And may we get comfortable on the same couch, all family members invited to rest together and watch a beautiful show unfold, hopefully, a docuseries, a binge-worthy one.

Chapter Six
Retreat or Rehabilitate

Retreat defined by Oxford Languages; To withdraw from enemy forces as a result of their superior power.

Rehabilitate defined by Oxford Languages; The action of restoring Someone or something to its former condition.

It appears that in the process of healing, coming back to remembrance of our truest self, there has been an influx of retreat centers being built around the globe, it's simply amazing. Teachers and spiritual leaders step up and share their wisdom and practices for humanity. I'm very happy to be a part of this era. I've traveled around the world visiting different centers and spas, I took notes along the way. My house began to change as I built, although my center is small, it is an intentional build. Built-in dedication to nature, for nature to speak through. I was very excited to open my retreat center, and I successfully did so in 2020. After ten years of building and carrying the inspiration and witnessing the Architectural beauty of over 15 countries I visited, Nature's Temple is birthed, a universal space to invite international teachers to be hosted and supported. Nature's Temple is a small facility, we are actively looking for sponsors to fund a much larger center in different locations. The vision is to build Nature's Temple on as many continents as possible. To share building workshops, skill shares, permaculture, meditation and inspire a way of life that our ancestors used to walk so gracefully.

However, the amount of retreat centers being built is low-key saturating the industry, and instead of sharing one mission, we are all breaking into separate spaces. I see this as both giving life and possibly taking life or at least more time in our lives. Our differences make it all more beautiful, and to see so many people stepping up and sharing their inner standing of how they have found peace and connection to self and nature. One observation I had growing up was that Crestone, home of countless centers and retreats, is catering to a certain audience, an audience of wealth and Western thinking, that is where the market is indeed. The organizations and nonprofits support their works, and many are sharing proceeds back home to their communities in Nepal and India. Crestone is a center for so many people in the USA today to come for rest and retreat, highlighting to me some of the most authentic teachers with vast principles passed down from teacher to teacher. It is truly beautiful. However, is there a space for the people who are lacking funds to access these spaces? Are we too judgmental to accept them as themselves, possibly smelly, and a little rough around the edges? And further without proper funds. It seems that the street people and the ones who have experienced more trauma in society are still going unseen and unsupported. We all know that the power of choice will end you up where you stand today, and your habits will reveal your future moments of life. So, it is somewhat fair to say that they got themselves into it. However, as we have been speaking in this book there has been so much negative influence pushed on humanity that I look at this situation and I find my finger pointing at the inner workings of the system.

For example, the war on drugs and the criminal acts to my knowledge was an inside job as powerful players moved mass amounts of cocaine into our countries and even worked with the police and other allies. They flooded the streets with drugs and then proceeded to arrest so many people. This is a smart system, of course, to make money on both ends of selling and distributing narcotics and then locking up people for carrying some. It became evident that once again we see them painting the wall a different color, as human rights for people of color and Indigenous communities are surfacing still, all of us in America are subject to mass brainwashing. We can look into how slavery changed, yet the oppression is quietly delivered in different ways. Still, a very nasty way, a clever way to lock up so many strong men, there are more people of color incarcerated than anyone else today.

So, the list goes on as we look into so many aspects of big pharma and the CDC control drug center. Or Control Disease Center, bought the same for me, as they oversee diseases and drug distribution. It appears that this is similar to the war on drugs, once again covered up to look like people are doing good deeds, whether they make it look like they are cleaning up the streets and locking up "criminals" which in reality they are locking up fathers whose children won't have natural direction from their dads, and the cycle continues of street kids getting caught in gang activity and street drugs. Or big pharma releasing new anti-depressants that in return have so many repercussions. How many drugs are administered that have addictive qualities, it's obvious that there are street drugs, illegal ones, and the "scientific" drugs, legal ones that are made from similar plants and processes. The process of making meth is very scientific. Just as adoral, and fentanyl, people are dying from these legal drugs even more than street drugs. Due to mismanagement and allowing them to become leaked into the streets from overprescribing. Pretty much supplying a lucrative drug business. They make it look like they are curing diseases when they are spreading more. Making up new diseases and then releasing new drugs that "cure." Don't get me wrong, I appreciate aspects of Western medicine and am very grateful for the good it provides today, saving lives all over the world. Big Respect to the doctors living in truth and authenticity giving proper diagnosis and speaking health into their patience. Just like in all early evolution, medicine is an actively growing subject and study. And is ancient to our early ancestors as well as helped birth the Western medicine of today, passed on and shifting throughout time in many variations.

It is very beautiful learning and sharing of knowledge, yet money is a powerful substance, and someone will sell their findings to get out of the system – simply, money is a way to get out of the game and enjoy your resort mansion. Many politicians, inventors, celebrities, contractors, lawyers, doctors, entrepreneurs, and anyone who made it to a point of power, may sell out or sell what they crafted or invented. You earned it, its every man for themselves, as they say. Gosh, sounds like a man-made construct to me. People have always been a communal species, since the first family arrived, they worked together, and all played their roles to be comfortable and in harmony. We already looked into the food industry and how we are literally seeing a large amount of our people eating their way to a comfortable and complacent seat on the couch, in their house. Fasting used to be a common occurrence in humankind, how will we survive when someone takes away some simple bare necessities? Building resilience and toughness is not as natural, many of us habitually do not carry tools and even lose jobs to machines, robots, or AI. We end up settling in watching the latest updates of world news and continuing to watch novel films and play games, as our elemental family gets lonely and farther removed from participating with human beings. Our relationship with our Earth is being shuttered with walls, industry, food, and drugs. In Ghana, the brothers and I would joke about the fraud nation. We see the system implementing yet another show, releasing another commotion, and separating people as we now are witnessing anti-vaccine people to pro-vaccine COVID-19 people. Simply race is not dividing us as much as it used to, they will always give us something to analyze to distract us away from coming together. Can we together lay these dualities to rest?

If they want to divide, why not give us the choice? This is one idea of how I can see a peaceful revolution. Giving the people the choice to move back into the village so to speak, allow us to garden and farm for ourselves, chop wood, and carry water, becoming reliant on our workings. And then allowing for the fast food, 5g, and other aspects of the modern world. That is arguably already dividing us from ourselves in a sense. To each their own, I respect the people who want the Western world, people around the world want this, due to what they don't have. It is no longer based on race or religion; it is based on a feeling in your heart.

Back to the agenda, due to freedom of choice, some people are drastically changing their lives and take the notion of isolating themselves in the walls and confinements of our houses. At the beginning of COVID-19, news of treating people infiltrated our ears, if we broke the "RULE," there was going to be a consequence. Was this a global control experiment?

Gosh, it seems to me that they were probing us as a collective, checking in to see who is complacent, or easily herded so to speak. We have all witnessed what happens to the ones who stand up and revolt, gunned down time in time again. COVID-19 was an amazingly thought-out experiment that they exercised on the whole of the world. We know that there has been and still is an amazing and very well-thought-out global plan. Simply, only light and Wi-Fi travel at these speeds, the evidence shows it is a true globalization. Kept quiet as well. Painted over again. It seems that this specific virus was also a great excuse and possibly a much-needed experiment. To see what the results would be if we stopped the world as we know it for a short time to see what would change. What did we see? We saw animals coming back into the streets, we saw fish coming back in population, and even the air quality started to shift as factories were closed and workers were sent home. Pollution cleared and stars were seen. In one view, this shows that the people devising these plans do care and are actively looking at the destruction of our Earth. Revealing they do carry love and empathy and carry a heavy consciousness, possibly repenting or wanting to do some good. However, it's too late to do good without doing more life-taking. Quite literally, I'm not sure of the number of deaths now but it is a global toll on the human population, killing people all over the world. The depopulation plan has been up in conversation in the last few years and could be part of this global plan. It could ring true that the world is showing signs of struggles, to support us. All our relations are dealing with displacement and have been for a long time, born into it even. Actively adapting to new environments and mutating new aspects of being. America today is the product of the most planned-out strategy of our age. For this could not just come to be so simply. Masterful minds, indeed. Yet recreated or taken from our early ancestors. A desire to mimic the magical qualities of such creations.

It may be to our benefit to brace ourselves and accept that a lot will be destroyed before a new, will take place. The talk of a global reset is projected for 2030, I hear, the agenda has been in place and actively working. If this is true, then we have 5 years only before the hype is real. Now, reaching a point of needing to change, I'm hoping that the great reset, if that is true, will help the planet and come from a place of re-evaluation of what has been put down in our past 100 years. Could the great reset, be a global revolution taking place? A shot of true love, or a fear of our demise? Or are we as common people going to stand up and speak out about making the changes? The first step is to expose the hate, as we are putting together so many pieces that many of us are aware of, putting into words and revealing the hidden truth, in a stance of peace, stating the evidence of a completely hateful and manipulative act against our family members, human to human. So sad to think about, most of my adult life I heard people asking what the fuck is going on in the world, I've thought the same myself.

So, the idea of revolution or great change will be brought up from time to time until we finish. Ideas and history, for in every cycle of human life we see a great rise, a renaissance time, are we now in the time of technological Renaissance, with many leaders leading us forward in their agenda, while we the people are struggling to find direction. We just continue down the rabbit hole until we get to the bottom of the pit. I think I've arrived at the bottom; it is dark and gloomy – it's hard to see a way out. The only way I can imagine is working together, standing on each other's shoulders to reach the surface, to get a view of what life was like. When we mentally time travel back to a day where no one was oppressed, a day that was shared amongst all children of the sun. Now, getting our ground back on the surface and looking deep into the pits and darkness, we can move forward acknowledging what was then and this is now. As we come from the bottom, we get to know the darkness well, the light is simultaneous, the powers that have been hidden from us, the power of nature that is our true identity, our birthright, that some of us don't even know about. The word guru means the bringer of light into the darkness.

For when it is so dark the eyes can't see, close your eyes and visualize yourself as a light. A light that emanates from your heart and leads you forward through the fears of whatever lies in the darkness, for in darkness the eyes may not need to see what is ahead, for the light in your heart lends a feeling of presence. The presence of great spirit and spirit will lead you on. With or without your body, your spirit leads you to the heights of nature of self, the source of creation.

Do we have to play their game? They may also know that life never ends and that's why they can easily kill and manipulate without turning an eye. Could it be that having faith in spirit and light is all we need to accelerate forward in a healthy movement of peace and mindfulness – movements together a movement as one?

I needed to go home to Africa, the original place of human beings, the place of so much beauty and resources, the place that humans sold humans, the place that all of this timeline could have stemmed from. After witnessing the world, the evidence is there, just as in India a strong past of deep connection rich in spirits and adorned by colorful culture. Naturally so beautiful that they were atop the list for resources knowledge and power. There is a light force and a dark force, a life-giving energy, and a life-taking, just like anywhere, like Shiva and Brahma, one God of destruction and one God of creation. We could look at this as a natural process of nature and sit back and watch the universe unfold, keep doing our meditations and breathing through our traumas and our stresses, yet turn an eye to the destruction of our Earth and our original DNA.

There may be some who think we can access higher power and keep moving forward as we are, yet that's similar to ignorance in bliss. How could you really access your higher power if you are turning an eye to a bully pushing so many of us around indirectly and quietly? The soldier in me says to get up go out and speak up, I've never been a fighter and I'm certainly not a killer, silence is a killer so I'm also going to avoid being quiet and watching so much die, at the least I can voice. Can you watch any more of this take place without getting involved? As I stated, before one's eyes can be the eyes of many, one vision can be shared by all. The more eyes on it the better, the more the vision becomes clearer, and a reality can become manifesting or accumulating.

It's crazy to think about how all of this has been planned from road construction, buildings, powerlines, plumbing, factory farming, clothing industry, food industry all of it, technology at its finest. A massive vision. Our DNA is shifting, as we ingest the environment of the new world. One interesting aspect about the "American dream," they say it is the land of the free, freedom to do as you like. Sounds liberating, sounds dreamy, however, the amount of energy or information they leaked to the streets, such as guns, drugs, and pretty much anything your money can buy you is here, even changing your sex. So, it is indeed the land of the free and freedom of choice. Yes, yet a downfall of simplicity of self and originality. I romanced the old days because life was simple, the information was less, and the energy was pure. We can look at ourselves as a body of water reflected as an ocean filled with particles of waste, and extras, literally the ocean is filled with leftover Gucci, Nike, KFC, lost fishing nets/floating fish traps, drugs, apparel of all things lost in the oceans. Whether we look at the human body of water or the ocean's body of water, we can see ourselves as we see her. These are all man-made contaminants, hopefully, the self is ingesting other things into our body as well, more natural and Earthly substances. I don't know how much longer our oceans can take without rehabilitation.

We have for so long been pillaging the land and emitting such life-taking energy from the world, resulting in human distress and uncertainty about where we go next. In my experience, it's better to just say flat out I've fucked up, take accountability, speak truth to the people or person. It's almost like a shy boy trying to tell his girl about how he feels, or that he was sleeping with someone else or at least thinking about it. If he hides the truth, he will go around thinking badly of himself, not being himself becoming colonized in the mind, forgetting his empathy and care for a royal woman. He forgets his honesty his integrity and his will to be the best. I'll talk a little more later about relationships between men and women later.

It looks like they are hitting us in all three main parts of a human being, hitting our spirits with drugs. Drugs made from plants and minerals usually invite the spirit of the plant to enter into our spaces and even get caught up in our spirit, starting a relationship with them instead of ourselves. In the end, finding our energy and self in environments that are not actively maintaining the temple of self, the home of your potential spirit coming back, potentially confusing other life-giving energies from reaching you because your body is confused about which energies to engage.

Hitting our mind with so much information and excessive thoughts that our mind does not know where to direct ourselves. We don't know who we are, over processing the amount of the modern world, have we lost sight of healthy manhood, society has made us out to be too much, forgetting about the simplicity of a divine being of man or womb-man. People are getting confused if they want to be a man or a woman, society today has made it possible for you to change 1/3 of yourself into something different. I'm a supporter of anyone's choice but that does not mean I understand or feel as they do. I could put myself in their shoes, I've thought plenty about what it would be like to be a woman. Or how hard it is to be a successful man in the world of today. What is healing without acceptance of self? With all the mental programming and projection of beauty norms, people are caught up in acceptance of self, not feeling good in their bodies simply because their minds perceive themselves to not fit the shape. Mentally confused about who we are.

Hitting our bodies with the obvious GMO foods, drugs, contaminated water, and concrete under our feet, holding our bodies back from resting on the soils of the Earth, making everything accessible so our body does not get to move through it. Our body needs action, or it will slow. Our body is the holder of our story, and they are actively scribbling on our canvas.

It's no wonder why we as a race are somewhat scrabbling to find our way back to ourselves, looking into books, community, Ted Talks, internet readings, and seeking teachers. We are all a part of this great finding of ourselves, on our way back home into our inner standings of nature of self. It really reflects why we are seeing so many retreat centers and people trying on different modalities of healing. I've been very invested in building myself into a facilitator of nature and building a retreat center to share the voices of nature, as I said. A decade devoted to finding myself and putting ideas into reality has been a very slow process full of ups and downs, as we all know feeling moments of inspiration and then lying down asking the creator why nothing seems to work. We need each other to make things work, together we can assist each other like in the good old days.

It wasn't till my fourth year of Sundancing, the final year of my first vow and commitment to praying for our relations, and dancing, calling for SSpommitapiiksi/WAKAN SKAN. I stated Sundance brings a lot of people who have been through a lot including myself, people coming back to the tree after getting caught up in drugs and altering substances. Realizing that the sense of temporary happiness from substance is not going to do it, for the purpose is not as strong. Each Sundancer has an individual reason and commitment for them and their families. It's one of my favorite times of year to come back and all pray together. I am just another dancer, dancing for our wounds to be healed, and our visions, our connections to bear fruits.

Nature is with us and the singers hold us up with their songs and drums. The days blur together as you stay present looking at the tree and dancing for your relations. It was in these days that a thought entered my mind about the need for rehabilitation. The contrast of how many rehab programs are available to us versus retreat centers. It made sense that this would be a message to change my trajectory, my mission in life was starting to reveal itself more. In my youth, I became close with users and actually enjoyed and loved their company. One interesting aspect of an addict is that they don't need much to feel good besides their substance of choice and their community. This is a curious look into general happiness, for when one is high on their supply, their problems dissipate, and a new energized feeling inspires. Of course, when one comes down, the feelings and potential sorrows are present again. However, it may indicate that one thing is all you need to be at peace or feel relief, other than the bare necessities of food, water, and shelter. One special ingredient, the notion of light energy that surrounds you, may be all you need to feel heightened, simply replacing the addiction with awareness. You would be a very impressive person. Especially with the addition of addictive chemicals put into tobacco. Curios to me is the breaking down of one's body through the journey of their highs and lows delivering many addicts to confront God or something higher. At some point, the high they know very well is found in another avenue, whether that's through Jesus or Sundancing, often very proud, rightfully as we stand in pride together. This pride carries us in life as it shows it helped us clean off. Making a way for us to come back to something that brings purpose. Celebrating sobriety is a true gift if you come from a drug culture or a poverty mindset, not referring to the financial aspect more so our energetic wealth. Sobriety is being in good relationship to all of our lives, to carry good energy and speak good words. cultivating a reality of health and happiness and sharing that with others.

I went to support at one Sundance located on a military base in Colorado, soldiers came to witness our First Nation people and see our way of life, how we pray, and how we conduct ourselves. Many Sundancers I've met and First Nation people fought under the American flag, were usually being drafted without consent. To see all Soldiers gathering around the arbor, honoring and hosting the Sundance ceremony, a healing sight to see indeed. My uncle had posted a page at the front entrance, saying: leave your crystals, singing bowls, tuning forks, yoga, and other spiritual equipment out. This is kind of a strong statement, but when I saw it, I laughed out loud. I found joy in this as I also felt that the spiritual community was starting to rely on too many aspects for their image and inner joy. It also stated that the Lakota way of life is powerful, and you don't need anything extra. As I've said, there have been real healings, physical healings that take place in the ceremonies. It's similar to how my senior priest explained about the voodoo spirits, he kept saying this is no joke, these African spirits are strong. There are tools we use in these ceremonies, made of all-natural material, animal bones, hairs, feathers, plants and trees, drums, and certain songs. It's all done according to the protocol of how the ceremonies have been handed down. This rings true for all indigenous rituals I've been a part of. It's no-show.

Outside of these ceremonies, we see a lot of people glamorizing and wanting to practice certain aspects of the spiritual works. This has produced a massive conversation about APPROPRIATION. It seems when someone does not understand what we do with feathers, yet they think it's cool to wear them, that is when we see people getting upset. The conversation has been present my whole adult life, as we see our traditions replaced with transient trends. The industry for spiritual accessories has boomed in the last 10 years. I know that many of my friends including myself, feel upset due to people not knowing what they are wearing, thinking that it fits a feeling they have. Now, of course, we are all connected, so no wonder, we are all having similar thoughts of wanting to get back to our spiritual selves. The authenticity of this exploration is the key. If you have not been blessed by another to do ceremonies, don't mess around, elders have said this can give life and take life. I witnessed this firsthand, holding someone as their heart stopped, and their spirit went back to the source. It is no joke as Kwame said and some of us have seen first-hand what happens when you play around it. The creator is gentle, and senses we are lost, so the innocence of our lack of knowledge keeps us like babies. Man will not scold a baby for crying, it is naturally finding comfort and crying out in hopes of receiving nourishment. That's all we are, babies crying out for attention, crying out to be seen. For one who sees himself in god and god in himself will not cry for attention, he will cry out to his relations so that we can all see god in ourselves. The remover of recognition, an unshakable conduction of energy. With nothing to prove, simply resting in awareness resting in the purity you were born into.

As I look deeper into this spiritual movement, I see that there are so many items people are wanting, which I'm sorry to say is also a consumption that is increasing, the more people come to. The woke movement is seeming to inflate even more. So, while people are looking spiritual and feeling good about themselves, the indigenous are sitting back with minimal need to buy spiritual accessories, with a strong oral tradition that carries us, unseen things such as songs and prayers. Not to celebrate drug use at all and with some humor. Almost makes me think that the ones who overcame addictions are more resilient and spiritual than the young ones pulling on a spiritual suit, not needing to put on much, and being able to withstand more difficulty. Most of the spiritual community does not have to work the same way we used to, enjoying similar to expats. I'm guilty of being a part of this too. Let's look at the impact that the spiritual community is having on the world. The need for Palo Santo, sage, feathers, peyote, ayahuasca, and many other things to enhance mental spiritual satiation. These spiritual plants are being produced and shipped all over the country, produced at higher rates than ever. I've seen footage of ayahuasca businesses that are looking like a cocaine factory. There are peyote deserts in Mexico that I hear more and more are being harvested rapidly. I can look into the near future if we keep it up, we may start to lack wild medicine. Palo Santo is a tree, of course, and sage is a plant. It could be that if Walmart is now selling smudge kits that's evidence of a mass industry of growing and supplying to massive stores. Now, I do believe we can produce all of these things sustainably. This is a look from above the border, I'd like to know more perspectives from south of the border. I'm just looking at our past and how we have been operating. We can see that we will continue to sell nature for money the global currency that we now rely on for survival. I'm sure the people in South and Central America are happy to be making money and supporting their families while working with their natural resources. A part of me worries that the power of the system will win them over and they will keep the supply going without recognizing the repercussions, just as the ones buying may not realize how others may be looking at them, not to say they are contributing to the demands of nature. I'm happy to see more natives and non-natives getting together and blending. That is how we can come to an understanding that we are all coming back to a healing place and the innocents. A lack of education is a large part of why people appropriate without even knowing it – there is sympathy.

While we can let go of our judgment and celebrate each other and even laugh at each other, "Golly gee, so you want to be an Indian, huh? We'll let me teach ya, aye." One of my favorite parts of a great Indian movie. I think it's Pow Wow Highway or smoke signals. Both are recommended movies. My Sundance brother jokes it isn't easy being an Indian. And that's the truth, we already went over why, always remember how far native Americans have carried their traditions and spirits. Through recent oppression and genocide, never forget how strong our global Indigenous fellow brothers and sisters are. For remembering and carrying these old ways of life, for remembering and speaking the voices of nature. The humility is effortless due to the environment, wisdom is found like feathers picked off the birds, arranged into beauty! Authentically and organically, only to share about the beauty, the simple wisdom that brings us into resting in our cells. One who waits patiently, with listening ears may be blessed by a winged one and the wisdom that bird kept. Nature will lead you to know the natural systems.

No native I know is buying feathers in stores or online. The creator blesses the ones who are ready to receive a message or a responsibility to carry these items or songs. Our early ancestors received songs from great spirits that have been passed down and sung the same way for generations. The Great Spirit is still communicating songs and messages to the people who are ready to carry them. That's a sure way to recognize if you're playing around with store-bought items or if nature graced you with a sacred object. To Wanbli Galeshkha, the spotted eagle may your offspring be abundant and your messages of heavenly wisdom continue to assist us, with gratitude to you.

My personal experience with appropriation has to deal with being lighter skin, or white the colonizer's name for us, and being into reggae and Afro culture. The music, the look, the feeling, I grew up always confused about why I didn't have an afro on my head and why my skin was lighter. I didn't feel so comfortable in my skin, not knowing why I wasn't browner, took me a long time to celebrate myself as I am now. Accepting my trauma story, being a European mutt with some sprinkles of world genes. I've finally found pride in my heritage, and I know myself. I know my indigenous origins to a degree, but I'm still listening and learning. Maybe God gave me this body and mind so that I can feel a sliver of what it feels like to feel unease inside, a glimpse into a person of color's life, say 50 years ago or even today. Distressed to fit in the eyes of white standards looking at you. Can you put yourself in her shoes, can you close your eyes and imagine the level of uncomforted sensation in the body? Saddens me and has enraged me on so many levels after loving women of color and holding space for them in racially disrespectful situations. I have grown in anger and awareness of the ignorant white man in this colonized whitewashed world. To know about Africans bleaching their skin to look whiter, and wearing straight hair simply because of colorism in a world steered by white culture, colonial culture.

In Ghana, I'd loved seeing a proud African woman flaunting her natural hair, we have to be proud, we have to fight through the constructs of systematic manipulation. They have got people around the globe thinking different things about their skin, even whites tan to look darker. Because they think it's more beautiful? Colorism is a huge global topic that I've witnessed in so many countries, for countries of color and people of color, I pray for your pride and your natural beauty to flourish and celebrate. I pray that the manipulators will empower us instead of disempowering us. May we all feel good in our skin, and may we all find acceptance in ourselves and celebrate one another. May we acknowledge the effects it has played on our grandmothers and grandfathers and may we smile at them with love, may we be gentle on one another. For all people are beautiful.

What I'm trying to get at is the plan to divide and make us all uncomfortable in our skin, and now people more than ever, are uncomfortable about their sexual orientation. Is there a connection. this vulnerable and hopefully transparent sharing, standing for justice. I've always known I am here to procreate a colorful family, a family that carries multiple lineages, engages and honors the beauty and differences of our songs, and cultures. A family of goddesses that inspires children to remember and grow in a way of life. As it is so important to pass it on in good ways. We imagine each race has its privileges. Now I've heard it a time or two about my white privilege. It felt negative at times but always with love, usually coming from a woman I loved and respected. I come to terms with my white privileges, The more you travel the more you will see all races have a unique privilege in this world today. There are things I may not experience duc to my lack of understanding of another's culture, it goes all ways. My friend in Ghana explained to me. He can access things I'm unable to. It makes sense that all races have privileges that others don't, that's why, I feel mixed families are strong families, sharing the privileges or a less loaded word, uniqueness of each race, identify their powers, hence we are all human beings and share the same birthright, By coming together and celebrating these gifts, I see us arriving at the heights of privileges. The spiritual privilege, knowledge of all origins of their Earthly ancestors and together will be able to speak to all ears and souls.

The biggest privilege, nature of self and conduction of universal energy.

 Racial privilege could be how we got into this whole fucked up situation in the first place, simply one heritage was jealous of another's and devised a plan to control them and revoke their power? There are four main races of man in the cartoon The Last Airbender. There are four colors of people all carrying different powers or privileges, they are at war with each other, based on the power struggle of showing who is the top – tiny dogs bark loudly, and big dogs chill.

Seems that many movies are helping us make sense, thank you art, comedy, and music. Another modern movie shedding light on this topic is 'Get Out' a movie based on gene manipulation, stealing, and re-creating. These are big topics, triggering conversations on all sides. I've heard that every 7 years our molecules and thoughts almost fully change, depending on what we ingest. It seems that 7 generations ago was a completely different time as well, no one alive now without a heart would stand for what has taken place, there are simply too many activists and journalists, and if someone was acting out of such evil they would be stomped. I've done my best to acknowledge the timeline from a global perspective. And I'm leaving some room for your inner gut to figure out what's what and make your way. I already feel like I'm sharing a lot of information in a time of very informed people. I'm intentionally writing this to expose the evils and hate and to bring some light. People of truest light step forward, ones who feel love and want to embrace each other are allies. I'm here as an ally to my fellow human beings, and conductors of light and love. Speaking on behalf of people of color in this country as a witness to the known facts stated, I must also honor the genes and speak up for a confused and possibly scared group of lighter skins made and named into whites, displaced also from our original clans as well. The system is strong and has pulled one over on us, shaming us for what took place over 7 generations ago – a time before the globe was westernized, recognizing that this is not just a trauma of the USA today but a global trauma and a way to wipe out our original way of life. We are slowly realizing that black-and-white separation is over, the man-made dualities can rest in knowledge. Yet still they try to keep us divided with the Pandemics and fear tactics. Cycles will help us reveal and prepare for more of what we have already seen. I'm speaking from an observational viewpoint. A view of looking at the Earth as a whole and hoping to address all our relations.

 I've been actively healing through the darkness, traveling physically by plane and then energetically traveling to look into the minds and realities of humans and animal's spirits, etc. We must not run from the wild but embrace the wild listening to the trees, and chatting with the animals. Seeing from the bird's view, and feeling what humankind is experiencing. When I was a youth, people used to say I looked like Mowgli.

People always feed your ego people joke around with me and tell me that I look like a Moses guy. In Ghana and Togo, people said I looked like Jesus, the response was I am a human being. Just another "white" hippie fitting the bill of a picture, a picture of a white man's savior. You have to watch out for people feeding your ego, you have to walk with humility, or a person will become confused with thinking they know too much, thinking they are something that they are not. Spirit will not see your heart because your mind is too big, If the true vision comes from the heart as the texts say, and we all know that a great leader does not elect himself. He is elected by his community, and trusted by the people. Adolf Hitler was said to be elected into that position of evil. Evidence tells us that makes sense, how can a man step into such power without the support of the ones behind him? Only through music, vibration, and awareness of the message and miracles will a great leader effortlessly emerge. Just like retreat hosts, everyone wants to lead the way. A good friend of mine said we are living in a time of false profit, a time of mass profiteering, a time of selling spiritual wear, a scam, telling us that we are in the dark and we need to pay money and do this and that to come back to ourselves. Then the pain continues because we are not at true peace, we haven't been accepting ourselves as we once were, and we are still navigating the trenches. We pop our heads out from time to time and see the light.

We are children of the sun, we are reflections of our father and mother, and we are the conductors of our birthing of light that affects all things in our lives. Light is love and seeing love in all things is the only tool we need to be happy; we simply need to practice, practice, and practice.

One church day, I enjoyed was at a small church, a church my great-grandfather attended from when he was born till he died. I'd say 90 years of praying to God. True devotion. My grandfather was a man of God and even if I didn't understand how he did it, he was a happy man full of laughs and cries, he prayed for us and said the blessing before every meal thanking Jesus for his food and the blessings in his life. He would often cry as he prayed in his older years of life. I'd like to go to church with him to show that I care and just to spend some time with him. I was surprised to hear one day the preacher preached to me. For the first time, I felt and heard him without my filter or translation.

I think he was speaking to me, there were only maybe 6 to 10 people in the room 4 or 5 of us were a family. I had my hair down, and I looked like an outsider kind of rough around the edges. At that time, I was still under the idea that I didn't care too much about how I looked. The preacher went on to preach that the shepherds were the wise men who knew that Jesus was coming soon. For they were not in the city, they were not thinking about money, they were not concerned with the local conversations. The shepherds were walking with their sheep, they were living wild, they did not care to brush their hair, the preacher said, they were nappy-headed bushmen who read the stars who felt the voices of nature. Starting to sound like my people!

The preacher went on to say they were the ones who heard the message of Christ coming. The preacher states over and over again, I know I said it once and I'm saying it twice invite the Father, the Lord, and Savior into your heart, for you will then enter the kingdom of heaven. Translated in the mind of a spiritual rebel once again, to invite the light of the sun into your heart, the savoir of yourself allowing you to enter the kingdom of heaven. A sight emanated from your heart. In the book Tibetan Yoga, which is full of color, to witness such beauty, you will not be able to deny the beauty of the essence of nature/God. Sun and Earth are the home to an energy so beautiful, a light that gives so much life, and welcomes what has been and always will be the kingdom of heavenly life. The only planet in our nine-planet solar system that holds this amount of diverse life.

The evidence is there that we once lived in a space of divine harmony with nature, a place of no judgment, a place where human beings conducted the energy of the sun and all elements. The original privilege of a human being, I like to believe that the indigenous people of long, long ago lived in the un-mantled Earth which is the kingdom of heaven on Earth and still is today. In my eyes and always has been, yet disrupted by an individual who becomes disturbed, taking it upon himself to go against his fellow, it appears, however, that this took place and took off, and the gears of evil cranking away. Naming and judging, hurting our fellow mates, taking an original painting, and changing it drastically. Reminds me of the art form called DADA taking a picture and adding to it, not erasing it but changing the face so much that you can't tell it is original. In the findings of the fraud nation, we decode and rewrite the old ways again. Calling out systems that are not of nature. Some experience in personal devotion and hearsay, or a story to mend a broken heart. Many have been killed in the name of a god. And many pray to be healed for their obvious sins. An odd exchange, to justify thought in prayer and then comb over the actions by stroking the personal god or deity for ease. For one does not need the blessing from Jesus or Buddha, yet the source of light that activated them in cellular remembrance is all you need.

But hey, my great grandfather took the name of Jesus, and many devote to Shiva, some to the self, some to nature and they feel good and full of joy. The essence of light, the essence of nature has been named hundreds of times. Many are called few are chosen they say. It appears if you choose then you are chosen. It's up to you to see love for you to see light, for you to choose what world you want to see. What you want to be connected to. My best human teachers would often guide me deep into a space and then I'd intuit what could come next and he would affirm my findings. You are the one you have been waiting for. Bob Marley sang there's a natural mystic in the air, the mystical energy has been here forever. I'm here sharing my relationship with nature and how it has been a mythical journey to arrive here. We are all human beings, if we don't massage each other and share a vision, of our liveliness, then we can waste away in sorrow and pain for what took place. It has been a dark time. Yet the mystical energy is indeed in the air.

I've been and will continue to be vulnerable here about my relationship to self, how nature found me, and how the nature of self is explored, I hope that my process does not offend others. I hope that I can be a living example of a person who highly appreciates and has worked hard to actively speak out for the service I feel for humanity. The naming game calls this line of work a humanitarian study.

Going through the struggle together and coming out in love shows us that a man and woman can become one, naturally starting to act and sound the same. The divine union of two beings in transparency, together exposing their light and dark. Moving into awareness of each other's depth. Sexual union is one of the highest forms of meditation and has been far removed from what it was, with the porn industry and the sexualization of clothing body, and even the act of sex. Simply our sexual relationship with self needs rehabilitation as well, men and women lack understanding of each other due to the influence of nonintentional sex. Both looking for fulfillment in the counterparts of yin and yang. Have we forgotten our roles? Are we struggling to be the men and women we once were? Are we addicted or assisted so heavily we can't stop? Human beings conduct royal energy of the kingdom of heaven and share that. To do so, it appears to me that many women are protective of their wombs, the evidence of an era of male-driven patriarchy has landed us in a world where men are becoming desperate for sex because they may not be tuning into their nature. Leaving women to be on guard for what else does a woman want than to share in the true nature of love? The reflection of the wild. A colonized mind will struggle to be still and build a healthy relationship with creation. Men's main role is to assist in healthy creation, as women birth new, men's role is to provide safety and security to direct and build healthy space for healthy life.

Music and vibration naturally bring people together. Love brings us together. I've found to not push love on others but be love in yourself, and love will find you. Don't try to sound like someone else per se, wait for your voice to come out, and allow your energy to expand into something that feels authentic.

Authenticity is the difference between appreciation and appropriation. That's why, I tell people I don't know how to play or sing reggae, after going to Ghana and spending time with Ghana Rasta and living and learning, I came home finding my voice changing and being able to sing in a reggae style a landscape that I experienced, I drank the river waters in Africa, I sat with the ghetto youth, I was invited to the slums, I got an up-close experience of African life, the life after Alkubelon. The African people called me white as they shouted abroni abroni, white, white. But as I stayed longer and got to know them deeper, they started to say you Ghana man, you African, you have this hair you are African. They said Africa has made you strong like us. Tolerant to the bullshit systems that they left us with. That was healing for me to be accepted by a place my soul had been calling me back to. As I entered back into the USA, I could feel the difference and feelings of judgment sometimes.

I think a large part of the healing of the USA today has to do with embracing each other. We are here now, there's no going back in time, as we all look forward together, we can choose to stay stuck in the systematic doings of the colonizers and the colonized mind, or we can recognize and actively start airing out what has taken place in this country and the world. No wonder why everyone is buying so much sage, aye. We are smudging down the grounds, this is all a part of the evolution that has taken place, as intense as it has been and as upsetting and angry as a lot of us are. I'm at the bottom of it. I've been peering into the darkness for a long time now up close and firsthand spoken from people who know about the darkness of the pits.

There's a big conversation going on about white people shying away from wanting to talk about slavery and genocide. It's hard to talk about because whites may be afraid of being prosecuted, indeed a true white to me, a planner or founding father of globalization, should be deemed guilty as charged. The majority of lighter skins still receive the same treatment as the whites. The prosecutor will in the end be prosecuted. I'd just say that I hope that based on what we have been through as a collective in the last 400 years, is taking a long time to heal – it's a big wound that has shed blood all over the world. Global colonization has occurred, and the bloodshed of our ancestors is spilled around the world. I don't believe we need to prosecute anymore. The true Whites are dying off, for they are not needed.

When I was in India I talked about the USA as not being a place I wanted to live because of the system and the tension at hand, I wanted to relocate and help out in India. I had met a beautiful Indian woman who was a young activist for women's rights and normalizing sexual exploration. Exposing the unhealthy patriarchy, and judgment placed on sexually curious women. I read a lot of this book to her. This book has been updated and changed and I've barely looked at the original text. There's just so much happening in my body, so much global information, information is energy, we will say it again and again. I'm so full inside; the writing is falling like rainwater nourishing the dry Earth. As I write this, I'm healing, I'm putting things together further. I hope that it lends the reader a sense of comfort and nurture that we are in this together. In Ghana, they kept repeating one family, one love. Truly embracing the people of the promised land taken from Mount Zion, a message from the center of the world as the Ghanaian people say.

What I was told in India was that I was born in the USA and today was needed there, why would you leave that place to come help over here, I was asked. Was I running from a place I didn't understand and felt misunderstood myself? Still to this day I feel like a stranger in a foreign land.

After going to Ghana, I realized for the first time the opportunity to be born in the USA, not because of the poverty and the struggle but because nearly every person I met said the USA is my favorite country. I dream I will be there one day. This tells us that America is the most desired place due to the extensive plans to comfort and assist us, nearly retiring all people from hard labor and straight into luxury. This has been a common theme in many countries I've visited, countries that are undeniably different. They see America on TV the "American Dream." Every time I'm in another country, I talk about the complexities of the country and let them know it is different than what the tele tells them. I tell you that it is a good country yet built on the blood and tears of the anguish of our global community. I share my anger with them. The other thing I've learned is that a large part of the world is watching the USA and what we are doing, what are leaders are saying, and what the latest trends are. Music is unity, music is connection, music is power. Part of my love for Afro culture was Bob Marley's music and the movement and feeling that spread through the world almost as fast as light and sound. The power of the message and spreading of history and spirituality. Bob's music is played in every country I've been to and if it's not, I play some.

Looks like it's time to rehabilitate ourselves and our environments. A lot of people are actively doing so. How deep is our wound and how much rehabilitation do we need? Seems it's not only addicts who need rehab but all of us do, we are all tainted by social programming. Many people push away therapy including myself, if I hadn't been looking into this pit of darkness without my meditation practice, I think I'd be toasted. I'm very grateful for my elders and my councils, my uncles I can reason with, my community is my council, and my mother is my therapist. Although she says I should get a therapist separate from her, to decompress how I was abused in her eyes. In my eyes, I've been blessed with two parents, regardless of if I may have been abused based on how society sees abuse, the personal lives of families breaking, based on different cultures and how they conduct family. After seeing the darkness and venturing into the pits, I no longer traumatize my trauma; I don't victimize my inner victim, I don't identify with my pain identity. These are all aspects that have helped me, not to say that I don't get down as I said, I've layed on the floor lost in depression and lack of hope for myself. Meditation has been one the biggest rehabilitations in my life. Yet my water is contaminated and needs even more rehabilitation. I'm carrying more energy/information than ever, and it feels heavy. I am currently rehabilitating myself back to my younger self with way less to think about and just a lot to feel.

I guess I'm referring to rehabilitation in a different sense. The sense of rehabilitation of each aspect of our one-thirds our minds, our bodies, and spirits could use some updating. Some say our bodies consist of 9 bodies, some say more. Energy is stored in our flesh, blood, water, and energy fields. To me, that's why, we attract the community we do, based on the energy or information we are ingesting we will usually find ourselves in the vicinity of similar people. If you are like me then you have a lot of energy and attract a very diverse array of people which makes you sometimes stick out like a sore thumb. People ask you what are you doing here. How did you hear about this? Are you mixed race? Are you a native? Are you a Hindu? Sometimes you don't even know how you end up in some places in the world.

So, whether the word retreat or rehabilitate, I think it's the same. We all need the same healing though some just landed in the depths of the pits while some helped dig the pits, and all in between. I think the heaviness is becoming too much to carry for the oppressor and the oppressed, we are on the rise. I come from a family of poverty on one side and then a middle class on the other, different stories, different standards, and different ideas, yet both sides can heal from the one thing they repeated in Ghana LOVE. In Ghana, we would talk about human beings a lot. We are all the same inside, I have no judgment, trauma is unique to each individual, and we all deal differently.

My favorite godly family member is Tapritsa. He has been a true inspiration in my life my energetic father/mother Taparitsa is nonbinary – a rainbow Buddha depicted as a being of white light. Taparitsa is depicted with no adorations or accessories. Tapritsa is sustained in the energy and information, breathing in light and exhaling light. A true teacher reflects the power of source energy and that we need nothing more than a relationship with light. To the sun, to the tiny sun that you are. Spending time with our elemental and spiritual family will allow us to disengage from the material world and the things that comfort us. Indeed, the evidence is there that we are not so comforted by the darkness of the night and the Earthly scares. The media portrays the woods as being scary and wild. Well, we used to be wild, we are simply becoming like domesticated dog. I hope you can laugh with me. Are we walking the dog or is the dog walking us, are we nurturing plants or is the plant nurturing you? Both are real. Both are funny to think about.

In Togo, I got to sit in a little smoke shack, on a friend's front porch, we would roll spliffs, and put on movies. The old TV is what we watched on, in the 90s, situated on a wooden box suspended from the ceiling. We smoked up and watched the original Jungle book about the Indian boy raised by wild animals and the voices of nature. I was so happy sitting there enjoying the whole experience of watching the original Jungle Book from 1994. It's a great film to watch if you are curious about our ancestors and how I'd like to think we used to live a little more in harmony with nature, not afraid of the wild but faced the wild and became stronger with the wild. Could be similar to the movie Dances with Wolves, another great American Indian story. Depicting another child raised in the wild, both movies depict a relationship with nature and how communication became about with animal, elementals and spirits. Funny to be sitting in the world today where that movie looks like a magical realm, and from the time-traveling venture of putting ourselves in those shoes. Looking forward to the world of today, it would look like a sci-fi film. The world we live in is turning into a movie plot. The characters are coming soon, featuring the great reset. Okay, enough joking around, this is serious.

I always admire how my elders prepare a sacred space to do sacred things, busting some jokes along the way. There's a balance between getting caught up in serious thought, which can lead to mass difficulty, and then the balance of joking around the seriousness in life. Missing out on some true depths of human nature.

I'm adding in these funny bits to give a personable feeling, attempting to create a possibility to read into the writer, and letting the reader know that as we go into the depths of darkness we can laugh along the way, as we are tiny suns we need not fear. As we are in communication with our ancestors, we have guidance, they are also laughing with us and possibly at us. I'm a simple mountain dweller, going through the culture shock of the world, adding another level of foundation to your special and auric awareness.

This foundation is yet another reflection of nature, looking into a toroidal field of the Earth. The two polarities are similar to our crown chakra and our root chakra. You can google a picture of the Earth's toroid to see it.

You can close your eyes if it helps you to see it better, in some view, this is already happening just like the Earth, and just by bringing our awareness to it we can simply feel and sense energy moving through our central channel and our toroidal field. We are going to use our breath, inviting movement to an orb we are going to visualize resting at our sacral chakra. We will also use the idea that our sex organ is a chi pump or energy pump, as we can practice clenching the muscles of our sex organ, our perineum, and anus. This area is called the VMA, a Very Magical Area as stated by my original meditation teacher.

Toroidal Breathing came to me one night. I used to sit in a tiny corner of my bedroom. I moved a shelf by the wall and made a very tiny sitting space where I'd sit at my altar, this was my most innocent time exploring the nature of self. One of the most exciting times of my life, as I was being guided by my teacher and then going home to do the homework. Exercising what I learned and allowing my body to become open. Naturally, I felt the energy around me, as I already knew the microcosmic orbit, inhaling energy up the spine and exhaling down the front, a new avenue opened, and on an exhale, the energy went out of my crown and moved around my body. As I inhaled, the energy flowed around to my root chakra area, imagining the light reentering my body, a pattern that persisted. A mantra came through as well. Reflections of nature. Opening Expanding Absorbing Transforming, that was the mantra OPEN EXPAND ABSORB TRANSFORM. I found later that this practice is known as toroidal breathing more commonly known. I named it dragon wings as I drew a picture of it and incorporated it into my awareness. I had around 10 pictures of different meditations I drew that were either given to me by my teacher or nature gifted to me.

Toroidal breathing

- So, rest in a comfortable seat. Allow your inner eye to look into the body and heart. Smile with a skeletal awareness. Light emanates from your heart's center. Focus on your sacral chakra. Imagine an orb of light, a tiny sun similar to the one residing in your heart. Inhale deeply. Allow the orb to travel up your spine. As you inhale slowly, observe the tiny sun climbing your central channel. Influencing your bones, organs, flesh, and all of your being. As your breath reaches the end of the cycle, see the orb arriving at the top of your head. Exhale slowly and see the orb splitting into two in a toroidal manner, controlled by the exhale. Observe tiny suns rotation around each side, slowly traveling in half circles until they meet again at the end of your exhale. Imagine the tiny suns rejoining. That's one full cycle. As you inhale slowly flexing your VMA or chi pump, imagine the sacral chakra pumping the tiny sunup the spine once again. As the sun rises to the top of your head and the inhale turns to exhale, exhale slowly and control the pace and movement of the orbs, as it extends out like wings of light. Circling as you exhale slowly observing them once again coming back to the sacral chakra. Rest in your awareness of the rising of the tiny sun and setting in every breath. Every sun cycle rests a little deeper into the comforts and warmth offered by this posture. Continue this breathing pattern and inner yoga posture until you feel like resting.

You can imagine your anus as a portal for light or energy to enter. That sounds very strange, I know. Your crown is a portal. The cycle of the tiny sun rising and setting in your inner verse.

"Just a mere reflection of the earth in effortless action."

Chapter Seven
Eyes of The Beholder

In the study of religion, I always find myself baffled by the perspectives and views of each religion. There's a level of judgment and disbelief of another's faith, seen in the spiritual community as well. Almost like a power struggle of whose religion or connection is more powerful or more truthful, although they all feel so similar. It seems to me that religion is part of the repainting of our original blueprints. An outline of how to live life. Contorting a way of fluid life into a regimented and outlined container, like nature as it is or science the study of nature, both are good. Both can bring a daze of thought, either putting too much trust in God or science possibly or not trusting our actions and the repercussions of our deeds. Religious and spiritual leaders carry the pressure to perform, and carry a healthy relationship with themselves, if they are true to the source they will indeed be great teachers whether deemed spiritual or religious leaders. However, we see many fall short as they are also configuring their human nature and fluid life. Just as we common people, all relate to human experiences. Our relationship with ourselves, the analyzing mind, rushes of hormones, all the emotions, and an instinct to procreate even though many people don't want children! With unregulated sexual energy, emotions, and human behavior. We see rape, molestation, manipulation, and emotional abuse, a very full spectrum display of trauma. Usually, steered by one's greed and desire, a lack to see themselves in another. Without proper love and attunement, our conduction will be hindered and even faulty, to say the least. It is important to recognize true spiritual beings, and more important to not get engaged with a spiritual predator, a more common aspect of modern-day spirituality, as everyone is dressing up to fit the bill of a spiritualist. I believe many spiritual gurus if you will, are getting in trouble because they are too shy about their human nature and experience. Only talking about solutions and how to feel good, boasting about certain ideals that entice the trauma mind with comfort. So, we ask does the one that speaks comforting thoughts also need comfort? Gurus also experience their own trauma story, appears they might need even more support and comfort it is all too similar to yours and my experience. We can feel pity for them and even see why they are just as common as us in our growth and integrity.

It becomes easier and easier to see the truth. The true guru will live only up to the meaning of the good word guru. The bringer of light into darkness, true peace into chaos, a brand-new sensation of energy, coming with lighter thoughts. A guru will help you drop the weight of your suffering, only because he or she has witnessed suffering deeply and understands the abstract spectrum and how a human being can feel about it all. A guru who has not suffered or will not talk of his demons may not be able to help the wide range of souls and trauma. See the words he is saying are truly comforting, but the fault is that the guru himself does not say he also desires comfort. Possibly putting himself above sex even or deeper human connections a friendly connection. Attempting to persevere the waves of testosterone and the natural male desires. He may carry wounds of hurt, the guru must have also struggled in darkness, to arrive in the light. It appears many guru types keep their sexual desires to themselves until they have subconsciously created a reality possibly perfect in their mind, but because it goes unspoken or without full transparency. The guru may be living in denial or not speaking his full truth. Let alone speaking on the simplicity of your being and your natural birthright to connect to your higher self and all our supportive relations, naturally filling a human being with purpose and connection to something important. That offers them benefits, in return, the mind can rest in the knowledge of our devotion. Without anything higher than you or any teacher. This is why I refer to Nature itself as the only source left, of true evidence. The sun brings new light each day, we are made in the golden mean ratios, and we are made naturally connected. Solar beings, water crystals, conductors or chi, avatars of Earth. These are simple sciences of human nature or in my eyes, ways of nature, possibly forgotten or unfelt in many generations. The real guru would tell you that nature will teach you everything you need, that he is just like you, walking the journey of knowledge of inner standing and the building of the light body our solar body or sun body, Religions refer to our Christ body or rainbow body. Ask yourself truly and honestly. Where are you?

Nature has nothing to do but rest in its creation, always in a natural flow state, always evolving, always growing. See the teachings of nature are simultaneously everchanging and also consistently solidifying and breaking down. Nature is unshakable in its display of creation and destruction with no remorse no attachment to change, honoring of a timeline, and living in the surety of Mother Earth's and Father Sun's legacy. Our mother Earth withstands the mindlessness and the altercations of the unhealthy implementations that humans have set course. So, I'm saying simply, to just reflect on what nature is showing you. Many reflections of nature are simple. Maybe instead of a guru we just need a good friend to point out some of the things right in front of us. I know I have, many things I'm looking for are right in front of me, my mind too focused on other things to even see my pencil is sitting just there. Our mind is the entanglement of all energy we engage with and delivers us with the sights to see as we do. Mind is so easily changed or influenced, this is why I say choose consciously what you wash your brain with. Maybe this is why gurus have been needed. I, for one, support gurus of nature and believe the audience is also at fault for allowing themselves to succumb to an individual of such stature, knowing that they are just as common as we. See the guru loop system can be just as obvious as the CDC or any other system that continually brings people back for something that we can argue may or may not be needed. Recently a large handful of guru types have been exposed for different reasons. It is a buffet of the human mind and ego on display. I think we can all relate to the human spectrum; however, we are not putting ourselves in a position of pressure. So unfortunately, the ones who have, must be accountable for their actions and own up to whatever they got themselves into. It is common to see, that many of us struggle to speak our truths, our raw animalistic thoughts that naturally rotate around procreation and sexuality if we are being blunt. A human being must speak their mind they must not deny their natural thoughts, we cannot sugarcoat or be too nice. One must manage and hold oneself in full transparency, thus the growing importance of a clean and clear mind. I'd recommend identifying as a common person before announcing you have found god. The godly pedestal that comes with the pressure to perform and many eyes watching. A spiritual leader's responsibility is to be unshakable in his understanding of the universe and all of creation. To be a reflection of nature itself. This is why we always refer to Lord Shiva also known as ADI Yogi the original yogi sustained by the source of creation, the great example of a human being overflowing with love and light conduction. You should feel the difference. Of course, the percentage of humans in that adapted level may be under 1% as I believe today a few of us humans are still remembering the simplicity and pureness of all creation. Yet those yogis are uninterrupted in their travels and devotion, some stepping out to let science study them.

There are many "spiritual teachers" and some will indeed articulate the art of chi/information in a way that is logical and practical for the listening ear. If a person is coming to a teacher for teaching there is already a sense of adoration for that teacher, a sense of vulnerability is usually offered from recipient to teacher to learn and grow. That is the point at which the pressure is put on the teacher to give the teaching he or she says they will. Unfortunately, it seems, many male teachers and gurus forgot that sex is the sacred part of human practice and acceleration, offering so much creativity and bliss. Carrying it in a good way inspires purpose and effortless joy. But some have allowed for the colonized mind to enter them. Their sexual energy starts to drive them. Funny enough, it may be possible that religion was partly put in place to regulate sexual affairs prompting people to wait till marriage and preserve the purity of their sex for the right conduction. While the spiritual community seems to be all about the exploration of sexuality. Yet possibly lacking components to attract a sexual partner or please them, or better yet explore meditative sexual practice. It seems as if some of the greatest teachers would just share the simple desires they had, their humanness, and how comfort helps them. They may not be on the hot seat, or even worse guilty of an atrocity. Today, we have teachers of all things. I have had the pleasure of being in the presence of some great teachers, common people, and dear friends. People who are more and more uncommon in today's world. We have also had the opportunity to witness the downfall of what we thought was a great teacher. I've seen Mooji Baba in India, and studied some of yogi Bajan works, I will always admire his courage, his temple is only 3 hours from my home place, and I have been to see for myself his success, and know a handful of people who know his medicine was strong and of origin. Again, the weakness of the mind, sometimes wanting to rule rather than surrender. In these moments of today, judgment and activism at their highest, only the real will prevail, and only the truth will be recognized. We just hope that the day a great teacher arrives, we will have the ability to see them and feel them. For in the days of judgment, it is hard to find true connections, our skepticism and analyzing mind, our association to society, the norms and triggers. An amount of energetic calamity has accumulated in mass thought and is felt from afar. I know we are all questioning and disbelieving in the idea someone could effortlessly deliver such beauty So, it is up to you once again, the eyes of the beholder will indeed reveal the energy that you will become. One teacher would say, 'Long behold; you are arriving at your destination' – coming back to remembrance he would say.

Maybe you will not need to see another Christ in the same fashion as before, and if you do maybe you can see yourself as him. Maybe I can see myself in Taparista la or Shiva. Maybe without the confusion of the mind, we would find infinite connection and simultaneous awakening to our higher cells. Just for fun, I want to experiment with the energy of this sentence, it is a pretend statement, please do not crucify me for it. Yet think how it makes you feel to hear a person say. "God has found me, I have taken refuge in the Lord's light and see the kingdom of heaven. Watching your mind while you read this, I'd imagine you are similar to me, feeling some skepticism and doubt. If you told me you had accessed god and were becoming like a god yourself. I'd probably shrug my shoulders and pass a joke, not thinking much. For even if you entered the kingdom it is mostly about how long you can reside, in a world of such challenges. For me, I will know and feel a true spiritual being and also, I see the one who wears the costume, playing with accessories.

So, we all are standing back judging slightly, and to me, we should. It is indeed the day to judge. Why??? Simply because the world is dangerous, full of people with hidden agendas, manipulators, and friends that are posing only to come back and be leaching off you, for what they see in you. Energy drainers are everywhere. My uncle would always say, "Don't leak your chi." Don't spew your words out for one it won't be received, and someone may use aspects of it for their gain. I've learned to hold onto my faith and speak when I feel is appropriate. For the most part to stay in my lane, and not get caught up in anything that isn't the goal. To respect everyone's religion and beliefs, even if I disagree. In a family, there is always a disagreement, yet you cannot deny the love and gratitude you have for your mother, the giver of your life, no matter the color of her skin or the god she may or may not pray to, the actions she takes – we must always love our mother and be in great respect and honor. Your mother is your first guru, the one who birthed you from the darkness of her womb into the world of light and color, of air and elements, she allowed you to live in the kingdom of heaven.

She shares with you the ins and outs of the world and prepares you for love, and respect for life, the evil that is at hand, and how to be diligent and discern. If your parents are not present or you were raised by another, embrace them as your mother. Some Reggae culture and music refers to the ghetto youth, the ones raised by many mothers, they are raised by their own experience, which is your inner guru. The voice in your mind that takes you from dark places from the bottom of the pits, we reach up and say, I'm happy to be here, I am so happy to be born into the kingdom of Earth. My mother Earth nurtures me, and blood mother, whether she is with you or not, she birthed you and may have had to give her life for you. And you should be so proud to carry her blood and to be a walking example of someone who would give their life for another. We can rejoice in all areas of life. We have so many family members, you can continue to invite more family members, the more awareness grows. Soon you may see yourself in a completely new light possibly seeing life more clearly, a full spectrum.

It's all based on how you see your life, holy or hellish, happy or sad, angry or content. The dualities are there, and the division and day of judgment are upon us.

Going back to India, back to the holy cow. The Hindus of India believe that the cow is to be honored and respected as stated, in the same light as their gods even depicted in many godly families, the cow is there. I love that simply because it acknowledges animals as a part of the holy family which this book is trying to paint a picture that everything under the sun is holy. The cow being holy is protected by faith; Hindus will never kill a cow or eat it. In Hindu India, cows walk the streets as free as people. The cows as we talked about earlier are being abused so heavily in the USA. We already talked about our animal families and the cruelty that is being done to them. Americans today have so many ways of chopping cows and eating them, it's a fancy man's thing. And we in America, well, we all want to be fancy and get that meat and cheese, that bread and butter baby. Not to generalize, however, it rings true for all of us, to eat well is to live well. So yes, if you believe in reincarnation, I hope and pray, that if you are reincarnated into a cow, you may be born in India in a Hindu part of town.

Say you were born into another animal, pig, chicken, or goat, not so "HOLY?" I'd beg to differ, of course, if you're getting to know me. No matter if you're holy or beautiful, or if you're in the wrong place at the wrong time, or if you simply don't have a choice because someone is dominating, literally steering you like a cattle herder – all we can do is pray and hope to escape. When I start my farm, it will be a misfit farm for animals that are unwanted or will be killed, my family farms, they milk goats and raise chickens, ducks, and turkeys. I'm not a killer as I've stated, so that goes for all living beings. Each time I've gutted a fish or watched animals be killed in front of me, I give thanks for their life, yet I won't be the one who does the act. Only if the creator gifts it to me. But I can support my tribe who does. I can help in the process, I'd like to strive to eat what grows around me and limit my diet to light and fewer foods. See, I am still adapting to nature as I quarrel with the thought of the world and my disposition. I've always desired to minimize my consumption to very little, breathing in the light, that good ass prana baby as YouTuber Ralph Smart states. That is an ideal yogic success to various degrees.

The vastness of India is spectacular, people told me you would have to spend years in India to get to know the place, it is full of so many languages, religions, and beliefs. A very universal energy lives there. Being the very un-picky and open person that I am, I found myself staying with some families doing some work in trade in the gypsy neighborhoods. I'd experienced some Hindu India and yoga India, some more commonly known things about tourism, and general information about India. I traveled to the state of Rajasthan, one of my favorite places I'd been on my trip. Staying in Jaipur, what seemed to be still very diverse in religion yet had an overtone of Islam. The call to prayer and the most beautiful mosques. It was in Rajasthan I found myself in front of a wall praying to Allah. All Muslims I stayed with were very kind and even though they may have had hidden wants from me, we found great friendship.

One evening, as I was outside of a hostel meeting some other travelers, they told me a man drove up on his motorbike and threw a pig over the wall like littered trash. They said the pig's feet were bound. Hearing this information, I jumped over the wall to see for myself. It was dark with trash littered ground, I walked around and followed the sound of a distressed pig until my eyes found him, and he found me. The pig startled as I got closer. I decided I was going to try and untie the pig's feet, so it could at least walk around. Yet every time, I tried to help the pig, he would become aggressive towards me. The pig was telling me that it had been mistreated and feared people. Now, I have been called a wild man before, yet I found myself afraid of this pig. I didn't know him well, didn't know what disease he could carry, probably none, yet the system had tainted me from being fully wild and holding him down and untying him. Scared by what doctors and parents say about getting involved with wild animals, the fear that media puts on us about animals. I still look back and wish I was able to do something, I could see its face, its tusks being surrounded by froth and foam of the mouth as it struggled for its life tossed out as an outcast. We pray that if you reincarnate as a pig, you can find yourself at my misfit farm with a no-killing policy in place.

It's always intense for me to witness these things. I always leave wishing I could do more to help. I was in a town that treated pigs the opposite of holy considered to be unhealthy to eat and were viewed as trash eaters. The sad truth is that there was no soil, no grass, the pig is stuck in a concrete world, left to roam the streets and pick through the trash. Like a hungry homeless person disturbing a neighborhood that does not understand them. Is this the pig's fault? Of course not, once again the man-made world indirectly creates suffering for other family members whether human, animal, ghost, or God.

India is indeed a universal place, rich in so much awareness. Home to more religions than any other place I've been. I'm sure there were more than I can list as I only spent 6 months in India and only visited maybe 6 states or regions. I toured the north, east, west, center, and south, I missed out on many places and hope to go back. India is a key component of spiritual wealth and a reflection of the heights of human nature. Home to more Maha Saddhias and saints than any were else I know of. India's population exceeds 1 billion, I do believe, consists of Hinduism, Islam, Buddhism, Christianity, Jainism, Sikhism, Atheists, and an array of Babas and Saddhus including the Agode Babas, Naga Babas, Brahmans, and as we would joke about the resting Babas, leaning Babas, street Babas, and busing Babas – for all peoples are our friends, we are all Babas in Hindi, meaning father or a wise old man. We are all teachers and students, we are all wise old men in some topics, and in others we are babies. So, I always say to my friends, thank you, Babaji, and bow in gratitude, for even resting Baba, street Baba, and standing Baba all have things to teach us. I bow to the Baba in you.

I am not religious, I am a free thinker, a spiritual rebel, an ally to the street Babas, and a Baba myself to the street kids. India and Africa are in my heart, the spirit of the land and the eyes of the people will never leave my memory. The things we witness individually are what we need to see and feel to grow our inner standings. My view is that all animals are equal. The same as we are in the human plain. It seems religion casts out certain people and animals, unfortunately, branding them as lesser or not as strong. This is one of the reasons I'm not as interested in the surface of religion, the twisting of the stories and the changing of the hands and the things in between, the merit that has never left the air. This is what we find interesting, this is why we have allowed ourselves into places many would feel worried or just uncomfortable to go.

I entered one mosque with my friend, arriving at the washing station, washing our feet, hands, and mouth, to get clean before entering the house of Allah. I am led to the carpet, in a massive room, completely empty, with nothing but the sounds of a fan blowing, there was only maybe 10 people in the mosque at the time. All faced towards the wall, prostrating and praying to Allah.

I felt alignment in this moment, as Allah is a very easy way for me to relate to how God found me and how I believe you do not need anything besides the presence of this universal energy, that is named hundreds of times. No statue, no picture to depict this energy of god, just Allah. I saw no pictures of what Allah is. It is the opposite of so many religions, and I love the simplicity of this devotion. There's no glamorizing, Islam is one of the most authentic religions I've been graced to witness, and feel the spaciousness that Allah offers the mind and the spirit.

I was quite happy to be embraced by Muslim people as well. I stayed with three different families, one of whom invited me to a family wedding. I got a tailor-made suit and got ready to travel to Tonk town. My friend said Tonk town was home to the largest book of the Koran in all of India. This was my first time getting an up close and personal experience of what Islam is. The call to prayer and the warmth of the families were really allowing me to embrace the experience. We stayed at a family house, we would watch the sunset in the evening skies, kids flying kits on their rooftops, and birds flying above – a romantic time in my life. One must wander off the beaten path to experience a full spectrum of human life in all forms and postulations. The wedding day arrived, and we all gathered at a large mosque, the quarter moon above sprinkled with stars. I found myself sitting at a table full of men, lined up 30 on each side. As the food came around, we washed our hands and began to eat together, wild water buffalo meat and freshly caught fish by a relative were served. It was a beautiful experience. I was full of gratitude.

I always appreciate people who understand the sacredness of animal life as our indigenous family does, taking of animal life is a spiritual action, a meshing of energy. I was raised alongside some of my best friends, hunters from young ages, we had been busting coals making stick fires, making bows and arrows, clay pots, and flint napping, making stone tools, my second mom, mama Robin, runs this program called Earth Knack teaching survival skills and wild things. Things that most people have forgotten in the USA today. At her second wedding, they had a buffet of wild meats including, bear, mountain lion, deer, elk, and rabbit stew. The wild meat buffet was all prepared and cooked with love, Mama Robin used every part of the animal as she taught me as a youth to tan hides and I worked with her black smithing and leather sowing. She's a woman of many talents and builds beautiful Earth homes. I have so much love in my heart for all these worldly experiences, that I often give gifts of hugs and words of appreciation.

There's a native story about a group of hunters, all warriors. They go out with knives and bows to find food for their families. There is one type of warrior, it reads that does not take life and does not carry a knife. This man is a space-keeper, possibly a guide or expert on the nature of animals. That resonates a lot with this story as I've always been around hunters and eaten meat with them, been present for the processing of buffalo meat at the Blackfoot nation. I've been on buffalo hunts in Lakota land, helped pull the organs out of the rib cage, and licked the warm blood off my arm - charging my body. In native way of life, we view animal organs as medicinal meats, all offering a different nutrient, I like to believe it was common for a hunter to eat a bite of the heart after the kill, while the blood is still warm and full of life force energy. I've even heard stories of a man killing a man and eating the heart of a man who had great strength. For the one who eats the heart of another may gain that strength, the blood of a human being and nutrients contained, just like the buffalo, help life grow. Healthy blood is used today to help cure unhealthy blood. If we are thinking in energetic formation, the blood of a being who is actively inviting light into his body will naturally amplify his or her blood. I'm not going to get into cannibalism, I'll let the imagination run with that, but it has been said that the harvesting of human blood has been going on for centuries and even some talk about it extending the life of people whose vital life forces have simply run out. Could it be that fresh blood is like a steroid for energy? Blood is a huge part of the human body and the most important aspect of human health.

It is also known that the Agode Babas are known for ingesting human flesh. I watched one Baba in India drinking some substance out of a human skull while another one was climbing a bamboo leaned upon a wall trying to rescue a stuck bird with a hurt wing, I'm guessing, who knows. As I sat around the fire and smoked chillum with some other Babas. Another lifelong memory I won't forget, there was a sight, a sound, and a feeling altogether, I heard that unhuman sound – the sounds of the unseen as I watched all this happening in front of me. I was being altered naturally.

The world is filled with so much information, it is truly up to you how you want to live your life. I'd just like to invite you to honor each other for we are all right in the sense of what we are doing and what makes us feel good – if no one is being harmed. Why can't we not worship each other and if we are going to eat meat, do it in a sustainable way? I mean the veggie factories are no better than the animal factories. All GMO-ed and sprayed with chemicals that then get into the air and spread to other organic farms show us that we have gone too far. We are all too sensitive and we need to be mindful of how our energy is transferred through the air and water. Space contains some crazy uncountable number of particles and diseases, unnamable and undiscovered.

So, it is important to give and receive as equally as possible, giving gifts shows that you are grateful and see the efforts of another person – another aspect of Islamic culture I really have grown to love. As defined "Dower (Mahr) is a religious and legal obligation on the husband, intended to provide financial security to the wife. In contrast, dowry is a cultural practice that involves the bride's family providing goods or money to the groom's family." A gift-giving to show the level of commitment and honor a man sees in a woman, I believe marital gifts can be given in many variations. I love these traditions and believe it is time to practice our traditions. Identify what practices will raise us to the heights we aspire to reach and gift that to each other as a form of recognition. Like worshipping great spirits.

However, we must also respect cultural differences especially if we are married to them, we must learn to love them. So that's all we're doing as we go through trial and error. As I was parting ways after the wedding in Tonk town, I wanted to show gratitude by offering a gift. I had collected some water from the Ganges and some ash from the Shiva fire in Varanasi, two very holy things in my mind, things I ingested into my body due to my belief that it is holy. However, my offering this to my brothers was not received. They went on to say that it's just dirty water, the only holy water flows through Jordan and Israel, the Jordan River of which Jesus walked along himself they stated. They furthered by saying that Jesus was the only one who went upstairs and came back down to talk about it. So, I packed up my dirty yet holy water, gave my usual hugs, and proceeded to head out. I felt bad I still lacked the understanding of their culture and I will probably lack so much understanding in this world. What we can say is that there were people who did amazing things, and miracles, and the places from which they originated are considered pilgrimage points. The promised land is a place to look for spiritual merit, as there are many versions of creation, some Earthly and some say out of this world, outside of the boundary of Earth. The Annunaki creation stories offer us insight into astral connection, another worldly energy. Stating the breading of our magical race. Two worldly energies come together to create human life. These ancestral recollections would offer strong support to the elemental magic of particles and atoms coming together, creating the oldest most original human life. The alchemical success of the Annunaki was Adam/Atom known as Adamu, the father of mankind. This evidence would support that the Adam/Atom gene is the origin of us all. The magical beings before us derived from Nephlem, Ini, and Inlil, the descendants of Annunaki. Birthing humans into a higher existence and with ability. Miracles were said to be more frequent and even to show power or exercise their spirits. Could all of us originate from the promised land, until moved or migrated? The original garden of Eden the garden of atoms, the garden that possibly all human life grew from. Have we not adapted to our environments around the globe? This Creation story is in line somewhat with the yogic success stories as well as the building of particles or atoms. The reference again to Christ's body and rainbow body are similar. They say we are the children of the sun, they say we are descendants of Adam/Atom. It has always been up to us to build and stack energy. Whether or not you identify with this creation story or the other, a recipe or guideline could help us in building or better yet engineering our light atoms. All religions and spiritual groups have these saints and claim them as their own, it kind of plays into the battle of power like the show The Last Airbender depicts. Some people believe Jesus studied with Buddha or vice versa. I read a text at the Bon monastery's library stating that Bon was the original Cult of Buddhism and originated in Persia or Iran. Geographically, this is intriguing, in context to the Annunaki creation story or a magical story of an Earthly garden dripping in the golden mean ratio. The Persian Empire is a massive and enriched land and culture, potentially boarding India, we could imagine just 400 years ago or bring up some biblical timeline for context, yet I will for fun just imagine a map of the Middle East and a special trail similar to the Silk Road. The trail would begin or end in Egypt or Kemet. The midpoint is Jordan home to the Lord Christ himself, onward through Persia and into the holy land of the Himalayan mountains, the home of many Buddhas. Imagining the culture of people the Bon Po people, our ancient Indigenous yogis. Still, today, represents the many spirits and Nagas the elementals, and the living color. I can see more clearly as I type this out a channel of imagination, a peer into the great mystery schools of the old. I can see these saintly beings in community, in study, in their darkness as they rose to royal perspectives together. Living and walking through raw nature builds toughness and resiliency, possibly having to create heat or comforts out of nothing. Due to rough and cold environments, many magical yogis persevere in the most extreme Earthly ecosystems. Taking some decades for Jesus and Buddha to remember the power of the genes, of the miracle of mankind of Atoms and particles colliding, creating life… we can see that the saints understood these sciences or ways of nature.

In my eyes, all the saints are a product of the same energy, whether we are descendants of more evolved species outside of our planet of inertia or are just simply a magical species in our Earthly rights and knowledge of this plane of inertia. Earth is a wealthy planet in this solar system and galaxy as it is home to gold and many precious energies and elements. It would not be over my head to consider the visiting of sereins, pleadians, or Annunaki-type beings. I'm also a believer in Earth being such a powerful conduction of life with the light of the sun, the frequency of the sound of Earth, and the will of human potential. I believe we are fully capable of reaching the heights of our ancient relatives. With the help of the energies of a hundred names. One can return to the reception of the sun and Earth of natural duality balancing in self. An opening to receive, and a great cultivation process begins, as we consciously inhale the plasmic energy from the sun, grounding to the frequencies of Earth, we can withstand the power and then cultivate with awareness and ease, we pray. See, one must let go of all the shit and return to the true nature of self, remember the essence of god before it was named and labeled. In my eyes, it is this aspect of creation that will allow light and love to overflow into the corners of the world. This world is all "lele wakan", a very holy place. As stated before, the only planet that holds life in our solar system, we are at the heart of our solar system. The other planets support us just like Chinese medicine describes our inner verse of organs, supporting one another and our heartbeat, our life living out their roles as a reflection of planetary contribution in our lives. So, the Earth is a holy plane, at one point the Earth may have been more of a disk, the plane the planet of inertia indeed supports this idea of the shape of the Earth and how it has grown over eons and eons. Regardless of Earth's shape, it is a magical place a wonderful place. The inhabitants here are all holy, all children of the sun. All human beings are holy as we breathe in the air, drink the waters, and walk upon the holy lands. Yet we have been tainted and disrupted along the way. Now claiming lands, waters, titles, gods, claiming our powers, and dividing ourselves from one truth, one community, from one destination, and one vital energy.

Could you imagine if all of our races were adaptations of one original race, and a simple yet complex natural energy, godly to mankind, that supports us through and through? If it was indeed all one, our journey home would be much clearer. Our traumas would all be one and all at once could be dropped. Is it too complicated to see ourselves in each other and see oneness in all things? It's like people love differences. Imagine we are all one, with one view, one god, and one purpose. People always say this sounds boring, sounds to me like too many egos and pride, but just for fun if it was all one love and one light, we would see that in another, and most importantly we would see it in nature. Nature is our leader once again, the one and only! Mind giving us this opportunity to squabble about literally everything. I'm laughing as I write throughout this book, stopping and thinking about the world as well. How silly things have become.

In this view, I'm scribing to support the idea that all waters are holy, and the inner constructs of Earth are mystical and sacred. All things are of godly essence, you can see the essence of creation in everything on our green globe. Still, we will ask where does all the water come from? So clean and so pure, I've heard theories that there is an infinite supply of water being supplied to the surface of Earth through underground water systems. Similar to the heart constantly supplying new blood, if you bleed out, your heart will supply more, like your semen replenishing always. Yet just like a human being and our timeline, the Earth also is on a timeline. Just as we see humans fall quicker due to bad choices and overconsumption, lack of self-awareness, well, Earth will experience the same. It is our choice to harm our self and is ok because the consequence is for yourself. Our Earth is shared obviously and so your actions will result in consequences for everyone if your actions come with power and mindlessness. Many Americans full of money and still complaining, still we pay taxes for things that we do not agree with or support. When our elements become contaminated or inflamed, we need to call for a serious sit-down and talk it out. We, as a collective, global community can share this knowledge and feeling about our water, air, Earth, fire, and space. I think Mother Earth can support an amazing amount of her human children, I don't think depopulation is the answer but a total life change, a total shutdown of mass industry, and a change of life. Letting go of the world as we know it, for it may not last much longer at this rate. When a human being runs out of their jing chi or special reserve, the vital energy can run out, life slows to a stop and the human being collapses. This is all due to our choices, we can add vital energy also, of course, a timeline is a timeline and all forms of life will run out of their vital energies at some point. This information I am not making up there is indeed a recipe for a successful death or transition. I'm talking about the actual steps or practices of each 7-year cycle, as we all near closer to our transition into the great mystery. To worry not, as honoring all timelines helps us accept nature for what it is and will allow for acceptance and even a smile of gratitude for one resting in peace and knowledge. Will only be celebrating this transaction or exchange of energy entering the plane of inertia and then exiting also. We will sustain as we are, however, in another 7 generations, another cycle of molecules infusing together and changing their shape. Changing the mind. Our continual habitual habits of the man-made world will change in front of us, instead of us changing the aspects of ourselves to see the change in the world. We may see the consequences affecting our Earth and lives.

In my eyes, we are too sensitive, we are too holy, and everything under the sun will continue to suffer if we do not rearrange ourselves and what we were told we need. Let us make these choices for ourselves, make it legal to garden and farm in the cities, and let us give it a shot at living wild. This world was born out of chaotic events and for some long time rested in the supreme beauty of stillness. Possibly we are in a time of stillness and luxury now. Maybe it is my thoughts creating this idea of reality, yes, and again I am only relaying what people think and say with an overtone and most importantly, the voices of nature. For the voices of man have continually steered us into complexity and overanalyzing our nature of self, simply, we are a reflection of nature itself. As we have been playing with our minds and traveling to see different people and places, it becomes easier to see through the eyes of all our relations and empathy for all beings, not allowing this to cripple us. So much suffering has happened but to affirm that the cow and buffalo are holy, the chickens and pigs, the Nile River and the Ganges River, the Jordan River, and the creeks in Cretonne. The 4 races of man are equally holy with different aspects of space, air, Earth, water, and fire. The god particle or the one with a hundred names is within us all and always has been. Whether it grew here on Earth or was brought here from an outside source. To me, it does not matter, its just here. Who is controlling our mind and keeping us back from our most natural and blissful conduction, who has sexualized us and sold us, the list goes on. Who is in the driver's seat, who is using the power of all things to keep us away from all things?

I ask you now,

In your eyes, how do you see?

In your ears, how do you hear?

In your nose, what do you smell?

In your skin, how do you feel?

In your voice, how do you sound?

Let's do an experiment my fellow alchemists, conductors of love and light.

Let us visualize the evil in this world, whether that is a group of people or aliens or something other, whatever is holding us back from our truest self. Use your imagination, and tune into what you really think. Who are they? And, where are they? How are they?

Invite yourself into their space or them into your awareness.

Think about them.

How do they see?

How do they hear?

How do they smell?

How do they feel?

How do they sound?

Maybe if enough of us do this, they feel an uncomfortable presence of being watched. Maybe they will jump and think they felt a ghost.

I think we are all getting a similar image in our heads of the workings of evil, and also, learning about energy, life-giving, or life-taking. A negative or positive conduction can move about the plane of inertia freely, we will say. However, we can keep our intuitions to ourselves for now. .

Let's focus on giving them an energetic slap of love.

The more people praying on this and doing this could affect some changes. The study reveals that everything is so sensitive and light or energy travels so fast. Energy can spawn at any given time. Can be manifested out of nothing and in multiple places. If we can see how we are all broke, may you not say we could reverse that. I've put myself together, I've healed myself and through that feeling you can see yourself healing alongside, together we can feel healing at this moment. Is our healing just held back by our egos and the comforting mind? In a narcissistic society of having things be your way. An indulgence of self through media or distracted by your physical self, so much that your subtle energetic self is wondering where you went. It can be looked at from many angles.

It's also an experiment to see if we can move into peace and energetically change the game, even if it's subtle. So, we will charge ourselves up, conductors of love and light. I see you in light, I see you empowered, I see you as human beings connecting to self. Let's turn on our foundations, the more we do these practices, the more it becomes like a light switch turning off and on. You will know when you are on, and you will know when you're off. Sometimes nature of self turns you on and sometimes it is easy to find yourself turned off. Yet the beauty of awareness is, that once it's there, it is there, you can always tune into your nature. By simply controlling or directing your mind.

So, with the lights turned on and the foundations in place, prepare yourself to share with light and love in tack, a prayer that they will receive this message and feel what we feel, and what we have been going through. Let the light that you send them, carry all of the anger and frustration, all of your sadness, and all of your emotions that have been triggered by systematic stress and oppression. Bring that into your solar plexus. See the conductors of evil and send them everything you got. See all the anger, irritation, sadness, and depression, let the true inner anger come out, the true stress that they have afflicted on you, and your ancestors. Send it to them and see it flooding their spaces with overwhelming emotions. Send your feelings to them enveloped with light. In hopes that the darkness, outsources onto us the difficulties find them in the form of feeling. May the light shine on them. May they feel the light enveloped emotions and suffering.

Dear Creator, we ask that this prayer and this action reveal the gears of evil and the suffering we have experienced. We ask that this light will find us as the oppressed and find them, the oppressor… We ask for the presence of all light angles and living color to be with them in their heart, filling them with visions of all of the suffering of the world Feed their ghosts and demons that follow them, quite their meek-mindedness, great spirits let them remember your presence and your glory.

Dear spirits we ask that you may hold them in love. We ask that they may come into love, we ask that they find a space to receive our energy and give back to us in the way we all deserve. Great spirit, we ask that we may gently smile upon them, that they may feel our global trauma and see that we are so strong, and we are still seeing love. Great spirit, we ask that this prayer will lift them to action, for them to hold the Earth in their hearts and begin looking out for our animals, oceans, and our fellow human beings. Great spirit, comfort us all and allow us to comfort ourselves. May the oppression be laid to rest in knowledge and power may we feel the peace

AHO AMEN ASE.

Remember in the native way of life, Buddha's light work, and voodoo are only to give life. I'm sharing a lot and I'm trusting in this process. I'm listening to my intuition as I'm writing creator is telling me to pray harder, to be more love, be more light, see more love, and affirm our strength and our ability to celebrate this life – and not be pulled down into gloom and the darkness of the pits! For the sunshine is so strong it reaches the darkest of places. My intuitions tell me it is time and its okay to share. For you all have shared with me whether you know it or not you have helped me get to this point of sharing. Therefore, it is my gift back to you! All the people who welcomed me and talked to me, made me think deeper or even helped destroy what I thought was me. You must know you were important on my journey. You have helped me alleviate the parts of me that were influenced by man. Killing the false character who has been supporting the colonized mind. It is the highs of nature that have allowed the distress of the mind to rest. So, I have chopped off my hair for the spirits. In my Priest initiation, I asked the creator to please help me help myself so I can help others.

Creator I pray, please help me clean off so that I may also help others to come clean. I prayed for blessings so that the blessings could overflow into others. Give myself to you creator so that I can give myself to others. In simplicity and surety of nature, I stand for the postures of light. Standing with nature in the unshakable position. We ask for your presence to keep us standing straight for you!

Chapter Eight
Pretending

In this chapter, we will be diving into the idea of pretending and the power of our imagination, including imaginary friends, as well as some other aspects of how we perceive things as real or unreal. How things may grow into simple ideas, and then into reality, we look into our playful imaginary self and the difference between fiction and non-fiction, some stories are hard to understand. Leaving us questioning a reality or a picture painted, starting as a mental image or fantasy. Maybe a feeling is there that you want it so bad you want to make it real. I'm not a physical painter. Yet my 15 years of meditation have revealed I am primarily an energy painter - an artist of auric fields, and self-imaged mandalas. Meditation was first taught to me as qi gong meaning "energy work" or energy yoga. Most exercises were rooted in Taoism and Tibetan practice, as I learned more about my teacher and the practices he shared… We are all energy workers, as all things in life carry information, and if you believe that energy is information. Then you can actively observe energy every day as you work through the energy of self, emotion, relations, and all things that enter your energetic field. See even a dog or horse whisperer is a specialist relating to an animal's energy in a very special and spacious way. Every relative including yourself listed in this book has a very special unique energy or chi, that can be consciously connected through vibration and frequency, sound and color. This is where we can see qi gong being much bigger than what we see in the spiritual community today. Most of us perceive qi gong as a form of movement or the inner or outer practices of chi work. Indeed, a master of chi will be able to corollate the network of chi, or matrix if you will, in a casual and practical yet abstract and phenomenal expression. Posing questions to the self and the reality that we create through the exchange of information or energy we share in throughout our lives. It is truly up to you to decide what is possible or to place limitations on what is real or nonreal. Qi gong is the oldest expression of interaction between humans and all of our Earthly relations. Lost in translation, revived, and handed to us today in doses. In fact, it is our most primal sense, that allows us to get here. With all the stories of saints, giants, dinosaurs, dragons, ferries, angels, ghosts, demons, and living color. We all have the same commonality, our energy/information is of Earth contained on our planet. What I am saying is nature has been present for all of us, holding us, and creating space for us. Nature is so magical, that there is no way of explaining the divine happenings, leaving many of us in question just like a book with a good cliffhanger.

Fiction, nonfiction, and fantasy, the network has boundaries or layers, the planet of inertia, the great organizer, all of creation in front of you. We have named a couple of movies for fun such as Jungle Book, Last Air Bender, and some other movies that shed light on a magical world that is said to be nonfiction. Of course, many of us watch these movies and ask ourselves could that be real, is that possible? Many of us may indeed want what we are seeing. So, I look at the stories of the Maha Siddhas, similarly and the stories of the miracles of different gods and how they were portrayed as mythical beings. As they do often sound like many fantasy movies. Sometimes seeming to be highlighted as aspects of nature or components of looking at different aspects of self and how one can start to feel if one acts in a strong devotion. I've witnessed people being filled with joy from all walks of life, Allah, Christ, Shiva, Guru Rinpoche, Babaji, and simply nature as stated. It seems in the stories; all these avatars were nature adepts to the fullest. Yet some of the stories are so colorful and beautiful, unseen in the modern world, that they pose many disbelievers, and could be viewed as nonfiction, stories to manipulate. In that sense, I have been manipulated yet by choice as I allowed this information to wash my brain, you could say I've been brainwashed by these stories and could be living in a falsity myself, we can only share the evidence of our study and our human experiences.

Buddhist countries being oppressed by Buddhism such as Myanmar used to be named Burma, when I went there they had just lifted the ban for travelers to enter, yet some regions were still unavailable to go to because of civil war still happening. This is a dominantly Buddhist country, the teachings of Buddha would never stand for that.

It seems that extreme religion has divided us, watching civil war and hearsay of different religions wanting to represent their countries as the one. So, when will we look at the oppressive part of religion? We can also see that it fills people with so much love and joy. While some of us look at them in disbelief and even pass judgment, I'm guilty myself. The ones who believe like my grandfather, in Jesus' worshiper of 90 years of faith and tradition, born into the great depression only to make his way to provide true wealth to his family, joy and peace, laughter and smiles. For his belief in something that I, simply, at the time, did not align due to my idea of religion and the oppression we have been speaking about in this book. Yet I was missing out on the simplicity again. The faith and the knowledge that is there without religion or an outline. The feeling that we are with God and God is with us. Naturally, that statement offers a person trust and good fortune. I'm very grateful to have spent time with my great-grandfather, who fathered the presence of God and love into our family. A generosity of love and care that lives within each of our family members uniquely. Although we see differently, we can also see the same. Christianity, a religion I've been angry with most of my life has filled him, and I know so many others who walk with the presence of the good lord. Once again, the amount of words and calamity can keep us from the simplicity of a prayer, and even keep us from a feeling of deep love or gratitude.

The mind is so powerful, in context to recognizing we are all manifest-ers of our destiny and reality through our habitual habits and habitual thoughts, again prescribed to me as karma. In that definition, we are the rulers of our outcome. What you think turns into what you do, and what you do turns into evidence and affirmation of your thoughts. So, this is why I say we are all energy workers and have the power to create what we want. Today's society is so full of so much that we have a diverse number of paths set out in front of us. They are so exciting; however, we get caught up in our passions of work and art, music, and all the beauty in life. Not to say that we are also passionate about nature and nature of self, as I can feel the collective mind, affirm most of us are arriving on the same page, regarding the reflections of nature, the beauty of sunrise and sunset, the peace and glory you feel, the stars at night and the wonderment they offer. The connection with another human being, and the relaxation and acceptance you feel. What a beautiful thing to share all around the world as we end our workdays and go home for rest.

However, I challenge you to look back into your day and ask yourself if you believe in the subtle impact of your qi gong foundations, we are sharing in this book or your mindfulness practices that you incorporate throughout your day. We need to know how to cook up our daily bread. Now I'd be in appreciation for nature and stop to view the beauty of the sky and life around, smell the flowers, find a direction, or a way of energy, and connect. In nature, we see beauty, yet it appears that our feelings of nature have been disrupted and the energy that has 100 names was replaced by WIFI and so many other aspects of energy that may not serve you the same way a recipe of true nature and nature of self would offer. Could it be as simple as breathing in Light? And letting the grief go? Sounds simple yet maybe a recipe is helpful? The recipe is important for any baked good, it could come out burnt or soggy, could come out too salty or too spicy, it could just be so bad it gets tossed out. This is the reason I give thanks to my teachers and the stacking of mediation/awareness that can be implemented in daily life without anyone knowing that you are actively painting your energetic field.

Business is to simply sell something, to talk it up, and to portray a successful story of the outcome. This is why in the spiritual community I often get turned off, because well, simply selling awareness of something that is part of us and a reflection of nature is lucrative. As society tells us how we need to fit the bill, this fuels the yoga industry, retreats, and all components of feeling like we need to pay someone to access this idea of beauty or perfection. People often say that nothing and no one is perfect. I agree, yet I could also say that the golden mean ratio shows us aspects of perfection. Like who in the first place said trees were not perfect, or a landscape, an environment. Human beings are the avatars of the Earthly landscape. I'll be the one to say it, you are made perfect. Every molecule, every ounce of blood is perfectly composed in you. You are a divine reflection of your environment. Sure, it's hard to believe due to struggles and cycles of thoughts, cycles of inner battles. From the purity of your birth till now, this is also a reflection of our environment.

So, I'll stop beating around the bush, I'll stop painting with words and I'll try to show how energetic painting and pretending has landed me into a bath of bliss.

Say we **CUT EVERYTHING MANMADE OUT** just for fun. My teacher used to say "Simply because we can." Simply for fun, because we want to.

Color Breath

Part 1.

- Imagine yourself sitting or lying on the grass, feeling as vast as the sky. Imagine that feeling… grounded Earth and lightness of sky. Visualize a tiny sun inside of you. As you feel the warmth of the sun above, the bright light shines down on you. Imagine a tiny sun inside of you reflecting the same sensations as SunRa. Affirm the heat and the light emitting through your whole body. Feeling into all light systems of the body. Imagine tiny sun in your heart or navel chakra, a tiny sun shining out of your skin. Imagine the energy of 100 names displayed in the sky, as lights and colors sparkle like stars emitted from the sun. Now imagine the energy of 100 names to be displayed within your body, sparkles of colors traveling through the body of water that compose you. Simply inhale your light environment, as you inhale imagine yourself breathing in through the nose and all pores of your skin, tiny particles of the light, the essence of nature. Inhaling more light with each breath exhaling the sensations of bliss with light.

Part 2.

- Continue breathing in color, inhaling and exhaling the living color, you can actively repeat and affirm the OPENING, EXPANDING, OBSORBING, and TRANSFORMING, "repeating this mantra can assist". Simply hold your breath in as the particles of light color enters your body. Engage VMA and pack the light atoms into your body and flesh by clenching all muscles gently. Still Imagining yourself as the vast sky, imagining your body full of warmth, full of light, and full of color, grounded to the Earth. Simply because we can. Imagine the light of the tiny sun and color penetrating your bones, blood, organs, flesh, channels, muscles, eyes, nose, ears, and mouth. Imagine the taste of light. Imagine the sound of light, imagine the sight of light, imagine the smell of light. Now amplify the sensations because you can and **feel** the sensation of light. **Let go of all other knowledge. Let go of all judgment. Let go of all fears**.

Imagine yourself in this way. You are simply a reflection of what you see, a reflection of what you taste, a reflection of what you hear, a reflection of what you smell, and a reflection of what you feel. This is your **daily bread**; you are the baker. You have the recipe. So, I ask you simply how does this feel? Maybe it is not I asking but you.

"Consensual Consistent Contact of light may Conceal consciousness in Colorful Containment."

Welcome to your own refuge of light! To all refugees of darkness! For the sun is always shining light on his children, SunRa gave this light to us all to carry and conduct. Hold strong in your posture.

The first step is becoming the baker, then the alchemist, and then achieving conduction. You are naturally already the conductor, baker, and alchemist. So much you can put in the oven and bake, too many recipes and steps, you may go to google for help. The original recipe has always been so simple, so simple it is right in front of you, it is below you and above you, it is inside of yourself. It's this evidence of a world that used to be so full of color, magic, awareness, and relationship to ourselves, and really still is. The networks of light and free energy of elements and polarity, magnetism and gravity, frequency and vibration, are present now. This is the perfect world that quantum physics and harmonics reveals, as all things are constructs of the 5 platonic solids, the shapes of the creation. Of atoms and particles colliding in space. In the old, there was nothing to know. There was just a feeling. Simply the sound of creation, the sight of creation, the smell of creation, the taste of creation, and the feeling of creation. The creation of the sun, the light in the sky that fathers us all to life. The new findings were miracles in the times of evolution and understanding.

Can you imagine the picture I'm painting? The greatest network of our solar system **pure light!** And the dark matters, in front of us every day SunRa provides all living beings the essence of life. The sky dancers or plasmic people of the sun and sky are merely the pyranic energy that all life forms thrive on. My environment allowed me to taste light, smell light, hear light, see light, and feel light as I built a relationship with the energy of 100 names, and let go of my wants to know anything else, I realize I'm merely a reflection. Without the guidance of very special humans in my life, I would not know the recipe and would have fumbled the voices of nature as the elements spoke to me, the nature spirits revealed themselves, it is the guidance of my community and the voices of nature that have merely told me to let everything go and be with them as we once were, to feel their presence.

If I were to do business in the spiritual world and sell my awareness, sell the voices of nature – not this book – but the teachings, some of which I'm sharing in this book. I'd simply be in trouble with myself and my ancestors. How could one sell something that is already yours? Well, by making an evil plan to deceive you, to tell you that you are not perfect, start feeding you your daily bread, creating a recipe, a system that would make you think that you are not fine, to put a taste in your mouth that you cannot forget, to make you feel so uncomfortable in your skin that it would be passed down in our DNA so that our children would be born into a world of confusion, always asking who am I.

This book is about the nature of self. To surface some truth, for the eyes of light see through the darkness of evil, for the sun's shine illuminates all darkness.

This relationship of energy, named 100 times is a relationship to self and changed my life. For years I fumbled around in myself, not knowing how to talk about this divine display of energy, I knew I felt the light, it offered me and for years I would push myself to sit on the cousin, allow myself to bath in awareness of this energy, to actively see myself as this energy, all the while recognizing my traumas and watching my mind battle with so many collective thoughts, thoughts of evil, that I wasn't good enough, that I was crazy, not allowing myself to be perfect, just for myself. I couldn't tell if I was stuck in my ego, thinking I was something I wasn't. Or if this display of light was changing me into something I indeed have wanted for so long, to simply be a reflection of my environment. Yet I still hold on to the evils at play as I watch myself attract so many others caught up in similar internal dialogue. As these conversations continue to find me, I'm actively bowing out, my interest is no longer. I must move forward in my conductions, or I will take on the conductions of the masses.

My meditation was the vocal part of my practice of my daily bread. My life became like a movie, struggling to decipher whether I was experiencing was fiction or nonfiction. All the stories I'd heard as a youth, are they real? In my innocence, naturally, I decided that it didn't matter. The colors, the rainbow filled me, the image of me. With no one to talk to, I'd find myself back at the Sundance tree calling the spirits for support, calling for affirmation. Calling to connect to their unique vibration, calling their voices.

Was I no more than a little kid in his or her imagination? seeing something that is untouchable. Yet felt deeply in my waters, as time goes on, so does the feeling, the reflection grows more real inside of me. The simplicity of life becomes apparent. All that is left is to practice and serve, to be in this awareness of color, to allow and to trust that it was growing inside of me. There is still doubt, there is still hardship, it is the daily work we need in the modern world we are in, that is if you feel you are being distracted. For me I ask the rainbow peoples to guide me, SunRa to guide me. Mainly we have to guide ourselves and keep ourselves on track to ingest the right recipe, to make space for the good and great daily bread/light supplements. As I've stacked qi gong foundations/awareness, a mandala of color, a display of light that I actively turn on. It is my life's practice to be in the awareness of the nature of self. However, I've been caught up in scams and frauds. Every trip I go on someone is trying to sell me something, wanting something from me. This has further confused me in some view, in another it formed my business. I built Nature's Temple to share my auric paintings. To organize retreats, to share the awareness of nature. To share an idea of imagination becoming reality, to assist in the awareness of your nature of self. Our shadow or darkness or lack of understanding or feeling reflects our inability to thrive. Grief and sorrow, judgment and self-sabotage, some say the nights of dark soul, bring us to the heights of our awareness. Humans are prone to naturally con themselves into thinking something is okay or not ok, justifying an action or playing it cool because others do. We can joke at ourselves some here. The me-too movement. well how about that! I'm mad too! And you're feeling disconnected, well, guess what, ME TOO. We are all prone to the human network the joys and the suffering. A con man coming with the con plan as Bob Marley sings, about the many Confusions of Babylon.

It is indeed an era of judgment, the era of the profiter men, the false profit telling you that you need to do these things to heal. I take accountability for planning a business around this exact thing, taking a decade to construct and a decade of meditation, a decade of craving success, to be seen and comforted in the ways my ancestors whisper to me. I've humbly arrived at a place of not wanting any of it. I just want to lay on the grass and be a little kid in the innocence of imagination. I've surrendered my wants, I know I to have been colonized in my mind. Yet the young light worrier in me was activated too young for I am becoming stronger than ever, through muddy lenses comes clarity as I continue to clean off the gunk of the world, the gunk off me. Cleaning off at Sundance, in my priesthood and remembering why the creator has shown me this way of prayerful conduction. I can see the destiny of our healings as a collective, people have spoken to me about my destiny as well, spiritual beings recognizing spiritual beings. In short and without detail, it is not to succumb to the colonized mind but to know their strategies to also know the power of nature and of human nature. To merely reverse the intention, or spell, to change the flow of energy again, for it is all coming from the same source with different conductions. As they have done this to us over and over again, to all of our early ancestors who carried such effortless love for all of nature.

It has been predicted by our native peoples that the warriors of light and love will come again, to confront the mass conductors of evil and life-taking power. This is why the relationship to the light network is so important. For they are here to assist us, the amount of love and light in the world will prevail, the more we remember the less their darkness affects us, no longer will they dim our spirits. With our collective knowledge, we can stand on our own. We will remain unshakable in our postures of light. I am a true believer of light and have spent some years gaining familiarity with the culture of light. The movements and colors are the sensations they offer us. I believe cults are merely an expression of a strong culture. In the old days cults or clans would share space to grow, protect, and keep the provisions close. We can joke about cults, leaders, and egos, and can expose them as such journalists like BE Scaffolding, writing for guru magazines, exposing what I hear to be an unhealthy culture. Such as love has won. A great example of a false profit and a conductor of manipulation is seen first-hand in Crestone CO. Be scaffolding the author seems to be doing good work producing many books herself and being recognized in the New York Times, HBO, and Netflix just to name a couple. This means that Crestone is not looking so good to the public. I am also making space from Crestone, which some call the promised land of America. A ruby in a haystack, an arch of safety, a refuge of truth. Crestone makes some big to do, as I grew up there I watched the story and clout grow. Watching in disbelief and uncomforted by people hyping it up but not living up to it or better yet even knowing what it is to be a spiritual being. However, I will forever and always stand and speak about the power of the mountains Crestone is built by, offering the rawest form of nature I've witnessed. The beginning of my journey around the world, pilgrimaging to places where the rainbow is recognized and consoled in. Crestone, unfortunately, now looking like a joke as we are referred to as the boneyard of the Colorado, attracting many drugs and crimes resulting in death, nasty and gruesome at times. However, Crestone still has the potential to create life-giving energy from these magical stories. I would not be typing what I am here without Crestone, I was conceived in the mountains near by the waters that flow down from the peaks, the peaks that rise high into the sky. Into the house of the great spirits of the sky- the sspommitapiiksi above ones and the mountain, a thrown to our highness to rest in the natural state of existence. That is how I perceive Crestone geographically, a less tampered location where nature is still dominating, a power point on our planet. A point of reference. Still a highly disturbed and possibly cursed land like the rest of this newborn country. Crestone is also home to many spiritual teachers who are self-proclaimed, giving people like Be scaffolding something to talk or write about. I don't like gossip and really, I'm learning to enjoy writing. I'll say if people are messing around naturally conducting chaos and even pain, it needs to be talked about. Be Scaffolding, Challenges Crestone, and anyone who wants to share teachings to be real.

We have been going over again and again the polarities of love and hate, truth and falsity. Illusion and imagination at the end of the day we will all suffer slightly; it may be more so how we articulate our suffering. Maybe it is not that we are suffering, maybe it is what we have been told we must suffer for. Or possibly we are just like elephants meant to remember, to walk around with our battle wounds as a map of our soul or energy field. The beauty in the struggle, I've ranted here about Crestone and brought Be scaffolding into the conversation. I hope we can work together as a community and as writers and activists, truth seekers whatever you want to label it. For I know who I am. I am Juniper Urieh Tree, born under a juniper tree and named after the juniper tree, a plant of protection and cleansing, Urieh named after the light or flame of God and tree, for I am to stand long and tall in my conduction and advocacy of the truth and light. My uncle always jokes may the forest be with you! I know whose shoulders I'm standing on. I know what I've seen, and more than ever I feel what I know. A true man of God if I have ever seen one is unwavering in his relationship to his father and mother of all creation. Man-made creation is tied to the colonized man that we all have to face. I have taken my face off and chopped my hair, my identity is still unshaken in the culture of light. No man has shown me the glory that nature has. This was why my childhood friends joked me, always telling me I'd be a fine cult leader. Sure, I like to joke with them and sure, my ego says that could be fine also. We are living in a lost culture in America, indeed a NEW culture is here if we like its presence. Yet I cannot deny the suffering that goes unseen for our pleasures and luxuries. I will always stand with the voices of nature and the cultures of light. They downplay cults for many reasons, and some are obviously not healthy in their culture. Resulting in a stench smelt far away. If America had been more open with its birthing of a new country and just how it became the youngest and richest in money, a cult that went unspoken till very recently, similar to the false guru, and still not strong enough to come out and tell the whole story, which may help us heal as a mass.

Honesty and integrity again are crucial for any leader and naturally promote trust and love. America is indeed a leader and an embarrassment around the world for its politics and ego, fumbles of power and ability. A puppet of the crown of England. That is why we see such things happening to us and not for us. Many pandemics in our timeline, many nations built on fraud and faulty intentions. Many times, we have been disregarded for our being. Many of us still looking to America for ideals and a new culture, a new way of life. Sadly, many do not know the amount of manipulation American people are experiencing, this country has numbered us like cattle and herded us into the land of the free, the oppressor cannot oppress the already free people. We are global trackers of oppression; these spiritual teachers are the least of our concerns and are just a part of a fragmented and lost culture of free people and free energy.

See Love has no con plan, love cannot deceit. Love is to put it all on the table, to smile and walk away. Love is selfless, love is to simply rest in light. Since we are all the same, all conductors, all free… The choice is yours, you are the baker, and you have your own recopies. We are all here to reason and to grow together, to share vision, to share voice.

Energy is subtle, it may take years for you to feel the side effects of the tiny sun that you can choose to reside in your heart, that you can imagine simply because you can. Me and you together or on our own, but WE are the people the spokesmen of Earth the forest is with us all. I speak from experience that it's a slow process, it all started with my eyes, seeing light, to then feeling light. It started from an innocence of imagination. Just pretending to be full of color and sitting with my imaginary friends. The many layers of the onion, the many layers of awareness. Boundaries and boundaries of beauty. The beauty in the struggle. The con man with the con plan has induced mass suffering, we are innocent conductors of love and light afflicted by a dark force, that smells and looks man-made. That is where forgiveness comes into play, if we are all of the same sun, we could more easily identify and take accountability for our emotions and desires. We can more easily look at the minority of greedy forefathers with compassion. Duality has been around from the beginning, the chicken and the egg need each other, does it matter which came first?

For each day as we ingest light and imagine ourselves in light, we may end the day with a less negative conversation. By the time we go to bed, what may have been upset may rest easy. It is good to mentally process the effects of chi in correlation to each other and the self. That's why I say meditation is the easy part of the day. Kind of like the 4 easiest days of Sundance, fasting and with staining from all things, being in prayer, being with the sky, and breathing in our natural environment. The morning meditation, for example, is the easiest part of the day. The minutes you get up and are confronted with thoughts of distractions is where practice comes in. We all need to practice. The act of staying aware of your nature of self and relationship to your environment, with staining from so much excitement around you. That is the pressure of a true devotee, to be moving in grace of awareness and simplicity of nature's reflection. People have and will continue to sit alone in isolation, so that it may be easier to do this great work. Showing extreme discipline and will, true devotion to their cells. I know now the avenue is quantum and destined to reveal its true nature. For I have seen this avenue in front of me the clarity that true light offers, the welcoming into the most beautiful culture. As I revel in my own duality, the desire to live a common life, free from many thoughts I am sharing here today. Or to accept this challenge, putting on my curly-toed shoes, my magical attire and just like any job, when you know how to do it, you will go in with confidence to the places that need your services most.

Even though I have seen that dimensional path of light and even pondered leaving it all behind for it. I would need a massive amount of support and comfort to walk such a straight and narrow way, with the pride of poor people and the sufferings of our ancestors. I can see myself going towards that natural call of nature. To give myself to nature as I do in Sundance. For we can all know and see the road to redemption, the practices are here the knowledge is available. It either takes one person to step up and sacrifice themselves and their cells, or all of us to recognize a healthy sacrifice and support global suffering to offer support and courage to do the work that the creator gave us all to carry. Some say one of us will come back to remembrance before others, helping all to remember the culture of light. There will be many disbelievers, there will be many ready to receive him/her and the light of the true sun. I know you are thinking I'm an egomaniac by now. Brainwashed by heroic stories, joking about cult leaders, challenging the eyes of the watchers and whistle-blowers. And lowkey speaking about my yogic success. I'm just like you though, my friend a human being. I am speaking from a disposition of experience. Take it or leave it.

Challenge yourself with the postures of light some of which appear in this book for you. Tell me how you feel after 10 minutes. Maybe try 1 year. Tell me did you even go deep enough to see? Did you even have the spaciousness to really drop in? Or do you just like the idea of it, maybe you strive for it. Simply not doing the work not having the environment that pushes you to go deeper. A natural friction that the street yogis or cave yogis had no choice but to persist. God gave them that life, not the life of you the reader of many books, the watcher of many videos, the seeker of yourself. I have met these people gifted by God, to watch and observe only the light and only the truth, tucked away far away from any distraction or naysayer. For this work is all too real and cannot be taken lightly I would not even suggest listening to me if I was not confident that I can tell you after 10 plus years maybe 10,000 plus hours of building a relationship to the culture of light. This has been my life! For fun, ask AI today the prediction of a human being that ingests pure light and elemental energy for their lifetime. Ask AI what it will think of a human in such devotion. Sure, AI can answer you the opposite as well. Like AI, please predict what will happen if humans continue consuming as we are! Try it for fun and let me know what the AI says, for the gods did not give this analytical mind to me. The creator gifted me these postures of light. In hopes, I will do something with them, to give my life reason and in my commitments and vows to be lived out. And still, I am also confident to say that I am a baby, and I have been afraid of what comes when you fully give yourself to nature or the essence of god. That is an experience I hope to speak about one day.

In the present time, we are looking down an avenue of awareness, practice, responsibility to the nature of self, and a conscious conduction of light and love. Kindled by the intimate relationship and recognition of the great power of nature and the spirits that walk with us on Earth. Leaving us to surrender our wondering mind, weak in power without the elements of nature to aid us in our growing sensations and build-up of chi. That avenue is already a straight and narrow path or hopefully an effortless way of life. Regardless, it will take attention and care to foster a fruitful presence and a future that would lead to total union with the sky peoples and healthy relations with the many spirits of Earth, and your cells. These spirits all have ancient names as our early ancestors sat with them just like Hector, the hungry ghost. This is why I say feeling is beyond all knowledge, it is what gives you the opportunity to know more, I do not need to know the name of something to recognize the feeling it offers. Then one can come to know or understand and offer the energy a name. For many, this avenue looks beautiful and special. I personally have wanted this opportunity majority of my life, I think many of us feel a strong connection to our ancestors and want to embody saintly energy, many of us already doing so in our own way. The work is very hard also, to simply sit in a cave or cabin in the mountains where you can bask in the light of the sun and the growing sun inside. To further the human study, I can tell you from experience as many know themselves, darkness is fun, as I have put myself into retreat, in the mountains, and caves. I'd find myself getting bored with practices, meditating for hours a day, and lying on the Earth. Day after day, I would ask myself is this it? Is this the romanced life I've wanted? I was simply unable to give myself to source fully, as in sitting fully in time and space effortlessly in bliss and sending out the vibrations of source energy or the good spirits of light. This tells me two things; I need more practice and willpower to sit still and devote further. Also, telling me that the temptations of our world today are so strong they can pull you away from these powerful points of Earthly conduction. we find gratitude in so many aspects of light and nature and also the human beings a large part of nature. Honor and respect to both, some people say they are meditating during their day, yet their day is filled with so much. How focused can one really be when naturally they are being filled with their environment? That is why the call to nature is so strong, I personally feel the great work of the building of your light body must be respected and taken seriously. In the beginning, especially, think of the pure baby again and how little it knows and just how much it feels. To do what Jesus did or Buddha, to leave it all behind for some small time, a sacrifice of their life to bring back the voices of nature to the people. To remind them that in the name of SunRa we all live in the light, breathe the air and space, and be free in our nature of self. We have everything we need and there is no need to take it. That sin is once again an idea that someone has wronged you, taken your life. For what if all we need to sustain is our elements and resiliency? Would one need to take if one was filled with the light of our creator the love for all relations? So, who scrambled our eggs? May be silly to think that we need to isolate ourselves to focus on ourselves. Or talk about ourselves, to be about ourselves. See I am not writing to tell you about myself per se although some may just think that, more so using myself as an experiment to convey some results. It is up to you to decipher the essence of the book, as well as all of life, your relationship to all of it. Do You need to be with light so that you can be happy, finding more comfort being alone and far away from all the other human life on the Earth? Allowing the light spirits to hug you and hold you! It's too beautiful, imagine light filling your being, it may be all you need to feel your life is thriving, a sustained orgasm if you will. Leaving a long-lasting influence on your presence and being. As far as I know a recipe, or a way will need to be paved for others to walk in comfort and clarity. And yet the hug of a human is an instant feeling and needs not much practice in context to the avenue we just peered into together of practice and devotion. To be held by a human is also orgasmic and can leave a lifelong presence as well. So, who is living a cleaner and fuller life? The one in isolation enlightening themselves quite literally, or the one who is only relying on humans for their connection? Seems that one could live in both realities. Some say that having a family brings the same amount of purpose and love that a devoted spiritualist may receive from building with their elemental and spiritual families. I believe I'm learning to walk the middle road and finding ease in practice and leisure in my recreations, A time and a place for everything.

Looking into the monastics of Buddhism, before my remembrances of the rebels and druids, I thought about becoming a monk when I was a teen. As my mother hosted many monks and Llamas who are now Rinpoche's. Monastic practices transpire great wisdom and chi to accumulate in a being, with the support and spaciousness of their clan. Many monks or yogis are recognized as Rinpoche also known as a precious one. All for good reasons, and with so much respect. I've been to the Menri Monastery, an origin points of Bon practice and where our Beloved Rinpoche, Tenzin Wangyal grew up, and into the great teacher and Rinpoche he is today, assisting many people including myself. It was actually Tenzin himself who welcomed me to Menri and set a course for me to Retreat, in a monastic context and setting. The Bon Po people are rich in ancient merit, with many magical displays. To me, any Bon Po is a rebel of the systems of today, no matter where his practices come from. A cave or a room, are just spaces. It is the rebel mind that will surrender itself to the Dharma. And let go of the common themes we see in the masses today. I've received good energy from both sides and have great respect for both yogic ways of life. Naturally, I grew up in the opposite of monastic life, seeing all the darkness and temptations a human can fall to. The mountains and the monasteries the caves are the reference point of stillness and purity.

My uncle tells his students, that it's time to leave the cave, leave the retreat, go into the streets, and be with people, for you were born a person, your people need you, and your families need you. Is it time to rehabilitate? Not only is it more fun when you can relate with human, animal, elemental, ghost, and God families but you are actively engaging them and supporting them, and they are you. Now if you can take your meditation from the cave or the cushion into your daily lives, the days of judgment, and be active in your practice. That is a universal energy worker, making time for all your relations. To identify the ones who are pretending to be happy, hug them, feed the animals, speak to the ghosts, share your energy consciously with them, sit in the elements and allow yourself to reflect them, listen to your relations and your true friends. To be love and to see love in all action and relations. Many of us struggle daily either not relating to other human beings or not trusting in the energy with 100 names, getting caught up in the present-day dogmas and stigmas. So easy to shun certain family members accidentally in our innocence of unknowing.

I don't think it's appropriate to beat ourselves up for things we don't know or feel. Gentleness is the avenue of appreciation. For what nurtures us we naturally appreciate. To allow judgment of self to be gentle. Judgment has been made into a strong word, a biblical word, simply, it is just to observe and make a life-giving decision based on how something makes you feel. It's a very crucial part of surviving. Although it could be how we got caught up in greed and want for more simply judging or deciphering, discerning our ancient ways of living and saying we want more. We all get out of hand or carried away at times, in context to complete stillness of self, sitting with nature. Well, you might get hungry and go to the fridge and aimlessly eat till you are satisfied. There's always beauty in the struggle, it is yours to judge, yours to see, it is your willpower and your openness that will get you where you can sit anywhere with people or animals, alone or with God or ghosts. Steer your life, manifest your life, imagine your life, and just for fun pretend that you are there, just make sure you do the work aswell!

My meditation teacher would always tell me to envision myself in my happiest place and see myself there. I used to imagine myself as I described lying in the grass observing the subtle living sensations of light particles, seeing them, hearing, them smelling them, tasting them, and feeling them. This has always been my happiest place; this has been my reflection and practice. This time, I think I'd be happier to see you on the grass under the sun with a tiny sun inside you, smiling upon each other and all our relations.

Worldly Breathing
Part 1.

- So, let's take a minute. Turn on your foundations. Imagine a tiny sun in your heart center. Imagine the warmth and light emanating through your being, imagine the functions and anatomy of your body. Imagine **light opening expanding absorbing and transforming** your cells. Allow your body to gently smile. See yourself from above, in a field together with all the humans you love, let's just say all 8 billion of us for fun, 8 billion smiles, why leave anyone out, imagine us all reflecting the same light that you are feeling, feel their smile, feel their light and affirm each other's presents. Imagine all the animals coming to see, sitting by your side, birds and four-legged of all kinds, all the animals you love, invite them. Imagine all of the hungry ghosts coming to see you, coming to bask in the love and the light of 8 billion conductors all reflecting light. Imagine your ancestors our relatives all coming to this buffet of color, just pretending that we are all on the grass together conducting and sharing love and light. Imagine our gods and our rainbow spirits smiling at us from above. Imagine the kingdom of heaven. Take some deep breaths inhaling each other's light and exhaling…

Part 2.

- **Opening, expanding, absorbing, and transforming** our molecules, influencing each other's energy as we raise the vibrations and amplify the colors! Affirm each other's hearts smiling, affirm each other's tiny sun, the warmth we feel from the shine. All your relations connected like the mushrooms mycelium systems all networks communicating through the effortlessness of nature, nature of each other, family of one nature, the natural forces of nature. Imagine even if you're just pretending. Just for fun, continue to place attention on the tiny sun in your heart center, taking long deep breaths as you open your pores and flesh welcoming in the energy with 100 names. The essence of nature inviting the living light. Inhale their presence into your being. Exhale and imagine light flourishing inside of you as the light dances and spreads through your cells. In the mind's eye, allow your vision to expand and grow, affirming the sensation this energy offers you. Breathe in this fashion for some time, allowing the self to relax into this inner posture of inner awareness. Imagine all your relations smiling and resting in the light of the tiny sun just as you are now Affirm that for your relations. Allow **JOLKA** Joyous Openness Loving Kindness Awareness into the ethers of space, exhale the love you feel into the ones you imagine yourself with. You can repeat the mantra and use the breath to add to the focus of the inner posture, or energy illustration.

This Energetic painting of worldly breathing is up to you to create In your imagination, for no movie or illustration nor the greatest AI can generate such imagery. It is the Abstract Imagination the original AI, it is the sensory sensations of energetic engineering that manifest such an image of reality.

A culture of conscious creatures, in conduction to all of creation! This practice is excellent for self-awareness, healing depression, anger, and low self-esteem, and helps create an image of a self-loving identity.

If you are like me then doing good deeds for others brings natural joy and gratitude, as people thank you for the service you offer them. This practice is a gift, you can do it with singular beings as well, someone you know may benefit from a light bath, it is also nice to ask permission. In this context of sharing light, globally, we are observing the lack of awareness that is key to the product coming out in a desired fashion. We can ask Mother Earth and listen intuitively. Mother Earth has been asking us to give her what she has given us. As the dominant species hosted here, it may behoove us to grow in light as our thoughts and actions shift, due to our daily bread. Finding that life becomes simplified, and we can rest in this space, knowing that our sun and Earth are with us, and their support is the main ingredient we need to be healthy. The idea is that if we are listening to the voices of nature, we will then be able to speak back in the mother tongue and offer our light conduction back to our elemental parents. This is where I have found divine purpose in my building of relationships with the voices of nature. The whispers of light coincide with all the material aspects of life. Making room for nature to fill, finding that our true identity is a microcosm of the universe we exist in – a mere reflection of elemental activity and processes. A greater expression of Qi exchange to all our relations, may the postulation of light find your chi, and lead you to your truth with respect and love.

Chapter Nine
Back to Nature

Looking into nature, we can see and affirm the beauty that is lent to us as we merge into nature. As our vibration slowly starts to shift, from a fast pace of living to becoming still, still as the natural environments of Wee Wu We stillness in action reflects to us, a space of peace, of preservation, divine movement. Allow yourself to just breathe, to simply feel the living sensation inside of your body, mind, and spirit. The stillness with bodily actions happening always.

Our body is our feeling and sensation.

Our mind is our awareness and our action.

Our soul/spirit is our connection/ love/magnetism our energetic pull.

To be a strong manifesto of our nature, we must clean ourselves, we must align ourselves so that we may see our nature turn into creation. For nature has created us, all we can do is to give the same reflection, to offer the same care, the same love, the same light that our father Sun has given us. The same support, the same nutrition, the same connection that Mother Earth has given to us. This is all we can do, to give to our elemental family. It is so beautiful to know so many of us are thinking and feeling the same towards our elemental family. It gives a sense of togetherness, as our human family takes courage we can all step back into the nature of self and give back to nature herself. As a collective, we are the co-creators of our environment, actively envisioning the world we want for ourselves and each other.

Meditation is such an important part of our co-creation as we can take time to sit with ourselves and see the thoughts that don't serve us. Giving those thoughts back into the ether, being recycled and actively inhaling the source of our heartfelt creations. The image that we can see in our mind, feel in our heart as we act it into reality, becoming the character we want to be.

Using mantra, prayer, and breathing, we naturally breathe in aware action and the visualization of the mind starts to reveal itself through our voice and senses of oneself. As we emerge from the depths of the pit of darkness, a 400-year stent of so much suffering, a suffering that started in the mind and actively was executed through the action of the spell castor. Showing evidence of what is possible, whether in darkness or light. So, we ask ourselves if we want to play, if we want to heal. To imagine a world of light and love. If we want to implement nature's recipe. Reflecting on the world of space and all elements, instead of making it into a man-made world. We surrender to nature to guide us so that we may work with nature and allow the voices of nature to speak to us, acting as the messenger of nature, so that we may live in harmony with nature itself. A wise woman once said to me how could a woman submit to a man if a man had not submitted to nature/creator. A man who does not know the nature of self will struggle and fumble the messages of nature. Or simply not be humble enough to listen. The purpose of a man will determine his relationships. It's time to let go of the control and offer direction instead. Time to surrender to nature and step into the stewardship, to become once again the shepherds of nature, like the whales in the sea. Naturally, ingesting foods and substances that feed us so that we may poop it out for other life to sustain and grow from. All gardens grow out of shit, plants and all of life grow from composting, changing structure, and turning into fertile soil for the next generations.

No matter what your belief is we all have to grow through shit to find new life, new information, growing our energy centers, and opening our channels for expansion. No matter if you believe or not, all people create their realities. I loved watching the Viking series, a show about Ragnar Lothbrok and his relationship with Oden and Thor his original gods of Pagan spirituality. The movie depicts him talking to Oden and asking for strength. As Ragnar surrenders himself, he begins having visions and through his devotion, he finds his purpose. He sees a bigger vision for his people, a way of giving life to his people, yet taking life from others, as he and his Vikings set out to find new fertile grounds for growing food and living an easier life. As they pillage the Christian territory, they find catholic monks, the Vikings laugh at them as they destroy their churches and kill their people proving to them that the lord and Savior cannot protect them from man. Ragnar spares the life of one man and takes him as his slave. The leader of a vision usually steps ahead of his crew to speak to his ancestors and spirits asking for guidance first. Ragnar allows for Jesus to enter his consciousness; he starts wearing a cross around his neck and becomes very interested in the powers of Christ. His Viking family then begins to judge him and even begins to cast him out, for most Vikings know the power of their gods and laugh at anything other. At the end of Ragnar's life, his journeys and experiences start to flood his mind. Traveling through all moments of his epic life. He reflects on his relationship with himself. He recognizes that all the gods were outside of himself, in personal to his inner voice. As he is dying, he realizes that it was his human mind and the vision, an image that came within him. A connection to an old spirit. Letting go of his life, he dies a man of honor in his actions, doings, and nature. Even if he believed he was supported by Oden Thor and even Jesus, it was he who imagined a life for himself and his community. So, was all that he destroyed and created an act of God or a great spirit moving through him? Possible nature led him or was it a belief that was felt so strongly that he acted upon it? Or was it the simple nature of self that he was talking to himself and possibly imagining something higher?

This story is so beautiful to me simply because it shows a man of God and his purpose, going through the inner voices of dark and light. God outside of self and God within self. For one who thinks he is something more, will fall, fall from the heights of the unhealthy ego. Consumed by the thoughts, I am greater than thou, there for one can rule nature. That is the beginning of an evil that can consume a human being, isolating them and exiling them from their community. We must walk gently on the Earth and know that we are all equals all a sliver of pie that fits into a whole.

All people are vision questers, allowing our gifts to reveal themselves, stepping into the roles that we know we were wore born into. Just like Sundance, some do not have the vision to dance, some lack the strength, and some may lack the body or the mind or the spirit. Yet they know their selves, they know they are amazing cooks, natural nurturers, and providers of sustenance for their people, some are supporters and space holders for the ones who are surrendering themselves as light warriors, the ones that step onto the front lines will always bring benefit back to the wise elders who extend their wisdom to the young warriors. There is always a need for a chief to direct the people, with the tribe's support and love for. A chief can be celebrated to be the visionary who is speaking to himself, asking himself how he can best be of service to his people. He has a council of medicine men and elders, his ancestors he speaks to. The chief is a man of nature a man of purpose and devotion to his people to his relations. He goes into the forest to listen to nature, to embody the voice of all his relations, considering all things all relatives, as he comes back home, he speaks to his relations. His wives and his children are the legacy of his blood and his visions.

Could this be why we are all struggling to hear and live in a world of true harmony because we are too jealous today? As I can see in myself, I want to lead myself, surrendering to no man, I ask myself do I follow him? I have not been able to take a vow under anyone besides nature. So, I can see that in many minds of mankind, we struggle to allow for the visionaries to be the visionaries and the helpers to be the helpers. The ego has been inflating into a selfish-centered mind. We all want to be recognized, and we should, that aspect of tribalism is so beautiful as we all can settle and celebrate each other's roles, as we all make surviving a bit easier on one another. Filling each other with gratitude, for life would not be easy if we had to do it all by ourselves.

Hence the world we live in today is ruled by the kingdom of self and mind, a woman doing a man's role and men doing a woman's rule. We see so many of us struggle to raise children on our own, to make money, find shelter, gather food, and find water. Back in the good old days, these responsibilities would be shared in a big family, you wouldn't pay someone to daycare your kids because mom or dad was there, your auntie or sister would fill that role, and you wouldn't have to go buy mass amounts of food because your brother was a great hunter and shared his meat generously. You would not have to pay for therapy if your grandfather spoke to you, the wisdom that his father shared with him. All the roles were in harmony with each other.

When this country of tribalism and nature beings was colonized and taken over, they divided the land, stamped it, named it, and branded it as a new world. The United States of America gave us rights after taking away our roles, only to rule over us. They gave us land instead of living off the land, they gave us numbers and began to count us, they created a system that is in place, if you are born on this land you will be a citizen of this land. Yet before we were a part of the land, we were the reflection of our environment, shepherds of the elements. Now we buy our water in bottles, we buy firewood, and we have no choice but to breathe the air that they polluted without asking us if we need more. We are left to stay on our portion of land, as a citizen in a "free" country, many of us are breaking the rules of gardening and growing our food. United States of America is a corporate industry that has replaced the roles of a tribal community, with the unspoken ownership of your social security number. Creating a system that you can pay into to be supported by. They did such a good job of designing this new world that one might not think it is too bad, forgetting the glory of pre-colonial times – living a simple life, of sweet love for our environment. So as much as we can embrace the world, it may take some cycles to see us living with the land as we used to, to have freedom to garden and to be free. In some look, we can see globalization has helped us organize and make for a more comfortable life. I think if all people had the same luxury I would not be speaking so much. If we can find appreciation for the old times and the new times, we could become full of so much happiness and joy, a mass healing of acceptance. A great sacrifice for a more advanced society? I'll leave that up to you to ponder. Where do you stand as we peer into global suffering together?

It seems one idea of revolution is to just globally accept! Be excited that we are living during this time. It is indeed the life that the old peoples prophesied to come we have arrived at a prophetic time of too much power, a technological advancement worthy of wiping out our original cells if not handled with love. We must realize the freedom we have. Most of us travel and find a place where we may settle and either live in nature or be happy in the city as we can still actively become gentler on Mother Earth. If we could slow down some of the fracking and some of the environmental issues, we could all feel a little better about our oceans and our air, actively giving back to our elemental family.

The idea of a mental revolution is interesting, as we see so many people battling in their minds about what we have to do or do not need to. If we could get back to nature of self, feeling the living sensations of our body as we become more intimate with our cells letting go mentally of all MAN-MADE DELUSIONS. Strengthening our connection to the energy with 100 names or simply empowering ourselves and stepping into our roles and celebrating them. This kind of revolution would simply help the human's internal environment and we could change our thoughts together, choosing to see love, choosing to be still and be with nature, for no matter where you stand or sit, the light is always with you. You can take your tiny sun inside everywhere you go; you can practice all day in each conversation, and in each difficult moment, you can always turn on your light. There is no need to fret for all comes and all goes. A revolution of divine Acceptance. It is curious to me that the American government was founded through working with the natives, even adopting structures and practices. Only then to perform genocide on our 1st nation people, the natural way of life that our people lived effortlessly. Early politicians took the life and the way of life performing DADA, re-scribing and newly stamping it as the American dream. An atrocity to say the least. My native brothers and sisters help me to heal even now as I have been enraged, I go to pray with them about healing and visions. It seems in recent history native way of life has been celebrated and even recognized as the original way. Bringing politicians and American leaders to their knees as they crawl back into the inipi or sweat lodge. These ceremonies are powerful for all peoples as we are coming back to pity ourselves, letting the creator know we can do better and listen more, we can surrender our analyzing mind. I will share a powerful vision from my Sundance, at the end of the book as I see it as another historical event in our healing of the nations. Bringing politicians, leaders, supporters, and all of the Earthly relations together as free people of Earth. What if we were all to come together in this way, we would be the end of a chapter and the beginning of a great time of recognition of natural power. A conglomerate of our past our present, and our future with all the energy/information on the table we could go forward together in clarity and understanding. Naturally outsourcing a sensation of peace, of forgiveness on all ends. Laying to rest the global atrocities, to learn to coexist and to respect each one of our ways of life, to know they are all current and spawn from the same source of creation. What a return to nature that would be. I sincerely pray for us all to feel the same peace I feel as I type this out.

However, there would still be a lot of environmental work to be done, the beginnings of a great rehabilitation. As we actively see climate activists coming to aid, I think we can do it together. We respect the roles of the firefighters, the farmers, the drivers, and the inventors, for if you are going to stay in the system just enjoy it. And if you want out take time and go find your place, no matter what god you believe or don't believe, nature is always with you. You will always be a child of the sun, a light in the world of so much sadness. In that position, maybe there is nowhere to go, maybe all there is to do is stand your ground and keep fighting for a better, more equal world.

Nature has been calling me back for so long and really, I've never moved from the foothills of the Crestone Mountains, for how I could leave an environment that showed me so much. I embraced myself and the world we live in. I pushed the system away for so long dramatizing the new world disorder! Longing for the old way of living in the community. It is still our choice how we want to perceive life in front of us, for the old days are not gone yet. However, I've had to work on my relationship with the world of today instead of making it wrong. I now find myself enjoying the balance of city and country. Consumption and minimalism. I'll never stand for how this country came to be, I will always pray with my Pikuni and Lakota brothers. I'll always go to the tree and humbly offer my ears to listen and my body to feel what to do next, I renounce my wants to be in a box and fit into a social norm. I no longer want to talk about the doom of our world, preppers and buggers can bugger off.

Nature is speaking to me, she has had my attention for too long now. Sharing her stillness with me. Her reflections of me, allowed me to speak on her behalf. My relationship with our mother grows, the nurturing that we have shared, the dinners we have shared, the vision that we share. The healing of our ecosystems, acceptance of our body, and the rehabilitation of our spirit. Mama is telling us to slow down to take time, real-time, practice and sit with her! Our Mama nourishes us so our Father can give us light to see and feel. Our mother is showing us how to treat her. You must listen to her, treat her as you would your lover, give gratitude to her, offer yourself to her, and Mama will grant you with even more than you know. Mother nature is calling you back, mama is speaking to you, allow yourself to lay down your arms, no more trying to control, or understand, stop trying to know. It is time to feel nature, the essence of nature, the quietness of nature, the stillness, and the color of nature.

It is a daily practice to carry your awareness of your connection. Play with yourself as you grow in and out of your awareness of nature and the nature of self. Attention is shifting from your spiritual connection to your human connection. Observe yourself for fun after sitting inside with your tiny sunlight turned on, observe yourself as you greet people throughout your day with your inner smile turned on. Just for fun pretend that you are an influencer of joy. For indeed, there is no pretending that you are a conductor, do not deny your sensations inside, become generous with the Joyous Openness Loving Kindness Awareness energy that you are. There is no doubt that you can become a living sensation of **JOLKA**.

I'm sharing a lot. Things that my meditation teacher would wait months and even a year to teach me. We do not want to go too fast or get caught up in an unhealthy ego. This is simply the nature that has been in front of you, with a revised recipe of light, color, love, and all the qualities of **JOLKA.** The qualities that you want to share with your, most loved ones. Now, in every teacher I've had in my presence, whether I'm studying Tibetan, Taoism, Voodoo, or Native way of life, it is all of nature spelled out by the old peoples from every corner of creation, naming the same things over and over again recognizing a feeling and saying its name. All my teachers say to only give life with this awareness. The awareness of JOLKA in short. This book is about exposing the opposite of life-giving energy as we go deep into the darkness of human nature and the diverse thoughts and emotions that can come, that have inflected so much harm. Now, I'd be naive to think that everyone who finds this book helpful and knows the magic of which I'm speaking will do good. I know Satanists who know mantras and spell castings that are also powerful. As we said before it is all of one source yet can be kindled in any expression. Any human being can give life or take life. Just know that the light of the sun, and the children of the sun outnumber the children of the darkness, the children of evil doings walking with demons/ghosts will always be present. We need them as the yin-yang or chicken and egg depict. There cannot be all darkness with no light and no light without darkness. We do not fear evil or darkness, for our tiny sun inside illuminates all, casting love and bliss so strong that no evil can make us feel as we already did. Their spells have come to an end, they are weak with too much hate and holding on to something that they stole from the beginning. Too many sold themselves to the devil.

There we are on the rise, and from here as cycles continue, it may not be easy to watch or witness but take courage! And when we feel sadness, we feel anger we don't understand. Go to Earth and sit with her, she will love you, sing a song to her, and listen to nature sing back. Nature speaks every day, even if one day is more difficult than the next, some days you get to chop food, and the next day you have none, fear not, for your Earthly community will feed you. If you are having some emotional issue, or feeling lonely, rejoice inside of yourself for you are never alone, the tiny sun is always shining, spend time there with light instead of mentally victimizing yourself. Knowing that you are a child of the sun, a connected human being, one who walks with nature, like an old mountain man exploring the hills. If you're dealing with relationship issues, take time to talk to your partner like you do with Earth, take time to lay your head on her chest, listen to her, and let her know that you are comforted by her breast. Before you engage in an argument, take a breath, turn on your foundations, and observe yourself in these hard moments – for that is when your practice is the most important. It is easy to close your eyes and visualize your perfect world. A soldier of land will walk into a chaotic space and with open arms absorb all negativity, and when he or she speaks, it will come out as gentle as a refreshing breeze. Not ruffling the feathers of one another.

I know all these things are easier said than done. I know energy is subtle and I know our habitual habits. As I quietly listen to your nature, your thoughts become my thoughts and mine yours. I can feel your emotions as if I am there looking into your eyes. For I see myself in you! All light and all darkness, I know it is not easy, big man. We must come to a place of embracing each other and our traumas. Even if we don't like it why let it get to us? Allow your material comforts to be replaced by your awareness of self. We have all come from kings and queens of the kingdom of heaven, allow yourself that royal perspective of self. My sister used to ask me what the difference between a queen and a non-queen is or a king or non-king. One who simply eats well, exercises their body their mind, their spirit, one who is listening to themselves, one who feels good and radiates divine beauty into their space is a royal being awakened to their happiness which is love for life. Loving and living in the kingdom of heaven, simply nature itself, such beauty here on Earth. Why do we waiver?

One who effortlessly supports another like an in-tune guitar vibrating the strings of another close by. My meditation teacher's wife had a vision of a healing modality that came to her that she calls resonance alchemy. The modality is offering the suggestion, similar to the guitar resonance. An in-tune human can apply energy to PowerPoints in the body, by chanting mantras, and syllables, and actively sending light energy there. The patient can feel their body shifting, her healing work views the human body as consisting of nine bodies. I had the pleasure of studying with her for a short time. The house we would go to was for qi going and energy amplification. Looking back, it was a house filled with more love and joy and funny feelings as my mentor would refer to different bodily sensations, your qi sensations. We would gather and sit in a circle twice a week and all imagine ourselves to be cycling light, looking deeper into our inner verse. Some students would have plenty of qi sensations. One good friend of mine full of laughter was saying that he felt like a giant, as his energy was so tall and big, he laughed explaining his qi sensation. These were the glory days, the beginning of my imagination taking off into the network of color. It was in this tiny room that we would go traveling through our body and exploring the vastness of our awareness, in this tiny room filled with love, awareness and light, my life changed. My auric painting project started there. 15 years of painting an energetic awareness, a compilation of dozens of inner yoga postures or qi foundations. Although the mandala is a lifetime project, and I have become tainted in my travels I'm finally finding effortless rest again. Allowing myself to bask in my karma, enjoying the baked goods, affirming my alchemy, as my uncle said there is nothing to do but rest, just rest. The pressure to meditate on the cushion has been released, I've carried my practice around the world, built my resiliency and now my practices carry me around the world. Giving and receiving of chi is my only soul contract. Everything else I experience in my life comes and goes. But these visions of light speak volumes throughout every day of my life. Keep me in love even when I am wounded, I'm healing simultaneously just sitting in the presence of Earth and the sun with water only.

My dad first told me about Taoism when I was a young boy, maybe 12. He told me about my microcosmic orbit and how to cycle my energy, this was paired with my first recalled sex talk as he paired energy work to lovemaking – the big draw and valley orgasms are all linked to energy work of course. My dad was into Mantak Chia, the Taoist master. He knew about inner smile and microcosmic orbit, I had been going to Buddhist retreats as I was 13 and 14 years old, but it wasn't until 16 that I really found the doorway into myself the doorway into nature.

The forest is really just a state of mind, you are the do-or, the one who does or does not. Do you enter the kingdom of heaven, are you doing queen things, are you walking, talking, and doing as a king, a royal being sharing awareness with your relations? Do you walk in the forest? Does the sensation that you gather from the trees and the elements follow you around? Does your awareness include the energy of 100 names, are you breathing these qualities actively? You are the do-or, the co-creator of your forest. You can open your door at any time by simply doing so. It's kind of like the light switch metaphor turning on, by simply do-oring so (bad joke, perhaps). Don't be shy, you are the one you have been waiting for, so get on with it, to me there is only one door left to open. Entering the forest of which we came, turn on your light, and allow for it to brighten your way. Conductors of love conductors of light it is time to do the thing. I think it will be appropriate to share a nature story and a nature meditation in this chapter.

At CHAC, Crestone Healing Arts Center the massage school my uncle built, opened, and facilitated in Crestone for many decades, is another room full of love, light, and layers of awareness, joking that it is the real-life Jedi school if you want to learn the forces of nature. That was the place. He and his wife take their time as they lead you through a yoga series, taking you deep into your bodily awareness, and also set you out into nature to build your foundations with the elementals. Elemental qi gong, the first element or relative we were going to work with was Earth, a tree to be precise.

Tree Qi Gong
Part 1.

- The instruction is to go outside foundations in tack as in qi gong practice on, lights on. Walk into the forest and allow yourself to connect with a tree. Feel the subtle energy of nature pull you to your standing relative. Once your tree calls you, approach with humility and openness. Once you get about one meter away from the trunk stop. Bow to the tree, bow to yourself. Then take one smaller step forward, planting both feet firmly yet gently on the ground. Bring your internal awareness up from the surface of the Earth's floor, feel your feet on the ground above, the roots of the tree, and imagine yourself connecting to the tree's roots. Allow your body to scan itself rising from the feet – legs – hips – lower abdomen – mid-chest – upper chest – into the throat – into the face to the top of your head feel your bones – muscles – organs, blood, and chi – feel your channels – add the gentle smile into the picture – providing the body with a sense of awe. Tune into the central channel, now. Allow your tiny sun inside to rest in your sacral chakra or as I stated before your VMA very magical area.

Part 2.

- Using VMA to pump the energy up the spine. Inhale slowly, and watch light travel up your spine. Acknowledge your connection to the tree. Exhale and with your imagination. Imagine the tiny sun entering the top of the tree. Like the sun in the sky in the morning warming the top of the trees. Exhaling still, slowly, slowly. As you imagine the energy flowing down the trunk of the tree until it reaches the bottom of the tree. Going into the ground, into the roots, inhale again, and imagine the Earthly energy to rise through the roots acknowledging you are connected to the root, you have tapped into the tree. Inhaling Earthly energy up your feet – legs – hips – abdomen – chest – neck – and top of the head, watching and observing the tiny sun the whole way until exhaling again out of the top of your head. Imagine the light climbing through the top of the tree as energy enters and flows down the trunk again. Flowing into the ground again. Continue inhaling the Earth's energy and exhaling your energy into the tree. This practice is done in a horse stance bent at the knees with a straight spine. Allow yourself to be in a comfortable position. Adjust if necessary. Rest in the imagination of Earth-flowing energy as you rest deeper into your being. You can breathe with the tree or any other aspect of nature in this way. In reverence and humility, open your inner ear and inner eye to nature. Listen deeply to the subtlety of the voice of nature.

This meditation can increase amplitude, the more you get into it. If you allow your imagination to grow, you may end up going on a profound journey of the inner workings of the underground world.

"You are a standing tree! Run your roots deep, into Earth! Feel her conduction and connectivity."

I named my first business Rainbow Chi Tree Healing after the experience I had with a very old ponderosa tree. So tall and strong, wise, and rooted in hundreds of years of growing in nature.

The tree was surrounded by water on both sides, its roots actively sticking into the creek as it flowed by. Drinking water as its branches reached high into the sky. I'd run to this tree every morning as we did tree qi gong for at least a week or two. As I approached the tree every day, I stepped in with a little more awareness. Coming close, bowed to my relative, and then stepped into connection, closed my eyes, and ran my microcosmic orbit with the tree. This day, as I saw the light travel from me to her, the light didn't just go down the trunk, on this day the light extended to all the roots and branches of the tree. In my mind's eyes, I watched the light reaching the tips the pine needles of the tree, the fingers of the tree, colors of light started to rain down as I breathed deeper into this and let my mind travel with the light. I watched the main orb continue down the trunk of the tree, till it reached the roots. On this day, I traveled deeper underground. I saw the light traveling so far, meeting up with the roots of many other trees. When I came to my inhale, I was mentally witnessing light traveling up the trunks of many surrounding trees all inhaling up our trunks, together exhaling out the top. I watched the trees exhale light into the sky creating a display of beautiful color, raining down upon the trees and the Earth. Exhaling and going even deeper this time. Rainbow chi travels through the underground networks of mycelium and roots. I saw in my mind's eye, a forest filled with lights of color. In my mind, I was standing in a rainbow forest inhaling with the trees, and the inner networks were filled with light, the forest reflected that back. I wanted

117

to stay in this place, it was a magical imagery, one of the most beautiful paintings I've witnessed. I stayed there for some time, 10 or 15 minutes of breathing with the forest, with the creek that flowed by the sound of water and light. As I opened my eyes and stepped back, I truly felt that the trees were feeling just as I did. It was an altering day that I will always remember.

Unfortunately, a volunteer fire department came along and chopped a large part of the forest down recently, they left mama ponderosa yet cut down so many of our friends. Sometimes we mitigate are relatives out of our fear of catching fire and burning us down. Another natural phenomenon of humans finding safety in justifying actions with feelings usually influenced or altered by others thinking it is also fine. In some settings, it could be necessary to mitigate. Humans have been interacting with fire since the beginning of time. Building a relationship with our elements in ways of intimacy, a way to carry water and fire with us. As elemental beings our relationships were important, we honored them because we needed them. Nature is, of course, bigger than any Hu-man and will burn, flood, quake, or erupt. Simply, it is the acceptance of it all returning to nature. Similar to the acceptance of the humans' mindless actions, taking too much? It is simply now a part of nature's timeline. We can attempt to prevent it, but in reality, Mother Earth rules our existence. This is why we must treat that relationship with importance, with reverence and sincerity. We are not meant to fear our elemental family members more so we work with them to feel safe and secure. However, looking through the eyes of business, instilling fear in us across the world with so many scare tactics, people justified the efforts of their work to make money. I understand we all need to eat. I just pray that we can find jobs to give back to nature. Instead of justifying that we are helping nature. Like so many false environmentalists and companies pose as water savors yet want to sell it, forest mitigators, waxing the landscapes becoming unrecognizable forests or jungles. My sister works with Crestone eco council as they are looking out for false profiteers, looking to profit from nature. It's time to communicate as a tribe, it's time to recognize each other and celebrate one another and the gifts. Some of us know what others are lacking. And vice versa.

Do not be afraid, have faith and pray for nature to be with us. And know that whatever happens, it's the will of our mother Earth. Creation and destruction are always present, I find rejoice in the constant light of father sun.

May the forest be with you!

And may you find the doorway into the depth of nature. Allow yourself to rest. There's nothing to do besides rest – just rest, for we are all in this rainbow forest together.

Chapter Ten
Natural Ecstasy

In the slow healing journey, we have stated a couple of times what my uncle described as "coming back to full remembrance" as we arrive together at the nature of self, our most authentic version of self. We will recognize and realize many new layers of awareness. Reading deeper into the story of self and the magical information that has been stored in our skin, bones, blood and spirit. Chi sensations will arrive us, furthering our inner standings of our cells.

One of my favorite chi sensations, I refer to, as natural ecstasy because of the feeling of bliss and happiness that grows in our body of water. Back in the day we liked to party, I'd smoke my ganja and enjoy the company of many friends as they elevated with molly, ecstasy, and MDMA, some common names of the uppers that lend the feeling of laughter, extreme happiness, and joy. Always having fun in their presence, sharing laughter, and getting contact high off their energy. Today, they use different variations of these drugs in therapy, calling it the happiness drug. I think in proper doses, like anything it could assist a person in depression, yet could also enhance depression, when you are not on the substance you can feel a lack of happiness. So, a healthy relationship is important to create with your substances, really any of them whether you're a smoker, a drinker, or dabble in drugs, all of these things can harm the body, of course. Yet they all offer us some moments of bliss and happiness, pictures of joy. Yet some more than others, and of course, can drain our vital life force energy.

If you know you know, and you can find your grace. My teacher always told me meditation is the slower route to living in a psychedelic experience. Let go of the substance and make room for your practice. In India, people said to me Shanti, Shanti, slowly, slowly, you will arrive at a constant state of bliss and happiness. I mean imagine yourself with a tiny sun inside. Shining light throughout the body, with an overtone of sensation and the qualities of JOLKA. We continue to repeat these statements and postures as it is part of the repetition and affirmations of the work. This is a simple recipe that has enhanced chi sensations inside of myself that I could relate to the highs I see in these substances. It's happened multiple days as I would wander through the woods running energy and realizing the depths of my cells. Sensations of fascination came over me, bursting out in laughter alone in the woods, feeling a growing sensation of happiness that erupted into blissful feelings throughout my body. I've talked to some users, and they describe similar feelings plus some more. Some heavy drug users I've talked to explain a godly sensation, and some people even start calling themselves God. This is a strong statement, of course, and possibly a joke, however I like talking to different people with different struggles, not only to see how they overcome their struggles but to see how they have felt, and if I can corollate similar chi sensations into my mediation. The mind is a powerful tool as we have been talking about. I know a lot of people, may be reading this book, and saying 'Duh, I already know that,' yet I think some information may be new to some and older to others. I feel it's just good to talk about our history and science and our human connections with different people around the globe experiencing and talking about different things. This can help us formulate a much wider spectrum of energy. Helps me connect the dots, the information is "Same, same but different," a statement repeated to me during my time in Thailand.

I like to believe that everything is stored in our body and energy, I'd like to think that a sensation someone experiences can be shared through imagining or letting go of any constraints, holding you back from feeling bliss. Sometimes, it can be hard to read ourselves, so going to others to read their energy can help us remember that life is blissful. Wouldn't it be nice if we could feel the sensations of ecstasy without needing the substance, the vision of hallucinogens, without the need to eat the fungi? Well, this is the study or experiment I gave myself to. I can't lie, I've never had a natural vision as strong as the immense amount of color I've experienced on LSD – mixing LSD and mushrooms is a godly experience, to say the least. Yet I'm happy to say that the vision that nature has gifted me is full of enough color to keep me off of these substances.

Being a seer of energy and a conductor of love and light, I'd often eat mushrooms in a meditative manner in my teen years, as my dad taught me. Side note, my dad was raised in a commune and started eating mushrooms very young and knows the magic and the downfall of overdoing it, hence, he educated me early. My dad educated me about substance, the sight of color I'll put it, the energy of nature, offering a meditation guide to ground me into experimentation not only with the substance but with my imagination, leading us towards energy painting. Most of my mushroom trips have been monumental and unforgettable, confirmations of my meditations, as things I saw in my mind's eye. I'd physically see an extreme shift as the trees start to breathe, the clouds continually crashing in on each other reflecting fractals of light and the blue sky. Wao! The sight of true living color spiraling orbs, arriving and disappearing by the thousands, a whole view of the sky dancing with color, the tigles or sky spirits. Some people say that your trips can linger with you, so stay in your awareness, 'Lawd, have mercy!' The beauty is so undeniable, I don't want to talk to anyone, I don't want to do anything besides just rest with them. The deeper I get into my cells and simply think about what is above? and what is below. what is without, and what is within. This simple concept allows me to close my eyes and see this display in the sky above, my body of water reflecting the same. Sky dancers, dancing in space.

It wasn't till I started tripping hard, referring to questioning my sanity as the world was becoming so beautiful and abstract. Getting caught up in heavy questioning if I'm hallucinating or if I am living in a beautiful reality and grounded. Different times in my life have confirmed my sanity. By that, I mean a sober-ish moments, no substance yet high on information and sensation. The gratification of oral tradition passing down knowledge through paintings and text. One of our Dharma family's good friends who helped organize and run the stupa in Crestone was having a yard sale. I already was helping her at the stupa, she asked me to help her at the yard sale. After helping her move all the things into the yard and looking at all this beautiful dharma material, of course, my fascination for these things actively growing. She felt that I was on a journey and she gave me a painting of a deity, that looked very similar to a statue that my dad gave me. A Dakini standing on one leg, wearing a necklace of human skulls. It was a beautiful piece of art. It was not until I got home that I read the text on the back of the painting. The text on the back describes the picture within the first couple of sentences, it names the sky dancers, as I've been referring to the orbs as dancers. Sspommitapiiksi the above ones dancing in the sky lodge. The more I read, the more my body began to smile, and the more I began to not feel like a crazy person. The more that I realized that auric painting is not at all pretend. Although it might be shanti, shanti, slowly, slowly. The more you sit with the sky dancers, the more you will be overwhelmed by color which offers effortless bliss. Now, I'm sharing some secrets of mine because, well, I feel it is time to share, and writing is a good way to express yourself and illuminate a recipe that is intended to assist in our healing as a collective, which I feel is overdue. I also feel comfortable because it took me years of putting things together and devotion to practice, finding the appropriate words to describe and share a very life-changing view. As humanity, we have come such a long way, seems like instead of keeping all this back, it would be better to allow the feelings to spread. True bliss, true color, and true groundedness take time. So why not share some vision and practice?

Growing up in Crestone has been like a game of clues, the hype is enlightenment, and the characters that lead you to light are the monks, the llamas, and the elders. The characters that lead you to confusion are the conspiring ones, the ones that will watch you as you watch them. The forest is the place where you find truth, the mountain is where you can reach the heights. The spiritual centers are the monuments of great mystery. The places to go and sit and give reverence to an idea that you can't quite tell if it's fiction or nonfiction. One other very complimentary clue to my sight and my feeling was the symbol on top of the stupa which in my understanding represents the Moon being feminine mother Earth MAKHA, the sun WI our father, and a teardrop-shaped at the top represents the birth of energy in the sky, SKAN or Sspommitapiiksi that this whole book is about, representing the tigly or sky dancers. In my study I see the Tibetan and Bhutanese indigenous people showing the highest amplitude of tigle energy. With many stories and successes of reckoning with the rainbow of living color. It is the mystery of my life, tigle is the only name Im familiar with from the Indigenous Asian lands and peoples. In Lakota, you call the sky network SKAN. Wakan Skan the holy or sacred sky, or SSpommitapiski the above ones. In Amskapipiikuni Blackfoot. We can call them in Adangbe language from Togo West Africa Inedo the great voodoo togbe, the spirit of natures rainbow. Correlating the names from Indigenous Asia, Africa and America we can see there are songs, prayers and names to call these spirits or relatives by. An invocation to share space and to embody a union with the spirit of the energy of a hundred names. Are these orbs of plasmic energy? Possibly the source of prana or source energy itself? Maybe the sky dancers are a nation of light particles, seems whatever they are our early ancestors formed a relationship and passed on many magical stories of the heights of human evolution and experience. You can call the spirits by these old names, they will remember you if you remember them. We can ask them to help us remember as we all know we appreciate when someone remembers our name. As I grow into my cells, and I find clues that affirm my vision, I can't help but devote myself to this growing feeling that lives all around us. It has been effortless, as time moves forward, I've rejoiced in moments of gratification, humility, and awe to the divine creation, Aho Mitakuye Oyasin, wakan tanka. To all of our holy and sacred relations, I give my thanks to you, For I am still learning and have been distracted by your holiness. In times of being caught up in my ego, having to go back to the canvas and clear my mind from delusional thoughts of always asking the question who am I? The older I get, the more I acknowledge that I am simply a conductor of light, just like my uncle told me, all humans are a part of WAKAN MAKHA holy Earth. My uncle also told me that the path of a true medicine man, one who walks with spirits and vision, is one of the hardest people to be. You are living in two different worlds, the spirit world and the human world.

Doing our best to stay grounded and not communicate to our fellow human beings a view that is ungrounded or just sounds crazy, being cast out as one who knows too much, or one who doesn't know a thing. A healthy medicine man is only here to offer a feeling and a vision that has come to him or her. To communicate in a way that allows for comfort and trust, to allow a venerable space to let your guard down to invite the spirits to flow into the bones and your body of water. A grounded medicine man will speak gently, and you will feel an authentic voice and language that is not only of his or her speech but also of his movements and body language. Many visionaries and medicines can come through a human being, depending on what energy we are using. A true medicine is given to heal and to give life, just like an herbal supplement or remedy. One has to become selfless in their service or they will fall into the category of a false profiter or a fraud, as they are not there to share just the medicine but to be an icon. As I stated before, in today's world, it is cool to be a medicine woman or man, people hashtag and post publicly about their position or the role that they play. Not to say that we all carry medicine and as my uncle said, we all can become sensitive to the energy around us and conduct ourselves in a healing way for the people. This is what Sundance is about.

Sundance is for the people; Sundance is selfless and without this ceremony, I think I'd be way off my rocker. If we do not speak gently, we will ruffle the feathers of the people. We will be misunderstood and lost in the vast amount of people who get written off for their egos or the want for more. For we are all subject and tempted by the colonized mind. Women are the best at seeing through a man. Woman is the natural flow of energy, if a man has no direction or is lacking, the waters of a woman will engulf him, and he will be flooded with guilt and shame, for he could not direct himself or have the ground or the abundance he needs to calm his sexual energy or his desire for more.

I'm kind of getting ahead of myself. In the next chapter, we will be going over this further. This book is like a mantra affirming what has happened, talking about it in different fashions, in hopes that if the reader was not already informed that different looks will help in the understanding of what took place in our history, our timeline, and our ability to manifest the world we want to see. I know I've repeated some similar topics and may have become repetitive at times. That is spiritual work though, to go over and over again and again to allow for the information to set in. This is how we change our molecules, this is how we see masterpieces of music and art, athletic skills, and this is how we become masters of self.

In a world where drugs and temporary feel-goods have replaced our nature of self and the power of energy that we cannot claim yet invite to flow through us, there are endless stories of yogis experiencing a world full of bliss and color. These avatars are living examples of the heights we are all born into. I am offering some awareness to you. Remember this is not well-spoken information regarding the orbs. I'm sharing this romance story of an innocent boy playing a game of clues, this is merely a feeling that is sensed and affirmed in his experience. A global game of clues, following of heart and vision, a pilgrimage to potent places where people have experienced such bliss and magic, that for hundreds of years have attracted people to come, pray and show homage. In the game of clues, we are looking at the land, the characters, and the deities. We look into their stories and images as they have been painted and sculpted many times.

This is how I came to understand auric painting, finding clues in the art, of the depiction of magical beings, as they are drawn in color and with different foundations intact. I'm curious if people look at them the same way I do. We all appreciate the beauty of the paintings just like we all appreciate nature. They are our reflections. When I look at a Tonka a painting of a deity' I see things that teachers have taught me, and I also see things that I can naturally adopt into my awareness. There is a practice in Tibetan yoga called guru yoga. Simply to see yourself as the deity, whether you see it inside of you or above you. In this practice, you are still working with a nonpersonal God, a god that is not of self, although in some looks the deity is a mere reflection of you and with humility and lots of practice you can imagine yourself slowly starting to look like them. These are some high-level teachings; I would suggest finding a person who has received this information from the oral tradition. I invite you to go to some Buddhist teachings, they offer the greatest number of authentic practices and invite you to step deeper into a guided image of what the nature of self looks like. They will invite you and show you a clear path to what they call the inner refuge or the natural state. Most teachers that come to the Western world come to help westernized minds calm down, teach about stillness, and give you tools to help you handle your emotions. Hence, preparing you for the playground of energy work. I'd definitely invite you to not rush and start where you feel is necessary. It has also been said to me by my auntie to not mix too many spiritual practices or beliefs. You see me doing that exact thing she warned me about as I'm weaving in and out of all expressions of spirituality and ways of life, from the four races of mankind. God gave this gift to me. Way of Nature, founded by John Milton, was our families plug to an international walk of life. With Hanne Strongs manifested vision of Crestone, an international pilgrimage point in the USA today. Offering young children, the opportunity to pray at Hindu Ashrams, Buddhist Temples, Native sweat lodges, and the church of Nature. I have gone all over the world continuing to pray and connect to even more universal Frequencies and vibrations. I, of course, do not want to disregard my auntie's wisdom as she has seen people short-circuit, simply it can be too much. It is true also that if you go deep into one way of life you will remember all the names all the songs and will be full of wisdom rejoicing in your remembrance of your ancestors. They will see you and you may become recognized as a great teacher becoming a Rinpoche equivalent to a doctorate in Dharma or a medicine man who has given his hallow bone for great spirits to travel through. For me, I have been working with what the creator gifted me with, although I am unrecognized today, I am grateful for all the magic revealed. In the end, I can sit back and say all of these walks of life are too similar and will deliver you to the heights, if practiced diligently and with sincerity, you will see the oneness I've been speaking of. Different names in different games, results all mirroring the same, all spawn from nature so no need to rearrange.

Only you know where you are at. As we are postulating energy together here. I am taking a wild guess that you are hoping to find peace of mind and acceptance of self, I'm guessing that you are like so many born, beautiful, and perfect yet tainted by the world of knowledge, I'm guessing that you are looking to develop a deeper relationship to self, that you have felt a feeling that you want more of. I'm guessing that you go back and forth, in between feelings that you know something is deep, and then arrive at a place of depth with no end, resorting to surfacing again. Indeed, a balancing of emotional narratives that you reside in, asking if it is yours or a collective story. Maybe you also ask yourself about your success story, even though you have mustered up your dream life, there may be a lack of a very important ingredient. Mentally, we are all going through very similar spaces, seeing an image of self, and how we want to identify for some time. Until we learn something new and then strive to arrive at what we feel is best for our cells. Our growth is continual like space. There must be something more, some cosmic chair to sit in that allows the mind to not grasp for more knowledge, a seat that you sit in, that feels so full of everything you don't want to do anything else. Maybe, everything that we want is much simpler than what society today says. Is it possible that less is more and really all you want is to drop the weights that society or you hold over and make room for your connection to nature and your nature of self? Simply to see beauty, and your elemental family to talk to you? Maybe letting go of media and human-created words may offer you more time to hear nature, elements speaking to you, a growing relationship that satisfies the soul, and continually gives gifts of connection and purpose to tend to our relationships.

I'm just generalizing here and experimenting with my telepathic nature. An ex-lover of mine and a wise woman of Mayan descent told me stories of her people and that they used little words as she did, they communicated with body language and mind, I believe she had telepathic abilities. I felt that she was testing me often as she would not say much at times, waiting for me to act, read the energy, and offer the proper support. Looking at our intuition, now it is strong yet it seems our fear of doing what is naturally felt is all too real. Usually not doing what we know would be helpful, waiting for the cue. Missing out on an exchange that needs no words.

This is fun to think about and truthfully, this is a developed skill as we come back into nature. We are all readers of energy. After traveling the world, and playing clues, I believe I can intuit some of what many people are going through in their lives. One night, I ate mushrooms with a friend, it was late, I had just bought a speaker with a microphone and was messing around with sounds, I was low-key starting my sit-down comedy act and the only person in my audience fell asleep. Wasn't too funny. I think we both had our eyes closed, I've enjoyed travel so much that playing with impersonations becomes natural, some of my favorites are Russian and Indian accents. In almost all of my travels, people shout at you, my friend. So, I was doing some of these impersonations in the dark, imagining the audience in the room. I entertained myself okay. As I talked in a voice that was not mine, I flashed to different times my friends had shouted at me, asking their asks, it felt like I started to channel people's voices from around the world as I heard and saw in my mind. It started as fun and then slowly the voice changed to a tired voice, 'My friend, we are hungry,' ' My friend, we are still here,' 'We miss you, my friend,' 'When you are coming.' The voices of people in other countries going through difficulties. My sit-down comedy was turning into a whole journey back in time as I stopped and opened my eyes in stillness, I could feel the difficulties people were going through. I can only say I feel because I don't know what people are doing, I can only imagine being by their side and remembering the lives of so many all going through similar steps in life, similar emotions, and desires. For we are all one.

I feel when people get home if they have family, they decompress and relax into the support the family offers them. For some, communities offer the same. Once all the body movement is done for the day, the mind becomes more active. I'd say most of us process our day, reminiscing on the good feelings and the feelings that were not so good. I feel there is a sense of melancholy in the world, a shared feeling that we are wanting more. We see so much on our phones and hear so much in the world, yet we are somewhat stuck, some more than others. I'd say most of us have small goals and some big ones, our thoughts consist of achievements and then feeling sadness when it is not happening. Whether you are looking for love or food, whether you are looking for someone to talk to or just a moment of feeling connected. Many of us are already happily married and living our dreams, dealing with some more minor issues, a lot of people around the world are stressed by money. Living in a world where our natural role or gift in life is neglected and displaced, many of us are just trying to survive. To get food, to feel full, and to rest well – you don't know what someone's struggle is until you have gone through it with someone.

Goes the same for the heights of life, the wisdom that one carries authentically. You may need to eat with them, work with them, or simply be their friend so that you can see how they move. Whether you are learning about global poverty or you are learning about global wisdom, it seems that the ones who struggle can endure a lot, the ones who are comfortable are quick to complain. I might even argue with myself and my telepathic ability to not be as strong as I witness so many situations a human can experience. The more people you know, the more you will understand their process, the more you can understand, and the more you can feel. Once you feel it yourself, you can see in someone's body language, are they shy, are they closed, do they want to be left alone, do they want support? In both Chinese medicine and Ayurveda, we are looking at bodies, and ways to diagnose a client, we can look into the sound of their voice, their body posture, their face tells a lot, their bodies tell a lot. Everything that we see on the outside of a person reflects their inside feeling. We are all different, but another tell is this intuition that we are all ingesting a very similar daily bread. Unless you turn your phones and screens off and simplify your intake, if you are baking for yourself, then you will have a different read. For many of us, I can see we are all struggling with similar issues, identity, body image, self-esteem, confusion, and a longing for something that is outside of ourselves. When it is merely ourselves we long for, all happening inside of the cells.

We all feel happy when we meet someone that we can relate to. We all feel happy when we eat when we get paid, we feel happy when our goals are met, and when we feel supported. This is the ups and downs, the ebbs and flows of a human being living in the world of today. So, I invite you to step out of your comforts to be open to your surroundings, it's so crazy to go so many places and see how many people are on their phones. Is life not entertaining enough? Is it a mechanism to shy away from the conversation? The movie Social Dilemma was released recently exposing behind-the-scenes of how a phone works and social media platforms as they have created a way for you to feel gratification from likes and subscribers. Technological dopamine and serotonin replacing our natural ecstasy and connecting with another person and what that offers you, let alone being in nature. Is this becoming a thing of the past? I'd say the majority of places I've been to, people are on their phones, this is a global happening, a public service announcement, the amount of sore necks from looking down at phones is higher than ever. You know when you see someone so deep in their phone their neck hasn't moved, just glaring at the screen? I'm still trying for some low-key sit-down comedy. I guess, I just miss the old days, I always have my focus on nature, I was born in the woods, raised in the woods, and stayed in the woods. I can't lie, I also enjoy the phones and would not have traveled the world with such ease as social media connects us and GPS guides us. The balance we will find, shanti, shanti, my friends.

If you are feeling good in yourself, if you're feeling royal, share that with someone bust a joke if possible, smile at people, offer the sensation that is growing in you to another, if indeed you are feeling great, overflowing with joy or happiness feeling it spreading throughout the room. You indeed are a conductor of love and light, my friend. So, as we get closer to the end of the book, there will be a few meditations left to share. One thing that I used to think is that I needed to collect as many meditations as possible like Pokémon I got to get 'em all. In my past, my Mayan lover told me that her grandmother was a Cud-Indera, a medicine woman from Mexico, steeped in Mayan mysticism, oral wisdom passed to her, she says talking to people is kind of like talking to plants. The more people you talk to, the more things you have to be aware of. You have to know your capacity to speak and serve up some sustenance or some people in your comedy act will leave the room or fall asleep. With comedy, I started with one in the audience and he still fell asleep. So, what I'm getting at, or well, what Abuela was getting at is to focus on four herbs or plants, really get to know them, listen to them, learn to nurture them well, know how much you ingest, and what they are for. The same applies to meditation world religion or way of life. You get all excited about all the different practices and then all of a sudden you forget about aspects of self, or simply do not give your awareness to parts of your practice. In my practice today, when I turn on my lights, I'm sitting with around 3 to 4 foundations. When you are ready to receive more, nature will bless you or reveal a person who offers you clarity in the next step of your magical self. I worked with my meditation teacher for two years until he transmitted the image of self, I knew I was already becoming, stacking foundations, building awareness until I could intuit myself, what was being painted in front of me and inside of me. Even what the next level of awareness will be, as we get to know ourselves deeper we get to know each other, identifying what stages of awareness we are at. I feel like I know so many of you, simply because I've been going through the steps and know that we are climbing the ladder to the heights of life. To the feeling of natural ecstasy, to the effortless action of bliss, allowing the tiny sun to turn on naturally when you are in a difficult spot. To remove all obstacles as they melt in the warmth of the sun.

We are all one mind, one collective, one body of water as we all are doing our best to keep our beaches clean. Be generous with your conduction and allow yourself to see people around the world feeling the same way that you do, simply because we can. Mainly do this because science, if not already proven, will be proven soon that our global conduction as in the average auric/magnetic field of a human is vibrating low, as we have been interrupted in our natural vibrations. Nature itself and nature of self will show science that the ways of nature and healthy conduction will naturally raise the magnetic field of us all, as we accept, that we are all of the same. And can all relish and bask in the bliss of our natural disposition. I am merely a good friend, an influencer of energy. If you can see me as simply that, then I believe we can work together quietly for the betterment of our fellow brothers and sisters and all Earthly relations.

Sun above

Part 1.

- Rest in a comfortable position. Invite your awareness into self. Imagine your bones, blood, flesh, muscles, and organs to feel the warmth of the gentle smile in your heart center. Amplify this feeling from head to toe. Affirm your inner joy and sense of awe. Simply place awareness on the top of your head. Imagine your crown opening like a portal. Imagine the pores of your skin, acting as a sponge as you **OPEN, EXPAND, ABSORB, and TRANSFORM** into a receptacle of light. Become aware of the light in your heart center. Imagine yourself glowing. Tiny sun shining in all directions. Affirm this inner posture.

Part 2.

- Invite into your awareness an orb above your head, a tiny sun shining in all directions. Allow the light from the tiny sun above to glow into your brain, into your flesh, and your entire body. Imagine tiny particles of light raining down upon you, face resting, shoulders resting, chest resting, hips and legs resting in light. Relax into the light. Allow yourself to surrender to any thought and just feel the sensations of your body as light pours into your body like pouring water into a bottle. Imagine yourself filling from your toes up to your crown. Imagine yourself overflowing with light. Invite all your loved ones and offer them this sensation of ecstasy, give them a pure feeling of bliss and awe. Give love to the light inside of you and the light above you. Offer this light to your loved ones by exhaling into space, seeing them in front of you becoming a reflection of you. Breathe in gratitude and exhale into your true nature. Mainly observe the tiny sun raining light upon you, there is nowhere to go nothing to do but rest in light.

"Enjoy your Bath"

This practice is good to quietly do on a bus or in line in silence, not telling anyone, experimenting until someone affirms to you, that your energy feels good. That is the sign of your tiny sun extending its sensation.

Good for all things potent medicine for mental issues and blockages, emotional turmoil. Pretty much everything can be dissipated or eliminated by light and resting in acceptance.

Chapter Eleven
Peacocks & Pimpoche's

We have gone over many complexities of the human being, looking at power in different ways and how it can benefit the self, the community, and the world. It is very important to acknowledge the intention of why we want to step into our higher self as some say. To become manifestos or co-creators of our reality, conductors of what we want to see in our daily lives. Getting very clear about what we ingest in our daily bread so that we feel inspired, clean in our energy field offering us an effortless devotion to nature more so. To be aware of our influence on our environments. We can arrive at a place of sympathy and love for the people who are struggling with the powers, as we said, we all want to be seen, and as we have been removed from tribalism and our roles, it becomes a growing difficulty to find purpose in our step. To feel that we are doing good in the world, so many of us have fallen into the seat of craving, grasping at things that satiate our thirst for being liked and accepted or to simply feel good, to support our emotions, our ego, and become financially stable. This is all part of the system that has replaced the original community where we once all found our purpose and were able to support one another and be seen in our natural roles. Now letting go of the desire for more; that is coming from Seva, selfless service to nature, our fellow peoples, and ourselves.

We have shared some practices in this book that are pretty high-level, the importance of acknowledging the intention is very important. When we step out of our cravings we can do our spiritual works for the betterment of humanity, instead of trauma-bonding and looking for something from another whether that is attention, time, money, or energy. This is all due to not being fed, not feeling celebrated for what we do, therefore, putting on an extra show, an extra explanation, when in reality, the healing that we are looking for is reflected in nature, as we have been speaking about. There's a fine line between being clean and dressed for success for the creator, our partners, or our community. Or putting on a show for your ego and your cravings.

As a youth, I was blessed by teachers of oral traditions and lineages, it gave me a sure look at what a real teacher looked and sounded like. I was also raised in modern spirituality, as many people innocently watching their egos and cravings for a role that was not passed on to them, showing us two very different teachers. This brought me to the understanding that there are two general facilitators, Rinpoche meaning the precious one, usually studied in a monastery or traditional location for 8 or more years, speaking from the teachings that were passed on. And then a funny word I like to use is Pimpoche, to identify a teacher who wants to be seen, wants to have his ego fed, or desires attention that naturally feeds the young child in them. The child that is living in a buildup of a mass story, that is hiding their internal wounds. One who is afraid to cry or say out loud I'm not sure why I'm doing this. The facade of a face that was not given yet was created through one's imagination. Many of these people still assist many people along the way of healing, I won't deny that. I celebrate them just as anyone, for I was once this person. I was a kid raised alternatively, tossed into public schools, it started for me. I cut my hair, I changed my dress, I changed my mind, all to fit in. I neglected myself but it felt so good to be cool and fit in. I took on the role of a joker and an athlete, going from a misfit to a cool kid. It wasn't till I was 16 that I got back into my hippie culture and stopped caring what others thought. I went back to the charter school to celebrate my roots, and that is when I met my math teacher who guided me into the auric painter that I am today. I was finding such beauty and life, getting to share meditation with other students. My story changed, I went from a joker and an athlete to a qi gong enthusiast.

By the time, I started building nature's temple. I had a whole story of myself and how I was going to find a way to be recognized as I grew up with many spiritual beings that were so celebrated in the community. I always wanted to feel that. Yet I was just a hippie, born into a commune of experimental anarchy, peace in chaos, ending in deaths, suicides, pedophilia, and substance abuse. We left with hopes of a clearer sky, I'll say simply. Although I did not experience any of the difficulties of the commune. It is still at the root of my being. There was so much light and darkness there, so much spiritual philosophy, a magical place for alternative minds. So due to being unseen and unnoticed, I decided to wear the mask of a qi gong teacher, for the satiation of being acknowledged. As I grow and continue to step into more Seva work and selfless service, I have put my mask down and shown my true face. Sundance as I've said is an act of letting go of material gain and ego cravings, it is to simply be with nature and self. Sundance has been monumental in my growth and the unbecoming of my masked self. So, I am just like anyone a young child exposed to the struggles of the world. Early on and making choices that I would live my life in happiness to choose my vision, iv felt everyone just stacking up their shit on me, wanting me to get into the shit too. I've had to actively support and keep my energy intact, for I know myself to be a people pleaser of sorts. I recognized the difference between pleasing people and pleasing to be accepted or to simply feel a part of something. Or instead looking at each person, reading into them, and then offering some pleasing information based on their trauma story. For I am so happy to arrive at the place of fulfillment of not needing to be social and to feel full when I am alone – to let myself be raw and real. I put down the want to be a teacher, I accept my trauma story, and I have nothing to hide. Creating comfort, creating a safe space for others to open, to be pleased, hopefully, we are conducting love and breathing it into the air.

So, with this being said, I've developed a discernment that recognizes when one has a hidden agenda, one who is still hiding the wounds and looking for someone else to nurture them, instead of sitting with the reflections of nature and adopting the ways of nature. That is the great work that one must do before one steps toward a person for love, connection, or even friendship. We have seen too many spiritualists suppressing their hidden agendas which then turns out to be a disruption of another's energy, becoming uncomfortable and even becoming violated energetically or sexually.

This is what we call the Pimpoche, a fun way to call out or discern a person who is making a story rather than carrying the teachings passed down to them. Now we all have a vision and I'll be the first to say that my main teacher is nature, my story is made up of nature confirmed by elders and traditions. The voices of nature have passed on a feeling and an undeniable vision, as I've fumbled my ego and trauma story in my days, I know now that this is medicine for the people. A teacher who also has a family is a sure sign that they are conducting love and already have a purpose, not looking for confirmation from another because their family is their purpose and their service, stepping into the family house as a family and sharing the medicine with others. The teacher who grows older without a family, or counterpart has their unique storytelling that their hunger for more could have gotten out of hand. Possibly, they choose to be in their energy for a good reason, maybe never meeting a reflection, or they were unable to do the work to support another due to their wants standing taller than the union between another lover or lovers. And if they adapt it may be due to the many distractions a human relationship offers, taking away from something so divine and a bit too mysterious to give a name to, that is a serious practitioner.

Being a world traveler is very fun, you're always excited to see who you will meet, to me a large part of life is finding your partner/partners and continuing natural procreation. Some people are blessed to find theirs around the corner, some are meant to love one person for a long time. I understand that I've been here to love many, as I learn more about my gift of qi gong/energy work, conducting the qualities of JOLKA and life-giving energy. These qualities can be shared in many ways, whether emotional, sexual, or simply to help one paint a beautiful image of self. Nurturing someone based off their traumas and stories from the past. To truly embrace the opposite and love them how they deserve, creating a safe vulnerable space to allow energy to move organically. There is usually an ingredient that you can add to an energy field to assist in moving whatever is needed. I feel that I walk my path to share awareness of love and expose the hidden agendas of men, exercising transparency and emotional intelligence. Nurturing aspects of a woman's trauma story with mindfulness and sensitivity. So many women I met are wounded from men's inability to speak the truth, truth does hurt, yet truth is love. If you can hold someone while you tell them your deepest desires, you can be your full self and be there to actively align with the correct ingredient. It may take loads of practice as it can be hard to even know what are closest family members need and how we can add to their experience in good ways. I used to feel shame and guilt for being in a relationship with someone and finding attraction in another. I'd get quiet and keep it all inside, then let that weight hold me down until there's already an inkling of non-celebration of your counterpart. Then letting it all out in that moment of them thinking something is up and you spilling the beans. Fellas, explore your ability to speak when you see or feel. Exercise your direction, don't let your mind steer you away from celebrating and being in full honesty to your woman. I've stepped into truth in self and spoken truth to my lovers, being celebrated in love and accepted for my natural wants and desires, while I recognize also the royals of a queen, sharing the view of her nature, her reflections of creation. No hidden agendas, put it all on the table just as we are doing in this book.

You can only speak on what you feel, you can only feel from the shared sensation another person is going through. I may be missing some things in this book of course, places and people I have still yet to visit. Around the world from Indigenous Australia and New Zealand to the Philippians and Oceana, into Asia and the Middle East and Russia, Europe, and Africa, to the Americas, today there is magic everywhere. Is it authentic and unauthentic? A guy on the curb ahead wants to test your discernment. It is your choice to see life-giving and life-taking energies. If you feel authentic grounding in a person, give it a shot and listen to the teaching or a simple conversation, but remember Jah is reflecting to you the deepest and most potent teachings. The teaching of nature.

At the commune, where I was born, there was always a family of peacocks. They would wake you up in the morning as their feet landed on the metal roofing and the squawking sounds traveling through the forest. I loved them, such beautiful birds, peacock has a diverse number of feathers as we all know the green iridescent eyes of the long feather. A royal feather, in many cultures the peacock represents royalty often depicted by gods and kings, true beauty, and a compliment to the royal house, a sign that you are in a special place. The peacock was my friend, and he would scatter his feathers across the 75 acres of forest, I would go and gather them. Nature had gifted me the opportunity to pick them as I walked through the woods finding an array of colors and shapes. As I mention, one of the spiritual tools we use in ceremony is a fan, usually eagle wings or hawk. I took what the creator had offered me and I created a peacock fan, little did I know I was dancing with a bunch of eagles.

So, I took my feathers to Sundance to the top of Montana home of the Piikuni, the Blackfeet Nation, every year my uncle and I set up camp. He would joke with me saying, "Nephew, those eagles are going to eat you up in there, there's no room for peacocking around in ceremony." To my understanding, the peacock represents too much glamor and a show-off kind of energy. The energy that a hawk or an eagle will see straight through. This made me think twice when people asked what kind of feathers you are carrying. I answer peacock, usually getting a response of a smirk and not much more. A Sundance brother gave me an eagle feather, so I added it to my fan. During my coming home to myself, letting go of even more material. Every year I go to pray I become humbled more so. I took off my earrings, and my necklaces and let my body be naked embracing Taparitsa, the deity of no ornaments, simply resting in light service to the people. Although I like fashion and some nice things to wear, I've changed my speech, let go of some of my wants, and got comfortable in my skin and my role in life. I am merely a conductor of light and in devotion to the **rainbow nation** of **Wakan Skan or Sspommitapiiski**. Light sees through the darkness. Repetition and refinement. A death or passing of an old self, a rattle snake shedding his skin. I've been a pimpoche and a peacock hiding my traumas wearing a mask. For those of us who are fumbling with a skill or finding our singing voice. Sometimes just letting go can allow our voice to harmonize our true gifts to surface, instead of pushing our voice out or changing it. Let your gifts come out naturally without pushing it on others, allow others to come to you and affirm your authentic nature, and relate to sharing the wisdom that you carry.

The more we disconnect from the new world as we know it, I feel we will find a bit more in-depth detail of being a human. The parts of you, you may glaze over similar to the fine writing on a contract, bottom left corner that we don't read because we are just speed reading through it. Signing the checked box confirming all is good. I think we can tend to do that easily as days go by, getting into flows where we are not checking in with the awareness of our body, it is easy to become overly occupied in the mind.

 Getting back to the reflections of nature, Energy yoga becomes more obvious through the practice of inner postures and holding awareness. The more you go into the image of your energetic sensations, fueled by the imagination, you could almost call it pretending. Mind is like wind and clouds, very easy to identify with and even take over. When we think of thoughts of frustration sometimes. We start to see it in our reality more, thinking about being nervous to go out, a mood can take shape and then hold us back from more connection. Not that you're pretending at all but the more of those thoughts form, the more they steer your days. Depression is a slow and long process sometimes that can end in a space of unknowing and lack of inspiration to do anything. Of course, they talk about the monkey mind, steering our thoughts a bit. Energy yoga is excellent for mental work as you are observing the mind and allowing yourself to focus or be aware of different layers of your subtle energy to your organs and flesh. In Ayurveda, the study of preventative medicine, they recommend you do things for up to a week and sometimes 3 or more. That's how energy yoga works, the more that you focus on the awareness of the self, and the qi gong foundations, the more those feelings will start to shape your reality and simply your mood. Looking at pretending as a platform to shape your field. I believe that with a healthy dosage of light, even 5 minutes a day of sitting with a tiny sun inside paired with an inner smile could make a monumental change in your day. Finding more appreciation for self and gratitude for the ability to breathe light, smell light, hear light, taste light, and see light. The ability to feel a sense of awe, these gentle inner postures are the foundation of bliss and love.

Energy yoga can be good for an array of different things assisting the mind to feel relaxed, calm, energized, clear, and happy and I believe it can improve organ health, blood flow and general body function.

I used to feel funny in the sense that nothing I was imagining was mailable to touch, the subtleness of energy is a growing sensation that takes some daily practice and quality time spent within the self and becoming aware of the surroundings. The more you believe and feel the sensations as they become more and more evident, the more sensations will affirm your postures. It is common in the beginning to not feel much and even be asking does this really work am I just pretending? The study is gradual as you actively observe yourself and the living sensations of the body. It becomes a projection of the mind; it seems that all we see and do for ourselves is projected through the mind. We see a goal in mind, and we project ourselves forward to reach whether it is a physical goal of getting in shape or a personality trait we would like to venture into. It's all a gradual process and takes time and attention to get there. Getting in shape or really anything we do making an album or a painting, you get the general idea of what you are going to try in paint or what sounds you will make. Then you lay overtones and blend the colors, so to speak. Looking into the finer points of the human blueprints can become fun. Once you get into the postures you will naturally begin seeing your skin flesh canvas start to take color and texture of your breathing and your postures of light awareness. It's like taking prescription drugs or as we just stated Ayurvedic herbs, making time and space every day to ingest your light and give time to be within yourself, looking at the sensations that are calming, and also observing the body and the feeling you may have of nerve or discomfort. Simply by taking notes of that area and then actively sending healing light to those places.

My first teacher told me lovely stories of people healing themselves through energy yoga ranging from physical sickness to energetic blocks holding us back from our nature of mind, the mind in reflection of nature. Due to the strength of the system today and all the subliminal messages, there may be more levels than ever to get back to the center of your inner verse. It all depends on what you want in your life, so many of us in the USA are migrating to more off-grid situations. While many of us stay in the cities and enjoy the amazing system in place. Many people I met on my trips living off-grid not by their choice and desire to have the comforts of a modern home in the USA today. Yet, energy yoga can be done anywhere. My teacher always told me to experiment in public places and to be active when I am waiting or just out and about. This is one of the reasons why on my trips I minimize what I carry, usually going with just clothing, toiletries, medical supplies, and my phone. Instead of bringing books and music and a laptop or personal belongings, I chose to go without, purposefully, so that I may have more time to challenge myself to go inside and spend time in my inner postures. Simply to build the resiliency and endurance for the great work. I've taken my high school backpack around the world for months on end, relying on my energy and prayer to help get me to the places that will best serve me. I also like to give away my clothes usually ending the trip with none of my possessions and finding myself with a whole new set of dresses – this is fun because you are actively wearing the world.

It's always fun to see the self before a trip and on your return, observing the subtle or strong shifts in your energy. When you intend on pilgrimage travels or even cultural submerging as opposed to just a vacation, you find yourself looking deeper into the culture of the place and different aspects of how it affected you. As opposed to going to the tourist beach and the places on the tourist list. Might feel too similar to home or just as comfortable. Sometimes stepping off the main trail into the wild helps us to find more depth in our relationships and how to navigate ourselves to the main trail. The more we get comfortable in the darkness, the more we will be able to walk confidently. I used to like to go out and still do, on the new moon when the sky is pitching black, the endless stars fill the sky, and the canopy of the tree shades you from the light of the stars as the moon visits the other side of our globe. You walk into the darkness, feeling with your hands out in front so that you don't take a stick to the eye. You move slowly and step gently, your feet guide you as your arms protect you, slowly your eyesight adjusts, and you begin to see the reflection of the trees and rocks that surround you.

This is also similar to your energy yoga practice, as your eyes adapt to see what you are imagining, the pretending, turns into an undeniable sensation. Like anything you cannot be afraid of your cells, slowly your body adjusts, and you begin to see things clearer. In Buddhism, dark retreats are very popular for advanced practitioners as they isolate themselves for days, weeks, and even months, in total darkness 24/7. An attendee brings you food and drinks to sustain your body, fasting may also be practiced. The idea is similar to the woods in the darkness. The postures of energy yoga have been said to amplify your sight as the living color you are visualizing in yourself starts to leak into the space and fill the room with the same lights that you are conducting. I've heard stories of individuals in dark retreats who with their eyes open are witnessing the living color of tigly the holy networks of light and space. We can visualize the tiny sun inside and the tiny sun above, imagine it when you open your eyes that you can see faint orbs of light.

These orbs are in many Buddhist texts and talked about amongst yogis who have been in deep devotion and were found with the sight to see them and feel their presence. As we open ourselves and become one with nature as we used to, I think they honor us and reveal themselves when one is ready. Just like anything if it's not in your awareness, it's usually hard to locate. So, one must be available for more. These texts and practices or not shared often, but I feel nature shared them with our ancestors and they passed the wisdom on. They are recognized around the world in indigenous communities and are usually spoken about in a way that shows their importance. You have to sometimes be guided to these places to reaffirm your pursuits. The common theme is to not try to know about it as I've repeated many times, as we are possibly talking about a part of creation, a godly particle named a hundred times, and how it has shown itself around the world. So, we stress what has been stressed to us whether you find these practices and relationships through voodoo, Tibetan Buddhism, Krishna consciousness, Christ consciousness, Allah, Native way of life, or simple, in nature. We should not play around with it, for all is WAKAN all is sacred. We should not misrepresent, or represent it in a showboating manner, for an eagle will see you stumbling, and swoop you up. We should not go around always speaking of it, be humble if you are to be graced by the company of any one of the many spirits of the Earth. If that day comes to you, you will know it. It will be a time to give thanks, a time to know that you are protected and full. When the connection comes, it will sit you down and stillness will feel easier than ever. You may feel comfort that you have never felt before. You will have to walk gently by its side or the spirit will leave you.

The distractions and the games of the man-made world will take you back, and you will remember the day you were visited by such a spirit. As you will celebrate that day till death.

You have nothing to do but rest, simply rest. The more I used to talk about the orbs in the streets and around, the more I noticed myself feeling silly usually being misunderstood, leaking my chi. As I write this book, I am choosing to share my story of being an atheist and how my relationship with nature turned me into a believer and a devotee of nature and nature of self. Removing all non-personal gods out of the situation, removing the person or thing that sells you some spiritual tools, just going straight to the source of energy. Energy medicine is real, and nature offers us naturally the ability to heal. It is always a theme I hear about how good people feel in nature, well, it's no coincidence that nature has always nurtured mankind and simply we used to nurture her back. In short, that is why we are feeling so dissociated from our nature of self. Instead of making sweet daily offerings to the spirits and taking time to sit at the same table, we have contaminated her, our mother, and taken too much. Imagine if corporate leaders came and sat with the native peoples and received the good ways of honoring MAKHA on this holy and sacred Earth. Allowing for reverence and appreciation for what is before we disturb. Every time we dig a hole, we ask for pity for disturbing the land, we let the elements or spirits know we are with them and want to work together to make some good conduction. The world of man has left a lingering energy with such a magnetic field that it will take global conduction of light and love to clear the grief and emptiness. To come back into good standings with all elements or spirits of the Earth. All together and with awareness, we could heal with the lands that linger with such sadness as all we see is atrocity after atrocity, a global happening. Our environment has been cursed, for hundreds of years now, with bloodshed without remorse, and a lack of sincerity and connection to the holy ghost. If we can all see the shroud together, we can reverse this curse. For all our relations. I ask you how much you need. Our environment could be simply why we are all trying so many things. Looking to access a higher self or nature of self. It is true anything that you believe will support your reality. Know your original environment, know it is holy. Know you really need nothing. Your mother Earth MAKHA and your father Sun WI have gifted you everything you need.

I arrive at celebrating everyone for their thoughts, of wanting everyone to heal themselves, and everyone recognizing nurture. We become planted as once before. Similar to how we see an old forest cut down and now nearly lost. Did we even need to cut in the first place? Then a human comes along and plants rows and rows of trees for his anticipated construction. A cash crop. More of a want than a need. See our old people and the old growth must be honored and remembered for things were different in those times. If we remember those old voices, they will assist us in our new life, our new growth. We can manicure or cut out some of these planted desires, giving away parts of ourselves even physical possessions to make way for new energy and new awareness. Holding and listening to the original voices of nature and now adapting to hearing a new voice, still of nature just sounding a bit different. The suffering, the story, and our life are at a peaking point on the timeline. The voices are screaming out and whimpering, there is more confusion and disillusion, and my ears have become full. Finding myself crying out as well for assistance. I rejoice whenever I realize the old is still present and my life is still original. That is why I am on the path, walking the red road. I give thanks to the creator for giving me the strength and courage to not only know but feel so much. My body is new, my origin of this awareness is coming from nature, old nature, constructs, and blueprints of natural things. Structures or postures if you will, a relationship.

People go based on what they see all too often, I always used to say nothing is as it seems. It will be always different than you imagined. Seems that's where many people's emotions come up when something simply does not go as they wanted. One will get upset and talk about the unsatisfactory feeling of I guess their disillusioned mind. That is the narcissist society of today, perceiving the world how you want and see it. Neglecting the natural laws of nature and the divine unpredictability of our solar systems. The less you feel you need to know, the less control you must have, and the more you can just sit back and relax, for you are part of the systems, in our instinct and natural self we can act without needing to control, arrive without timing, eat without starving, drink water without panic. I have never felt a need to fit myself into a calendar or a schedule. I grew up with father time. Without fear in the mind, the Earth and sun will let you know, you might even be doing it naturally and then the thought comes into the mind. For example, waking up with the sun is natural, no one is making you it just feels natural. When you realize you are coming back no one can tell you how to be or what to do. You become your teacher your student your elder your youth you become circular. You will see yourself in others around you, you will see them where you once stepped, and you can even step towards them to confirm they are on their way.

I've stepped into my 4th cycle of 7 years, arriving at an understanding and a sensation of newness, a strengthening, and affirming of what is in my past, what has got me to now. Starting in on my new cycle, I am asking for the support of my ancestors and guides to further my molecular structures to crystalize in color for myself to continually be OPENING EXPANDING ABSORBING TRANSFORMING into light fully embodying the qualities of JOLKA. Imagine yourself for fun ten years down the line of actively feeding yourself in Joy Openness Love Kindness and Awareness, think about how you would feel. Think about 10 years of turning on your inner light, think about your next seven-year cycle. As we age, we see our bodies changing anyway, based on our food activities and thoughts we carry, will either age gracefully in health or slowly start to see the body decline. In construction work, I constantly have to remind myself to not victimize my pain and to actively not grunt and groan when I move due to sore back, hips, or knees. It's easy to watch yourself slow down at the end of a full workday. It's a daily challenge to talk those voices down, to shake their hand to meet them as they arrive. And to affirm that there is light there, that the thought is temporary. Mentally, moving lightly and keeping our youthful motions in action, not allowing for the inner old man to come out, or that weird thought that tries to stay too long. My grandpa's simple wisdom stuck. I don't see the man much and I'm learning a lot about him and his sisters, sold in adoption to the Good family. His roots are interesting, as his DNA dates to Iran as our first origin point, sounds like a migrant already. Nathan Good's original mom was said to be a Comanche woman. We do not know much about her and can only really go off the DNA of my grandpa. I've been caught up in wanting to know where I come from and who I am. Why am I dealing with these things?

It's so easy to watch life go by, so easy to engage in the things that we can see, the things that people bring to our attention. I believe we are all healers as we all are healing, remembering our original story, looking into the flesh, and recognizing the magic we are made up of. The Earth was so perfect, so clean, so serene, and so full of natural happenings, miracles to the human mind until our greed and or forceful energies started to control and rule the day. Now we are scrambling back to a place of trying to help the Earth, and ourselves, the timeline got filled with so much extra. Yet I'm so happy to see things happening, conscious festivals full of prayer and intention, full of workshops and activities that help us connect to our cells again and connect to the Earth, laughing together as one family. I'm so happy to see so many people stepping up for our animals and our environment. I never think it's too late to get the energy back in order, as long as the trauma has not been too severe, as long as you didn't hurt her too badly, you can always take time to set intentions and let her know how much you love her, by your words and most importantly, by your actions. We must celebrate her, celebrate the loves in your lives, the Earth that holds us up, the people who keep you together, and your community. Give them love and see how synergy will come back to you.

Permaculture is the idea of creating a very diverse garden that supports each other plant to plant, giving nitrogen and potassium, magnesium and so many other nutrients. Each plant offering to the other creating a garden of health, trees to shade the undergrowth allowing just enough light to come through to give optimal growth. Through stacking functions, a garden can become very sustainable. The idea of human permaculture used to be very natural for human beings, as we all supported each other, similar to how we talked about the natural roles of healthy tribalism. If we can let down our guards and our want to grow alone, we can actively grow to the heights together. The communication that goes unseen in the soils, mycelium, and roots is the network of love and support throughout the forests, everything is reflected from space, planetary support, tree support, and human support. Our neural pathways mirror the mycelia and mirror the solar systems. In all golden mean ratios, all the constructs of creation come from an infinite source of energy. Running through the world is similar to electricity running through wires, connecting a whole country in light or the WIFI signal. As I said, it's an amazing reflection of how man has created a system to send information through the clouds, signals, that go from conductor to conductor, or satellite to satellite. I know a lot of us already know this stuff, but for those who don't, I hope, I'm painting a good picture of the world of reflections of hard work and how you can truly simplify. We can cross-pollinate, sometimes talking about things over and over can bring about a new way of thinking.

138

You are the conductor you have been looking for, you are a receptacle of the frequency of the forest, you are an antenna for source energy, you are a body of water that is a magical elixir of color and sensation, held in a special container of your flesh. You are a walking temple of nature, you can see the kingdom of heaven simply by seeing beauty in nature and of self and becoming very aware of the unseen system that connects all people to all trees, to all animals, to all of life. It may be true that you may need guidance, a facilitator to assist you in finding your nature of self, yet do not waiver in the thoughts that you are a child of the sun. Mushrooms and teachers can definitely help you find new neural pathways as you start to view things a little more organically and rudimental. These are the fundamental practices of getting grounded, you are merely a plant, a tree, a flower blossoming, run your roots deep into the ground extend your arms up to the sky, and speak light. Give light to all of your relations. Energetically, see your elements and your spirits, your animals and your fellow human beings all embraced by the warmth of the tiny sun that you don't need to tell anyone about. Let them come to you and tell you thank you for being a light in this world. Be humble, this is why my teacher told me this is a hidden practice, these are exercises you can do that no one will know simply because you are sitting normally at the restaurant, or you are in line. You are the alchemist everywhere you go there is energy to alchemize, simply sitting still and in awareness, be playful and light, gentle on the self and your surroundings. Only give life, it is no joke, I would not repeat that to you if it was not repeated to me. Any mantra and practice of anything produces results, we don't want to go back from the darkness of which we are currently healing. It is the time to visualize the world that you want to see, more so than we need at this point. To act in the direction and manner that will give life – it is time to simply give life – as so much has been taken.

May we walk in sincerity

May we speak authentically.

May we act for our relations not ourselves.

May we pray for our connection.

May we smile upon each other.

May we see clearly.

May we hear our environments.

May we taste our truest selves.

May we feel what is coming

May we sense the need for change.

To all great spirits we ask that the connection we share may be felt, and we ask that we may all support each other as necessary. We ask that you continue to guide us, we ask that we may hear the voices of nature as you speak to us, great mother. We ask for forgiveness for our ill actions that have wounded us – we ask that you be gentle on us – Mami Wata, Mini Wiconi, We ask for the strength and inner standings to carry you in a good way. We ask that our elemental family and all spirits will be gentle with us and us to them so that our relationship can flourish. We ask that the animals grow in populations that our systems of mycelium and the ways of the water will sustain. We ask that we find our way through the maze of mind and ego to arrive at a place of coming home. Wakan Tanka, we ask that you welcome us back home as we start loving you again, as we start listening again. We ask that we have the humility to hear you. Pity us, creator, for all the holes we have dug and the contaminating of your waters, for the pollution of the air, for the mishandlings of the fire that burnt the human heart. Pity us for scorching your lands with oil and waste. May you see us in our accountability and help us to do better. Great spirit, may you be with us as we want to be with you, thank you to the above ones for your presence in our life – thank you for honoring us and showing us the light. We pray that you will find your way into the hearts of the people who need you the most. We ask that the hands of the holders of evil, feel this prayer and feel the light inside of their cells. We ask that your presence be strong with them, becoming so beautiful that they can't turn away. Great spirit, be with the ones that are hungry and lonely, the ones in pain and disabled. Great spirit, smile upon us as we are here to smile at you, as we see you may you see us in the good light of our father Naapi Naatosi or Wakan Wi

AHO AMEN ASE

In this chapter, see in your mind, reflect on your mindfulness, practice your meditations, engage the foundations that I've shared in this book, and stack them just like the idea of permaculture stacking your foundations. Feel into the body, feel into your bones, your blood, your organs, feel into the spaces that go unlooked. Invite your tiny sun to turn on, allow yourself to smile throughout your whole body, and laugh at yourself for feeling silly. Amplify the sensations in your body and then open yourself to what you want to do next, what you want to conduct, and what image you want to paint yourself as. Allow yourself to play, allow yourself to not care what anyone thinks, take some time painting your perfect environment, your perfect view, and see yourself in it. The choice is yours, the image is you; the action can become effortless, resting in your cells, relaxing into your nature of self.

Just don't be a pimpoche.

You are beautiful, don't flaunt it, act in it.

A true spiritual warrior has nothing to say, just a lot to do.

Chapter Twelve
Time is Now

This chapter is named in dedication to the first Sundance I attended the Tasunke Witko bloodline of Crazy Horse. Me and my uncle knew the time was now to step up. For Crazy Horse and his people to dance for Wakan Skan. To let the networks of light know we are here to dance with them, to be with them, and to share with them in a good way. For it has been too long that we the people have called their names.

To the remaining tribes and clans carrying their language and ways of life, we honor and respect you, for without you, all of our peoples, lands, and relations on Turtle Island would be vacant in deeper connections. These ways that were nearly beaten and sold out of us, are still present and getting stronger as we continue to pray in the ways our original fathers of this land did. There is a great reason why it was not fully wiped out. For in these coming times our connection to spirits and the old ways of relating to nature is becoming more and more important.

The general sense is setting in about now for most of us, it is becoming easier to predict what is coming around the corner for the human race. The Hopi prophecy exposes the elements coming strong and as human life is getting more and more distracted, we can see easily the doom of us, if we do not take some action. To become aware of our present actions and the next 7-year cycles that are coming and for the next 7 generations of our children's children. It is very easy to look back into the 90s till now and see how fast we have accelerated from the home phone on the chord to flip phones to now small computers in our pockets. Phones are beneficial to the world sharing important conversations and teachings all over the globe. We can share at a global capacity. We can also see the world becoming more and more accelerated in these new ways, which could play a part in the downfalls of our awareness and or forgotten sensitivities to nature.

In my vision, observing my struggling willpower to do what I know I need to become stronger. My 7-year cycles are benefitting me and also hurting me as I gather so much information/chi and talk to people around the world. Constructing so many new thoughts in my head, yet smoking still as I go, my way of breaking bread. Feeling the destruction, I know I need to slow down the pace and I can still learn and enjoy social life without it. Yet I press on simply because I enjoy it. This is my prediction of myself, that I will adjust my willpower and quiet it, continuing forward with less pollution in my body and becoming stronger in the breath. Buddha said one must have clear lungs so that when one speaks, the air that comes from his or her mouth will be refreshing to the recipient. I can see myself going in two directions and honestly, I'm happy with both the recipes I've been baking with the main ingredient of light. I'll either go forward cleaner and healthier, or polluted and coughing, finding myself in my later years with difficulty breathing and falling sick. It's good to find peace with your addictions, yet it is also good to be harsh and say I have to quit it before my body makes me quit it.

So that is my simple predictions of the human race and the world as we know it, as we all deal with our inner management of what we need to feel comfortable and happy, buying into those things, as a race we may continue in these ways, it has become so comfortable to just sit in our house, eating the food given to us not grown by us, watching the news that is given to us not created by us. Getting more and more addicted to our phones and the replaced serotonins and dopamine that our phones give off, we will become unaware of the world diminishing in front of us. We could say that we are headed for a time of stimulation. In one decade, the smartphone has the attention of a global audience, getting individuals caught up in themselves more, and forgetting about the original connection before WIFI. Our awareness and roles that we seem to not care to see, unsure of what we are and what we should be doing. In the 7-year cycle alone we are seeing this magnetize more and more. Listening to people talk about nature and meditation, shows us how far we have come from our timeline of nature of self. Something organic and effortless in the days of the old, a way of life that went unspoken for eons, the stillness and stoicism of natural life. Now turning to the nature of technology, if we struggle with cigarettes, phones, and a handful of other vices, will we know that Mother Earth is speaking to us? In the next cycles, we could go in many directions, one direction is a society lacking basic common sense and basic work ethic because we have been enamored by the man-made world. We could all become victims to the power of man and although we feel we are doing good we are just talking and going on about the latest creations and man-made ideologies. In one prediction, we can see humans getting more and more removed from nature becoming their environment of technology, complacent in entertainment.

Unknowing of their inner voice due to such a strong and exciting time that we are living in, there is no doubt that it is hard to not want to get involved with the new world. It's hard to not want the latest and greatest, yet if we all want it, the gears of production will continue, and the Earth will continue to be exported from its raw form and slowly changing into another. As we see our atmosphere kind of like a snow globe, the more particles, and the more burps and farts, the more upset mamas insides become, as humans continue to contaminate her for our privileges and wants, naturally she will start to get sick and start excreting her insides to the surface. Fire, water, gas, and many things will start to affect our lives just as we have been affecting her. It is easier to predict what will happen because we are an image of our mother, she made us. When we get contaminated by smoke, gases, viruses, and growths, we start getting sick. Our mother Earth is so strong yet in the next 7 generations, I could see it becoming more in more toxic for our humanity. As we see people wearing masks to keep contaminated air out of their lungs, drinking out of tiny plastic bags because the water is contaminated, littered Earth and oceans that people and fish have to start living in, sorting through trash, the skies of many cities in a haze of fossil fuels, chemtrails and planes. All these masks, water, materials, and trash management are all delivered by trucks, which is, of course, run out of fuel, which is why we go to war so often to settle on oil, to fund our massive consumption. The world is pumping the insides of Mother Earth out, drawing the blood in a sense, changing the structure of her insides, so that we can fuel the gears of material gain. The American dream has jump-started the want for so much. A global consumption that is extracting the Earth's inner resources at a higher pace. We all know how it feels to be dehydrated or lose blood, we start to feel wobbly and hazed, we start to lose our strength, sometimes it takes a lot of love and care to get back to our normal selves. So instead of predicting this world, I hope we can diagnose the larger issues at hand and manage them accordingly, for the world, with love and support. It is going to take a lot of care and will, to give back what we have been taking as a global hand. It seems that if we don't make some massive rearrangements, then we will be in for an upsetting elemental family reunion. Some of us won't know what to do, panic when the waters and fires come, the tornadoes and the Earthquakes. Some of us will be in peace as we have been waiting to see the hand of nature take us back to the land.

I predict that if we don't make some efforts like now that we will, and already are seeing the results of taking without giving, in an unequal world of man to Earth – we are going to be in danger and many already are. It is time to make a way for a healthy relationship. I'm hoping that the great reset will be an act to start making a global shift to rehabilitate the world and different populations that are suffering obviously more than others. However, we don't know who those people in charge are, we don't know the agenda of the minds behind the mechanics. We are the people who are working for them as we pay taxes and pay into the system for them to support us and play most of the roles that our uncles and aunties used to do for us. We are just the peasants outside of the kingdom walls. We are the pawns, the ones that walk forward first, the ones that are experiencing the experiment of the new world. We are the ones who have been manipulated by the hands of the ones who show no faces. Hiding behind the news that we can't tell is fake or real. Dealing with stress and extra emotions makes it harder to process the world as it goes by, and inevitably, staying caught up in the loop of the cooperation that we are essentially working for. Fear tactics in a high form we could ask? It's kind of like the chicken and the egg, the flower and the seed, which came first, and which is creating which. By playing into this industry, we are indeed affected by them and will continue to work. In some sense, they are working for us. It seems that the power is in their hands mainly, they are the chicken laying us as the egg, to be scrambled where we sit. It's like we are domesticated dogs, a tracker friend of mine just told me the difference between a dog and a coyote or wolf. A dog runs around sniffing everything, getting out of the house and off the leash, and has so much to explore, it already has food, so it is not looking for anything in particular. The coyote goes in a straight direction as it picks up on the scent of his next meal and is after it. I feel like we as a human race have been like dogs wandering around looking for clues to where the biggest shit is. It's time for us to be coyotes, to be the tricksters and trick the main tricksters. It is time for us to make some decisions. Is the dog walking us or are we walking the dog I asked earlier? Are we working for the system or are they working for us as they have brainwashed us into thinking that we need so much, that we become the reason why the system keeps pumping it out because we need it?

Because they said we wanted It? What if I told you, you may want something else? Something you don't buy. Something that is already in you. Everything else in front of you is extra all of the material is simply material.

What if that was no longer the case, what if we simply did not need so much, what if our happiness was restored with nature and simple things, what if we decided we didn't need 8 of everything and became happier with less, what if we gave things to each other instead of buying a new, what if we grew our food, what if we built our houses, what if we stopped going to the stores and started making things ourselves? What if we could fully sustain ourselves as we once did? If we did as our ancestors did and found our roots, found our source of true happiness, and found our roles in life. This would inevitably change the industry if people stopped paying into the systems, and stopped paying into the man-made world and let the lord handle it, as usual. Sure, the roads would not be as maintained and life would be drastically different. Some may say what the heck happened here, while others would rejoice in the idea of letting things be. Some eyes see beauty in creation, and some see pain in creation. The same goes for destruction. As we see a big building being built, some are happy about all of this. While many feel sad for all the wild that was removed for the sake of construction.

Let's just say we unplugged for fun, we would then be walking them in a sense, the roles would change, and it would be a taking back of our world, a changing of what we think is a success. We would be doing this for ourselves but mainly our Earth so that we can sustain and create a more natural world for our children to live in, building homes out of all-natural material, that may not last as long but decompose back into the Earth, straight back into the garden. A home that was once for a person then becomes a home for other creatures and mushrooms and plants to grow. Instead of a building to last 100, or 200 years, we can build temporary houses that are less impactful, we are now seeing the powers of Earth hit us. Some buildings are already falling due to elemental powers.

So, these are the two main predictions I can see around the corner. We get with nature and listen to her and make some active changes in our minds and our realities, allowing for harmony and spirit to guide us.

We may have to embrace the systems at hand as science is reaching heights that may make it possible to advance with more sustainable and ecological practices, we could surrender our worries if we knew our leaders were truly caring for this Earth. At this point, our leaders are too rich with money and seem blinded by power. It saddens me that a man such as Elon Musk would not use his millions and billions of dollars to assist millions and billions of people. Even just a 1/8 of the man's money could clean up mass amounts of countries lacking infrastructure, trash piles, slums, rivers have stopped flowing due to trash build-up. I would challenge Mr. Musk to a debate on science and history. For I trust in the faith of our Father in the sky SunRa and the Earth Mother who nurtures us. That we must not fear. She is stronger than the fear tactics lead on. The elementals and the spirits are the relatives that are consistent and ancient. The foundations that have held life here for millions if not billions of years, will prevail in the laws of nature, therefore, do not fear man-made law, and do not let these weak-minded fear loathing leaders affect you. Maybe we should stop referring to them as they. Maybe we should name them just like in prayer, inviting their names and energy/information into our conscious field. These people are human also, we can go sit in our energy in front of them. We can speak to them quietly; we can infiltrate their days with love and light. We can ask them to truly consider their life. Like my uncle said the history books are still being written. Elon Musk will go down in history as a powerful leader of our times. I'd ask the man himself if I could, how he wants to go down in history. Our leaders have the same choice as us with more pressure and less empathy, possibly more ego and more royalties, leading to selfish and outlandish actions. Why would we be shooting rockets to Mars and building a space center when our Earth is so beautiful? The fears of living on Mars completely outweigh the fears of living on Earth if the planets were like our gods and influencers of our realm, Mars would be the grumpy creepy uncle. Mother says you must go stay at uncle's if you been misbehaving. He will show you what cold is he will show you how dark life can be.

I pray for our leaders to find balance. Or step aside and let someone who cares and knows what to do with such power, for our people, oceans, land, and animals around the globe. They may look like buffoons now, but I know they can act as revolutionary leaders if they choose. To do good for all our relations. With all the money Musk owns, he could in himself nearly change the entire world. Giving equality and benefit to all, supporting all agriculture and farmers, allowing us to be farmers allowing us to also help and have a role instead of following a rule. The man-made world has been making us weaker. We must show them we are still strong. That we deserve a say in how our world is changing, the people's voices are strong. The ones that have not seen the mass struggle will not be able to devise a solution-based plan, simply because they have not been to see the problem.

We must find a middle ground. All working together as one, including the ones pushing the buttons, in the control seat. As we hear of new technologies, ways to continue forward in life. We are finding new ways to fuel cars with hydrogen and hemp. Finding ways of turning plastics into fuel, creating waste management systems that can create in an equal fashion to the destruction. Equaling out our consumption with renewal and rehabilitation. There are many people today who are actively working on new ways to sustain life as we know it to be and give back to Earth as she has so generously shared her resources with us. There are so many topics to hit on, and so many things we can do to support our environments and live in a world of comfort and convenience. So many people around the world are looking for comfort so that they can sleep easily, and have money for their basic needs. There is a global epidemic of hunger and lack of resources that we easily take for granted in the Western world. We can actively engage the world and start to rehabilitate each other and the Earth that supports us. The fear-mongering has no power in the knowledge of nature. Know that you are a conductor of pure energy you are a Tesla coil in your cells, become unshakable in your postures of light. For we can all resonate with the frequency of the Earth and find comfort in her constant consistency. And bask in the light of our father, his constant and consistent living color provided to all our relations we share this reverberation.

I think it is possible to live in harmony with nature and also embrace the new world of today. I respect Mr. Musk for his developments yet I know he can do better if he wants to. For we have found comforts in evolution and want to make things easier so that we may rest deeper. Yet what is it to rest deeper if many of us are still struggling, can we rest while many of us are not receiving the same resources? It's time for true equality, time for true freedom, and time for us to act to sustain our loved planet. It won't be easy as we have been going on for so long without looking back. I hope that this is a time that we can stop what we are doing and take a look around, looking into the details of ourselves and the world, and ask ourselves if this is the world we want to live in. Ask ourselves if there is anything more for us to do besides help.

For me, there is always more to look into, to look deeper into the fine print of our environment, and to take time to read what is there and to embrace what has been harder to see or to hear. We have to ask ourselves if we have the energy to change. The world as we know it would be drastically different, many of us, are already complaining about the workload and the tiredness of survival, for it is so easy to just sit back in the comfort and watch the time go by. So easy to not know how someone else is feeling simply because we have not seen how they are living. The questions we have to ask ourselves will create a challenge, a goal that we may want to go for. Or is it a dream of a better world that is just so far away that just residing in acceptance is our best shot? My dad and I used to talk about the world's happenings as they are, whether it is our doings or the destiny of man to create and discover until we destroy ourselves. In either look, we can benefit ourselves from saying I am at peace with what is in acceptance for the world we live in, for I am just one person, what can one do? Yet this is kind of a hall pass out of the work that I feel in my mind won't let up. After seeing what I have, I can't help but be engaged with the world and the feelings of our human family, wanting to speak on their behalf, on the behalf of global suffering. It is not easy, and it may never be easy, there is so much beauty in the struggle. Are you willing to fight for the beauty of your loved ones? The feeling a man has when someone is posing danger or discomfort to his wife and children. When you travel the world, you will be greeted with many different feelings, you are inclined to give love back, as you are embraced as a brother, as an uncle, or as a Babaji. How can you not embrace others as brothers and sisters, for we are one big family, thinking similar thoughts and dealing with similar issues and daily questions of self? Will I be okay, will I get the money, will I be able to support my family? These are worldly struggles.

After all of this, it is very clear that we are all family and it is so hard to rest when you know your brothers and sisters are dealing with adversity, pushed on to them by another, no wonder it's so easy to victimize the self, being filled with feelings of doubt and uncertainty, shame and sadness. When you step outside of the self and look at it from a bird's eye view, you can see we are all the same. We are connected by a system that is overrun by man-made information. Scrambling the mind and dissociating us from our nature of self. Is it time to change? Whether that's a choice of people living partly off-grid and part of society on-grid, or if it is a mental peacemaking with self, or a global effort to act for our environment and our relations? Global activation of light and love travels as fast as Bob Marley's music. None of these will be easy or instant. I believe in a global miracle if we all felt life-giving light together who's to say it could not be instantaneous? Simply remember the voices of nature and call their names, bringing them offerings of peace. It is a slow and gradual process of finding oneself. Not only finding oneself but being able to actively make the changes in your life to live better for you and your fellows. Even if we have found the light and know the sensation that light offers us, the hardest part is incorporating it into our daily practices and living in the light as we go about all the things that we do.

This is indeed the topic we all have to check into and ask ourselves, do we have the will to change our emotions and our view of the world? Do we have the will to adjust our diets for our globe, the animals, and our health? The burgers are so good, the drugs are so nice, the cars are so convenient the emotions are so deep and the growing pains are unique to you. Only you know best, what you are experiencing or growing through I speculate for fun, and to help myself, of course, I do not want to peer into your life without the consent of agreement. Can you see yourself living in a world where you have to work/survive? Would it be fun for you? Like the work we used to know, the work that it took to get us here today, the sweat on the brow that comes from days and months, years, and generations to create the world we want to see. Do we have the ability? Do we have the same passion? Do we have the same dream?

Is it a time of renaissance again? An age of awareness and mindfulness. May we be stepping into the age of remembrance of spirituality and technological peeks. Are we merely fumbling around with ideas until we understand the whole planet Earth the plane of inertia we exist on? At that point of understanding, would we not be taking a large step forward for all of humanity to simply live better? We can consider them reparations to the countries that have been stripped of resources to give back to them now. The relationships we have with each other and the millions of jobs that need to be done around the world. Could we let go of the day of judgment and step into the day of acceptance? Working/helping to manifest leaders that lend correct action and correct justice. Can we celebrate each other and hold together, by the community that builds together, that prays together, that farms together, that creates together? Have we become so domesticated that it's hard to imagine a world where we live outside under the sun in devotion to the elements that have welcomed us, the ones who reflect beauty and restoration to all of us? The elements that have supported us till this point. We are seeing climate change; we are seeing species go extinct. I believe our species changed so much that our original physical DNA and blueprint are altered and still changing. We simply know different things than before. You can see the difference in our looks, conversations, and a whole bunch of things that are just seen or rarely spoken about. Are we even the same human beings we were 100 years ago, say 500 years ago, not long ago we were stronger, more of an animal more like the cayote than the dog. Human beings have changed so much in our timeline, what do you think of our collective?

Are we ready to accept what has taken place, and simply do we care? Are you able to smile at the world and say that you can envision a world of love and forgiveness a world that does not need to deal with man-made ideology? Realizing that we are perfect just the way we are, accepting that we have been told so much and have been suffering because of it. Where do you stand, even in this conversation, we could see how it could be dividing us further, as some are happy to continue forward, and some are ready to leave the city and head for the hills to make a new life. Instead of looking at the division, maybe we could find acceptance and honor in each other, maybe we could celebrate the differences, recognizing that there is not a right way or a wrong way, there is a choice. The voices of nature speak loud to the ones resting their ears on her breasts. As do the voices of the machine, as we continue to listen to the gears crank out so much material.

Do you think that we may not need what has been prescribed to us? The baker has created a recipe for a product that is so impressive you can't help but ingest it, it is always nice to have someone bake for you, no matter the ingredients you are being served. All humans want to be served, loved, and held. Yet in that do we forget how to hold ourselves, bake up the foods that feed our soul. It boils down to what the man at the Ganges River said. You must spend time with the gods, with the spirits, and with the self, if you want to have a good relationship you must put in that time. The stillness of nature has shown the true colors of man, the true colors of what we do when we forget our inner stillness when our mind needs more to become fulfilled.

Do you want to spend more time with the machine, with the comforts of the new world? Or with nature? There was a time I've romanced often, a time before all this. There was a time that was referred to in another look as 'herstory.' The time of the matriarchy the time of nurturing, a time of loving, of submission to nature, a time of harmony, for all men know the glory of which a woman offers him. Her-story was a time of the feminine, the time we listened to our hearts, a time we listened to our elements, as we lived in harmony with the land, allowing the woman to create and foster life. This time era is not even put in His-story books, another hiding of our capacity to love. They replaced our original heart and connection, Our Indigenous family, the ones who listened and lived in closeness with great spirit. The ones we are still connected to.

History has been written by the victors of patriarchy, while herstory is not even talked about. It was a time of such beauty, such perfection, they didn't want to tell us about the Shangri-La that is still the same, yet a veil, a shroud, a spell cast to keep us outside the mental walls. Outside of the kingdom of heaven, outside of our inner verse, stimulating so much on the outside that we forget about the divineness of a human being, forget about our hearts, as we are a society of the mind, a society of individuality, the heart is the brain of the body. The receptacle of your spirit, without proper attention here, the mind will rule the day and you may forget the love you have for so much in our world. The love you have for stillness the love you have for peace. If we were not asking these questions, we would just be a subject of experimentation. As a collective, I know around the world, people are standing on both sides of the riverbanks, asking the question, why the world is like this, as others look onward and say what a wonderful world. Not thinking about the suffering, it took to get here. Not acknowledging all the heavy energy that is present around the globe. You can pilgrimage to spiritual locations, and you can also go and feel for yourself the heavy energy of 400 years of bloodshed and pain, you can hear the sound of people crying out, losing their minds, from being captured and contained.

How can you go forward without accepting the past and repenting of the things that were done? The world is full of subtle energy, do you feel it or are you caught up in the flow of technology and find yourself captured and contained in your manifestations and dreams? Stuck in the house on the screens, longing for connection and love.

As we find clarity of nature of self, nature itself becomes clearer, it becomes easier to be in love with the surroundings. Whether you believe in the process and creation of the Constitution for the USA. Or you stand with the 1st nation, love will keep us together. Even in my own family, we are divided between religion and political views, I've been threatened by my family to be disowned for not being a proud American, in the sense of Not standing for the US Cooperation or the finding of such Constitution and the fraud fathers. Love keeps our family together, owning our differences and seeing ourselves in each other. I am not celebrating these Western holidays. As I take a knee and respectfully disregard the national anthem, Mount Rushmore, Columbus Day, and so many things I just don't align with. I've always been this way. I've never understood history books, and even science has seemed to be a labeling game in itself. We could agree Science is indeed a huge reason why we are here today, I cannot deny my appreciation for science, plane travel, global communication and so many of the things that allow us to move more freely in a global look. But it is nature again that science derived from.

People used to take years walking to get to their destinations, and even die along the way sometimes, it is indeed beautiful to be able to see family and see the world with ease. So, we can discern what is helping truly and what has just been straight-up lies or false information. I've never been one for Westernized traditional living, I was given a mind for nature, a heart to feel and conduct. To be in community everywhere I go, it's time to be in the heart, the mind is the image of self, and the mind is the action to move. Without checking in with the heart, our direction will be mostly for the self. As the mind thinks to share, the heart is the effortless feeling of love that connects to our spirit. When we are listening to our heart we are listening to our spirit, leading us to the places we need, to put the pieces together. Some places call to us, some people call to us, some say that we were together in past lives, and some say we are from the same planet. Whether you believe in reincarnation or not it's hard to deny the energy that people carry or the place you feel into. Their energy tells a story of where they come from and the energy that they come from. The Keys of Enock talks about the rainbow prophecy, not the rainbow family or the idea of all people coming together as the color of man uniting. This is part of another prophecy; I'm speaking of the rainbow nation, the spirits of Wakan Skan and Sspommitapiiski presence. The rainbow prophecy speaks about the orbs of light, the above ones coming down into the hearts of human beings. The Keys of Enock depicts orbs of light from the nation or networks of the sky beings coming down to reside in humans, a connection to nature of self, to assist humanity in healing. The humans who are here to help remind humanity about the importance of the spirits, light, and making clean to prepare for the rainbow spirits/energy to work with us more, for if a human is not connected to nature of self and nature itself then how will he or she recognize the living color in the air. How will one build a relationship with the sky dancers if you do not recognize their existence? Well, I guess I'm here to remind you then. The Spirits of color are here to unite and share the understanding of the source, the great networks of light. The rainbow people or sky dancers are the children of the sun, the babies of Maka/Ksaahkoom Earth and Anpetuwi/Naato'si father sun, the coming together of polarities, the birth of the trinity, birthing of light. The ancient ones that have witnessed mother and father since they came together, live in the elements, their children dance in the sky. Once you witness their presence, you cannot look the other way, you are invited into your heart, into your lightenment, to make this so, you have to reflect the same union that your mother and father did. They came together in union and created life. They birthed you as the 3rd, all humans born into the divine trinity children of the sun and earth.

Yoga means to yoke, to unite your masculine and feminine, your mind and your heart to mentally see yourself in love and rest, in surrender to nature, to ground into the Earth, connecting to your mother, and your heart. By nurturing your mother as she nurtured you, your father will see you in reverence to your mother, see you coming back to her, the long-lost children of the heart, the vacancy of our spirits. Father sun will kiss your forehead, a Shakti pot of sorts, a blessing from above. As you open your heart to your father, invite your mother and father to dinner, and invite your mind to balance with your heart, you will start to engage in a beautiful reception of self. Becoming a receptor of Earth and sky energy, befriending the spirits. A mere reflection of your heavenly parents.

When you go to church, they tell you about a book of man, a false message that you need another being to save you, you need to take Christ as your lord and savior to see the kingdom of heaven. When in realness, you may simply open your heart to the WAKAN the holy and physical sun in plain sight, and receive the source of light, to merely reflect our father. Jesus Christ to me is like our big brother, the one who went upstairs to talk to the above ones, the light angles, the living color, he came back down to talk about it, to show us the truth is real. A human being who understood the dark and found the light, one who walked with the elements one who became elemental. He is a great example to all of us. The church never shares Jesus's recipe for success. They give glory to him and praise him. Shoot, I will too as I look up to him just as Taparitsa la, Guru Rinpoche, Shiva, Mahavitar Sri Babaji, all rainbows that entered into the human flesh. Is kept secret or is simply

150

unknown? Is the information hidden from us? Would it be too powerful to live amongst a race of light beings, even if we were just pretending, even just the mental image of us all together, tiny suns turned on, inner smile amplified, radiating light in all directions, just the image of that is powerful? This is indeed the kingdom of heaven, by surrendering to nature itself you find nature of self, preparing for light to enter the flesh, you can rest assured that you are supported by your nature's parents. Take time to be with them, and take time to arrange yourself accordingly. So that you can be rejoiced by the most beautiful, and infinite amount of bliss and light that can be received by your body of water, your water-crystal that is you! To amplify your daily bread and your daily light medicine.

So last meditation of the book, the beginning of the end – bridging the Earthly plane with the sky plane. My teacher always said, that before you start working in the vertical vertices, you must become very grounded and feel the sensations of Earth, you must tune into the senses and receive Earthly energy. You want to be humble and grounded before the sky dancers will come down and dance with you. Coming only when they know you are strong, sincere, and ready for that relationship. I've heard rumors that monks are simply preparing themselves for a relationship. Taking one to two lifetimes or more to prepare themselves for a woman and child, to effortlessly father in good ways. Maybe this is true and maybe this is similar to any other relationship you desire to cultivate.

Sky Breathing

Part 1.

- Tune into your qi gong foundations or turn on your lights. Imagining all the life-giving sensations in your body gives a little more attention to your VMA or sacral chakra. Imagine a glowing orb of light resting on the pelvic floor. Now Just like we breathed with the tree, inhale the orb of energy up your spine, and exhale the energy down the front of your body. Breathe in your microcosmic orbit for some breaths, inhaling up the spine, your governing vessel, and exhaling energy down the front of your conception vessel. After some time, observe your tiny sun rising with an inhale and setting with an exhale.

Part 2.

- On your next inhale, as the energy rises up your spine, actively envision the energy of the sky and the sun entering your body. On the exhale, allow for the sky energy to meet the insides of your body… Inhale the energy up the body and exhale, setting back into the sacral region… and again inhale the energy of the sky, the particles of the sky, the source of light… light traveling up your spine at the same time, energies meeting at the brain, as the energy gently rains down to the sacral region. Staring at the sky, with open eyes, not staring at anything particular, a gentle gaze into the sky, a mere reflection of your mind and spaciousness of body, making new room for the light of the sky to enter you. With each cycle of tiny sun rising and setting, of new energy entering you, rest deeper, relax further. Affirm the action taking place for giving gratitude to the rainbow nation, give gratitude to the Earth and sun, gratitude for the elemental family, and give thanks for your breath and your ability to breathe in this way. Recognize your conduction recognize your antenna. And allow yourself to conduct pure energy whether you see it or not, the beauty is in the finer details. Inhale the sky, and allow yourself to feel vaster, allow your cells to smile more.

"A culture of light..."

All relations all connected as one awareness. Do this practice anywhere you can see the sky, blue sky is my favorite, yet grey sky, cloudy sky, and night sky, for the sky dancers are dancing. The spirit of the rainbow is around. Offer them the same attention that you do your favorite activities, invite them to your temple, for you are Nature's Temple, a conductor of nature, the reflections of the sun and the Earth, an elemental being. No need to talk about it, there is nothing to do but rest in this image of self. Practice, practice, practice. Shanti, Shanti. Slowly, you will arrive at the do-or of the temple of your nature. The kingdom has been waiting for you to break the rules, jump over the walls, and see that the peace and harmony of 'self' have always been available, just been made so difficult to see due to the excessive world that we live in, creating quite the maze, before finding the door. The beginning of an end. For now, we have explained the inner refuge, the nature of self whatever you want to call this neutral space in mind and love in the heart, your true journey begins. The journey of building yourself, the journey of painting your aura, the journey of walking in the mandalas that you see in yourself. The living sensations of the body. You are back to the state of being a happy innocent baby, you are now able to go into the playground to explore the planes of energy, the malleable feeling of your source of creation. Play at your own risk, know the power of the mind, the power of thought, know the power of great spirits, always play with love, always be in love. Don't try and know for all there is to do is to feel. However, know what you need to know to keep it simple and true. To me, less is more in this world today.

This is the story of a young boy, innocent in nature itself, stumbling upon the nature of self, a story about all the nations coming together. A brief of global history, a look into many images. A self-help book, a reminder of your essence and the essence of nature. Live in the qualities of **JOLKA! OPEN EXPAND ABSORB AND TRANSFORM** into the cells that you want to see. You are the light amongst your darkness. When in doubt be love, I've done my best to speak gently, to speak clearly, and to speak from my elders. I've done my best to whisper the voices of nature to the listening ear, for I know there is so much noise. Do not be upset with the self yet laugh at the idea that most things that we are looking for are usually right in front of us, especially stoners. There's nothing to do but rest. You are the conductor of your life, you are the baker, you are the alchemist. Take action and serve the people, the animals, ghosts, the gods, the spirits, and the self. Your time is NOW!

The Beginning of an End
Disclaimer & Writer's Not
Comfortable on Concrete

This book is written to expose the evils in the world that suppressed and tried to wipe out our Indigenous peoples, our original peoples. The Original thoughts, the ones who walked with the great spirit's. The ones who understood the powers of nature, the ones who worked alongside great spirits, the ones who listened to the voices of nature. To all indigenous peoples across the world from Turtle Island as a whole, to Africa, to India, Europe, Asia, and Australia, the Kingdom of Hawaii, I thank you for the teachings and reflections. I thank you for your strength to persevere the hand of the oppressor. I thank you for your songs and ceremonies, for your traditions and ways of life. Our old people of the First Nations our big brothers and sisters. It is time to be humble, it is time to listen. It is time to once again let the voices of nature whisper the words of great spirits. It is time to clean off to get ready to conduct love and light for our world, for our Mother Earth and Father Sun, and the elemental family. It is time to come back together.

We are highlighting the power of indigenous spirituality and way of life as it has been discouraged and even made illegal to practice in the last generations. The people who cast us out and tried to replace us with a new one! For you cannot erase the people of the Earth for the spirit walks with us, the spirits that walked with our ancestors are still with us. There is no way you can break us and our connection to nature, great spirit's, and creation. It has already been seen, it has already been told, and it is just a matter of time before we can all hear the voices of nature. **SANKOFA** Time now to take back what is rightfully ours! For it is not a taboo!

The book paints a picture of oneself, the original self, the children of the sun, and the simple reflections of nature. I hope that these energetic postures will affect you as they did me. I trust that only life-giving energy will be conducted, I hope you take it as seriously as I did when my native elder said don't play with this, it is powerful, can take life and give life. When my Voodoo Sr. Priest says the African spirits are strong, this is no joke. When my meditation teacher told me to only share light and uplift people, I trusted myself as a conductor, I knew to only share the light in a good way. I trust that the majority of us on are the same page and are ready to get back to our original cells. I've shared so much because I feel it is time to heal, to remember who we are. We are bodies of water crystals, we are walking conductors of love, light, and color. Be the change that you want to see.

Close your eyes and visualize the self you want to be and the reality you want to live in. You are your karma, you create your destiny. You are the one that you have been waiting for, mama Earth is ready to receive you and ready to love you. We must take time to spend with our spiritual family, with nature. Nature of self is awaiting you.

A Vision

I had a vision in the Sundance that we were Sundancing at the White House, many tribes gathering together and with mass celebration and respect to our ceremonies. Recognized by politicians and world leaders. Not only welcoming these ways of life back into the day but a movement of tears and rejoicing of our First Nation people, being honored to lead the way as they once did. A vision of all people praying under the sacred tree. On the lawn of the white house, recorded for the world to see. The giving back and honoring this original way of life, I saw in this vision our First Nation people leading the country again. A full circle of creation and destruction. Letting the rest of the world know that Americans as mixed up as we are, can listen and come back to listen to Nature. A vision of all people listening to our original nature of self, our indigenous root whether yellow, red, black, or white. May our differences be seen whether we were Pegan Indigenous, African Indigenous, Asian Indigenous, or American Indigenous, for each carries a sacred view of nature and relating to it. We are all here together in knowledge and sensation. This is the power of the people when we come together as one.

Do not allow yourself to get comfortable on the concrete, the subliminal messages, the casting of spells, the buildings rising so high they block our sun, the seclusion of living in walls, the devices that put one another against each other. No matter if I hear a Christian, Hindu, Muslim, Buddhist, Sundancer, or nature lover, if they are in true understanding and in devotion to their way of life, they all speak the same. For it is love and kindness that will awaken us from this day of judgment, it is acceptance and action. It is a feeling that once is recognized in all people, we can come back to our original identity stated over and over again in this book. One who is connected to spirit, one who is consciously conducting love and light. We are all made up of the same elements. Stand in your heart, not in your trauma, lay the crouches down and stand on your feet with your senses activated. Rejoice in the great reception of connecting to Earth and Sun. Allow the birth of your true self to come out of the darkness. Is it not true that we all want to live in peace in love in harmony with ourselves and the Earth we inhabit? Is it true that we are frustrated with what has been taken from us? Is it true that we can make subtle changes in our lives to see greater change? May the number of comforts we find on the concrete be the wake-up call! Take steps back to the land, step back to the tree, coming back to the voices of nature, your mother has been waiting for you, and your father has lightened the way – welcome yourself back home to the nature of self. If you are already there, challenge yourself to go into the concrete and share your conduction with the world.

E MA HO ; O How Marvelous

Thank you for taking the time to not only read, but envision, feel, visualize, and imagine a cellular shift, a change of awareness. I hope I spoke gently and thoroughly; We are here to offer guidance in the return to nature of self. We are actively looking for sponsors to build more Nature's Temples, retreat/rehabilitation centers, where we can see a community of people growing food, raising children and animals, and practicing our original ways of life, all guided as one family, one community, and one love.

If you feel inspired by this grassroots vision, please feel free to donate to our works.

Our contacts are:

Email: naturestemple108@gmail.com

Facebook: Juniper Urieh

Website: Naturestemples.com

YouTube channel: Voices of Nature

This book is written in devotion to the rainbow nation, to the sky dancers, thank you above ones for delivering me with a good relationship with you. All that I have done in my life is for you. Rainbow, thank you for guiding me to build nature's temple physically and energetically. Thank you for your presence in my life, thank you for receiving the love I offer you. I smile back at you as you have smiled at me, I am in selfless service. I'm here to share the voices of nature, as you whisper to me, I am in Seva, devotion, and praise to you.

Great rainbow spirit, we ask that you continue to work with us. We ask that you guide us into the field of living and breathing light all together. We ask that you will be a blessing to all of our relations. Great spirits of living color, may we be humbled by your presence as you continue your revealing, we ask that you help us to reveal our nature of self and nature itself. To all our relations we smile the good smile and send the good energy of Sky and Earth.

AHO AMEN ASE

www.ingramcontent.com/pod-product-compliance
Lightning Source LLC
Chambersburg PA
CBHW080126150626
46550CB00017B/2732